D0761011

Robert Frost

Robert Frost

The Ethics of Ambiguity

John H. Timmerman

Lewisburg
Bucknell University Press
London: Associated University Presses

Associated University Presses
440 Forsgate Drive
Cranbury, NJ 08512

Associated University Presses
16 Barter Street
London WC1A 2AH, England

Associated University Presses
P.O. Box 338, Port Credit
Mississauga, Ontario
Canada L5G 4L8

The paper used in this publication meets the requirements of the American National Standard for Permanence of Paper for Printed Library Materials Z39.48-1984.

Library of Congress Cataloging-in-Publication Data

Timmerman, John H.
    Robert Frost : the ethics of ambiguity / John H. Timmerman.
        p.   cm.
    Includes bibliographical references (p.) and index.
    ISBN 0-8387-5532-1 (alk. paper)
    1. Frost, Robert, 1874–1963—Ethics.   2. Didactic poetry, American—History and criticism.   3. Ambiguity in literature.   4. Ethics in literature.   I. Title.

PS3511.R94 Z595   2002
811'.52—dc21   2002018610

Contents

Acknowledgments

I WRITE WITH APPRECIATION FOR THE GENEROUS SUPPORT OF CALVIN College for sabbatical leave and secretarial support.

The following sources are hereby acknowledged for use of quoted material:

Excerpts from "The Constant Symbol," and "Education by Poetry," SELECTED PROSE OF ROBERT FROST edited by Hyde Cox and Edward Connery Lathem. Copyright 1949, 1954, © 1966 by Henry Holt and Co., copyright 1946, © 1959 by Robert Frost, © by the Estate of Robert Frost. Reprinted by permission of Henry Holt & Co., LLC.

Excerpts from letters #46 to John T. Bartlett, #53 to John T. Bartlett, #55 to Thomas B. Mosher, #430 to Victor E. Reichert from SELECTED LETTERS OF ROBERT FROST edited by Lawrance Thompson. Compilation and editing © 1964 by Lawrance Thompson. Reprinted by permission of Henry Holt & Co., LLC.

Excerpts from "Mowing," "The Tuft of Flowers," "Mending Wall," "The Death of the Hired Man," "Home Burial," "The Road Not Taken," "The Oven Bird," "Birches," "Putting in the Seed," "A Time to Talk," "The Hill Wife," "The Star-Splitter," "I Will Sing You One-O," "Nothing Gold Can Stay," "Lodged," "Bereft," "Acquainted With the Night," "Sitting By a Bush in Broad Daylight," "Neither Out Far Nor in Deep," "Design," "Afterflakes," "To a Thinker," "All Revelation," "The Most of It," "The Lesson for Today," "Directive," "Take Something Like a Star," "A Cabin in the Clearing," "Kitty Hawk," "My November Guest," "Ghost House," "Lost in Heaven," "Desert Places," *A Masque of Reason, A Masque of Mercy* from THE POETRY OF ROBERT FROST edited by Edward Connery Lathem. Copyright 1923, 1928, 1947, 1949, © 1969 by Henry Holt and Co., copyright 1936, 1942, 1947, 1951, 1956, 1962 by Robert Frost, copyright 1964, 1970, 1975 by Lesley Frost Ballantine. Reprinted by permission of Henry Holt & Co., LLC.

Introduction

THE EARLIEST SUSTAINED STUDY OF FROST'S ETHICS APPEARED IN George W. Nitchie's *Human Values in the Poetry of Robert Frost* (1962). Nitchie's study held, and continues to hold, value primarily for locating axiological truths about human nature discerned by humanity's engagement with nature. But Nitchie also detected a trait of Frost's ethics that is central to his study: "My immediate point is simply that Frost tends to shy away from explicit statements of a theory of nature, or of man's relationship with nature. And this is interesting because, paradoxically or not, one of the cardinal errors according to Frost's scheme of values is going against nature or natural processes; at least, man does so at his peril."[1] In fact, Frost not only "shies away" from explicit ethical statements, he adamantly refuses to reduce his poetry to such. His poetic world is rich with implication, and devoid of direct pronouncement unless surrounded by undercutting ironies. Ambiguity shapes the common denominator.

Subsequent to Nitchie, several studies, most notably Dorothy Judd Hall's *Robert Frost: Contours of Belief* (1984) and Edward Ingebretsen's *Robert Frost's Star in a Stone Boat: A Grammar of Belief* (1994), have pursued Frost's ethical thinking through religious avenues. While religious beliefs and issues suffuse Frost's poetry, Frost's presentation of them is often contradictory and ambivalent. Religious and biblical influences are patently clear, as both Hall and Ingebretsen demonstrate. Their influence upon Frost's ethics is at best partial.

As one follows Frost's ethical thinking through his body of prose and poetry, a conflicted and often confusing world unfolds. Some apparently overt claims are shaded in context by tones of cynicism or skepticism. Values he apparently lauded in his work are violated freely in his life. Ideals he longed for are often crushed under a bitter sense of a reality that erected barriers as tense as taut barbed wire. Consequently, the important questions to ask about Frost's ethics are whether any systematic patterns emerge; what influenced such patterns; and, most importantly, how they are manifested in the poetry.

The danger of any study of ethics in the work of an author is to impose one's own set of beliefs upon the work and author. In her study of reader-response theory and Frost's works, *Toward Robert Frost: The Reader and the Poet*, Judith Oster puts the conflicts like this: "This [reader-response theory] may result in resistance [by the reader] to being so entangled; in the case of poem or poet, to being read. I take this to be a central conflict in Frost: the need to be read, and read well, against the *fear* of being read well coupled with his possessive need to protect his creation from appropriation by others."[2] One might restate the issue like this: at what point does the reader own the work, forcing it to his or her *meaning*? If there is ambiguity in the work, must the reader resolve it on internal evidence, or may the reader consult outside evidence (the life of the author, for example)? Such are dangerous questions. They attach themselves to reader-response theory in particular, but no studied critical appraisal of any author's work is free from them.

I find such issues particularly cautionary in a study of Frost's ethics. Here more than ever the temptation arises to read his ethics in the light, for example, of theological issues in his personal life, or, in fact, in the light of events in that life itself. Conversely, the temptation arises for the reader to impose—or even bring to the poem—his or her own values upon the poem. As with reader-response theory, the reader is an active participant in *uncovering* meaning but refrains from *determining* meaning.

With such cautions stated, an alternative course is to engage a study of Frost's ethics in a contextual fashion, refusing to extrapolate the work as some independent entity that appeared as if by accident at some point in history. Several important contexts come to bear upon a study of the ethics of Frost's poetry. The primary one is the nature of the work itself as we examine some fundamental influences upon Frost's art and the way he shapes the poetic work to engage an ethical issue. The first context, then, is artistic form.

While few scholars place Frost fully in the mainstream of turn-of-the-century Modernism, none would leave him on the shore as a disinterested observer. Although Frost adamantly held to his own poetic way of doing things, his awareness of the poetic and aesthetic culture of the time was particularly keen. Such is undoubtedly the case with the seminal thinker of the time, George

Santayana, who, I argue in chapter 1, may very well have influenced Frost's aesthetic sense. In chapter 2 I apply his philosophical sense of the artistic work to Frost's actual crafting of the poetic work. The argument here, central to later chapters in this study, is that Frost deliberately crafted ambiguity into the very form of his poetry. Form, in this case, abets the conceptual ambiguity of the work, energizing the dialectics and tensions that Frost holds forth.

The second significant context entering this discussion is historical/biographical. While it is not the aim here to read Frost's poems directly in the context of life events, it should be understood that, as a poet who is so often narrative in style, Frost's own life inevitably and indisputably enters the story of the work. Furthermore, the understanding of ethical situations and responses is significantly enhanced by an understanding of the personal and historical details behind the work. For example, the purchase of the Derry Farm for $1700 in 1900 bears significance at several levels. It was indeed an escape from the huge sorrow evoked by his son Elliott's death. Frost did indeed enjoy raising those first chickens and bringing in some much needed money. Derry Farm was restorative of his own health (he had left Harvard for health concerns). But Derry Farm also permitted him time and space for reflection to write nearly all the poems collected in *A Boy's Will* (1913).

The third context comes directly from the philosophy of ethics itself. The primary purpose of this study is to demonstrate that a consistent ethics, even though intrinsically encapsulated in ambiguity and ambivalence, does in fact appear in Frost's work. Rather than observing an accretion of clues through that work, however, we might better understand Frost's ethics by holding them up against five leading ethical theories of the late nineteenth through twentieth centuries. These chapters briefly introduce and define the particular theory. They then examine several of Frost's works within the contexts and directives of that theory. The effort here is twofold: to see with which "school" Frost's works best compare, and thereby to demonstrate and define Frost's own "Ethics of Ambiguity."

Abbreviations

QUOTATIONS FROM THE FOLLOWING BOOKS, WITH ABBREVIATIONS AS shown, will be cited parenthetically throughout this study. All quotations from the poetry of Robert Frost are taken from *The Poetry of Robert Frost*. Ed. Edward Connery Lathem. New York: Henry Holt & Co., 1979.

Selected Prose	*Selected Prose of Robert Frost*. Ed. Hyde Cox and Edward Connery Lathem. New York: Collier, 1968.
Family Letters	*Family Letters of Robert and Elinor Frost*. Ed. Arnold Grade. Albany: State University of New York, 1972.
Untermeyer	*The Letters of Robert Frost to Louis Untermeyer*. Ed. Louis Untermeyer. New York: Holt, Rinehart and Winston, 1963.
Selected Letters	*Selected Letters of Robert Frost*. Ed. Lawrance Thompson. New York: Holt, Rinehart and Winston, 1964.
Interviews	*Interviews with Robert Frost*. Ed. Edward Connery Lathem. Guilford, CT: Jeffrey Norton, 1997.

All quotations from the Bible, unless otherwise noted, are from the New International Version (NIV).

Robert Frost

1
Aesthetics and Ethics

IN HIS *MODERNIST QUARTET*, FRANK LENTRICCHIA MAKES AN ADMIRA-ble effort to tug Robert Frost into a modernist mainstream of Eliot, Pound, and Stevens. However entertaining and stimulating the effort is, and it is both, its success is questionable. Indeed, Lentricchia is wise enough not to force Frost into any one camp, like some concrete slurry left to harden indefinitely. Frost's thinking and work are far too protean and flexible. Yet, they also bear markings that separate him cleanly from the nineteenth century and into an undeniably unique position of his own in modern letters. If Lentricchia's argument does succeed, it does so both for circumstantial and evidentiary reasons.

By historical circumstance Frost was born into the poetic legacy of the American Fireside Poets—Whittier, Lowell, Bryant, Holmes, Longfellow. The full bloom of Romanticism had long passed, but the Fireside Poets were doing their best before their deaths (all within a few years of each other) at the end of the nineteenth century to keep some blossoms alive in the withered soil. They could do so to a large degree because of the cultural power they had obtained. They were Men of Importance. They had dominated the general tastes in poetry for the better part of a century.

Frost was avaricious for the fame (and fortune) these poets held. In fact, he courted fame like a lover from his earliest poetry writing. He found it nearly impossible to turn down a public reading, even as he became increasingly afflicted with respiratory ailments and illness in his later years. In what proved to be his last public statement, published by Robert Peterson in a syndicated news story on 10 December 1962, Frost commented:

> Maybe it's my general lack of worry and ambition that has somehow enhanced my longevity. I didn't make any particular effort to honors and prestige folks have heaped on me.

> Money and fame don't impress me much. About all that impresses
> me is human kindness and warm relationships with good friends. (*In-*
> *terviews* 294–95)

That is the sort of thing one can say after having won international fame. (Frost had just returned from a reading tour in the
Soviet Union in September.) It is also the sort of thing a poet can
say after a lifetime of writing the kind of work he wanted, and of
defining for himself and also his reading public a style and a narrative form. In developing that form he remained suspicious of what
he considered an overblown and simple artifice of the Fireside
Poets. He wanted a seat by the fireside, but he wanted his own
chair in which to sit. The Fireside Poets represented worn-out poetics, but also an inauthentic set of values.

All of the Fireside Poets came to prominence during the collapse
of the Age of Reason. Unknowing was accepted; spiritual incerti-
tude, as with Bryant's "Thanatopsis," seemed inescapable. They
turned instead to human experience where the human record
might shed some light upon humanity itself. Human experience,
then, shaped the poetic epistemology. Then as now, the effort pro-
duced a poetry wildly popular but also, at times, philosophically
impoverished. When Frost found himself coming of age at the end
of the nineteenth century, when the memory of the Fireside Poets
was receding into the ashes of the past, Frost faced the same poetic
issues confronted by Joyce, Stevens, Eliot, and Pound, among others. What stories would be told now? What epistemology would appear in them? And, if the new poets discovered an epistemology
of a fragmented and emotionally flattened humanity, how indeed
would it affect the stories they told about humanity? Such were the
issues confronting the young poet on the cusp of the twentieth century.

A second item of circumstantial evidence should be added, for it
leads us directly into Frost's poetics. Frost, as Lentricchia points
out, was a nondegree candidate at Harvard from 1897 to 1899.
This period also saw the appearance at Harvard of three leading
"modernist" philosophers—George Santayana, William James,
and Josiah Royce. Of particular significance was Santayana, whose
1896 *The Sense of Beauty* developed an aesthetic theory that, while
classicist in many regards, departed radically from theories of art
that had prevailed during the previous two centuries. His strong
emphasis upon narrative, character, and idealization in particular

may have influenced Frost and the other young modernists of his time.[1]

Santayana set himself no mean task in this relatively brief work. At one level he pursued the traditional task of the philosophy of aesthetics: an inquiry into the nature of beauty. But a more subversive level quickly emerged, for Santayana wanted nothing less than to deconstruct historically received notions of beauty in order to provide a definition that was contemporarily significant and operable. His first step, then, was to strip beauty of all its traditional honorific titles. In particular, he was intent upon clearing out the nebulous fog of notions left by Romanticism. "Beauty is truth," or a "symbol of divine perfection"—such familiar slogans he swept away as phrases that "stimulate thought and give us a momentary pleasure, but . . . hardly bring any permanent enlightenment".[2] The focus of aesthetics, argued Santayana, should be on the conditions under which beauty appears in the object (or work of art), and upon the beholder's sensibility of beauty.

If, on the one hand, Santayana began with a broad, backhand swipe doing away with Romanticism in favor of a much more concrete aesthetics, on the other hand, he pushed out of the way traditional notions of criticism, a word "still retained as the title for the reasoned appreciation of works of art."[3] The difficulty with criticism, in its effort to cast art into categories, is precisely the opposite of the Romantic aesthetic. Rationalist aesthetics risks the danger of pure formalism, thereby imposing constraints upon the imaginations of artist and perceiver alike. Thereby Santayana appeared to have jettisoned over two centuries of thinking about aesthetic matters. But such was not wholly the case. He attempted to achieve nothing less than a reconciliation—or at least an accommodation—between the historically pitted camps of Romanticism and Reason. He does so by arguing that aesthetics is essentially "concerned with the perception of values."[4]

Ethical values, Santayana was quick to point out, arise from the individual human consciousness. In aesthetic terms, they are shaped concomitantly by the craft of the artist and the perception of the beholder. The key point is that art is not some neutral matter. Nor is it entirely a rational construct, as Pope would have had us believe when he stated his purpose in *Essay on Man*:

Laugh where we *must*; be candid where we *can*;
But vindicate the Ways of *God* to Man.[5]

That vindication, for Pope, occurred through the rational intellect that could in fact ascend to and make known the ways of God to humanity. For Santayana, however, the artwork is a living means of communication (some might use the stronger term *communion*) between artist and perceiver. The technical means by which this occurs—euphony, character, and so forth—Santayana wasn't to work out until his later literary essays, but the germ of it lies in *The Sense of Beauty*.

Where, then, do values inhere in the work of art? Surely not in didacticism, implicitly an aesthetic defect for him since it imposes the author's judgment upon both work and perceiver. There are, Santayana pointed out, aesthetic merits in art that are pleasing, but not necessarily matters of values. For example, an understanding of facts and relationships may be worthwhile information, but these lie essentially within the purview of criticism and merely at the fringes of aesthetics. That is, it may be important to know that Frost insisted that his two *Masques* be placed at the end of his *Complete Poems*, even though they are far from the last works he wrote. Facts (e.g., the dates of the first publication of the poems—1945 and 1947) and relationships (e.g., placement at the end of *Collected Poems*) are valuable tools, but not aesthetic issues.

If critical tasks and aesthetic values are related but dissimilar, moral and aesthetic values, while more closely allied for Santayana, are similar but not identical. At its simplest level, he means that art is not a vehicle for moral judgment (didacticism).[6] Moral issues are, in fact, subservient to aesthetic merit: "Art is the response to the demand for entertainment, for the stimulation of our senses and imagination, and truth enters into it only as it subserves these ends."[7] The relationship that Santayana does observe, then, is a curious one, simply because it lies in a contrast. The highest aesthetic merit clearly is pleasure; the issues that involve values are essentially ethical ones. Nonetheless, the aesthetic merit of a work intensifies when engaging an ethical issue:

The sad business of life is rather to escape certain dreadful evils to which our nature exposes us—death, hunger, disease, weariness, isolation, and contempt. By the awful authority of these things, which stand like spectres behind every moral injunction, conscience in reality speaks, and a mind which they have duly impressed cannot but feel, by contrast, the hopeless triviality of the search for pleasure.[8]

Santayana weighs down with immediacy the abstractedness of both romantic and rationalist aesthetics concerning the realities of the human condition.

Such a view also might have kindled the imagination of young Frost. In fact, a statement such as the following from Santayana may seem to have been spoken as a poetics by Frost himself:

> The truth is that morality is not mainly concerned with the attainment of pleasure; it is rather concerned, in all its deeper and more authoritative maxims, with the prevention of suffering. There is something artificial in the deliberate pursuit of pleasure; there is something absurd in the obligation to enjoy oneself. We feel no duty in that direction; we take to enjoyment naturally enough after the work of life is done, and the freedom and spontaneity of our pleasures is what is most essential to them.[9]

If a reader were to place that statement as an epigraph to such poems as "After Apple-Picking," "Home Burial," "The Death of the Hired Man," "Nothing Gold Can Stay," or any of a dozen others, we would have a pretty fair perception of the poetic aims of Robert Frost. His poems often serve not as means to prevent suffering, but as a means to engage and understand it.

Beyond question, the ethical issue of understanding suffering was also a profoundly personal one for Frost. It was well entrenched by the time he attended Harvard as a nondegree student. Born in 1874 to a deeply religious mother, Belle, and an alcoholic and violent father, Will, Frost's early years were a string of unsettling events—sporadic schooling, moves, beatings at home, and gangs on the streets. Nor did life improve significantly when Will died in 1885 and Belle, with eight dollars in her bank account, was left to care for Robert and his younger sister Jeanie Florence. She packed them up and headed back to the ancestral home in Lawrence, Massachusetts, where poverty was going to be their constant companion. Life in Frost's grandparents' home was a reeling succession of contrasts. Jeffery Meyers observes that, "The cold, cheerless and depressing home of the grandparents, then in their sixties, epitomized everything he disliked about New England. There was a striking contrast between his grandmother's well-organized housewifery and Belle's domestic chaos, between his grandfather's careful and cautious way of life . . . and Will's recklessness about his health and future."[10] Over all, lay the pall of poverty. Frost worked a seemingly endless succession of dull and dreary jobs, nearly all of which he hated. Despair seemed never far from him, pointlessness his constant companion. All he had were his ideas for poems, and a wondering about how poems could address the life he was living. In 1891 Jeanie was afflicted by what we would now diagnose as anxiety disorder and depression. Frost was acutely aware of his own tendency toward the illnesses, and fought them off by a nearly obsessive—or perhaps hypomanic—immersion in his studies, a pattern that remained with him throughout his life. From an early age, it is fair to say, Frost was attuned to sorrow, and compelled by the effort to understand its presence.

Without claiming a direct influence, one observes a similarity between Santayana's aesthetics of values and Frost's experience that may have paved a way for the young poet. On the one side we have the artistic theory; on the other, the life experience and its enactment in poetry. Both theory and art-making share the ethical urge to make sense of things in this world, particularly to engage the issue of suffering, to ask why it happens, what its effects are, and what can be done about it. But the commensurate inquiry remains of how, exactly, art does this. What properties must it possess, what ends does it pursue? Here again, further inquiry into Santayana's aesthetic and literary theory evokes remarkable similarities to Frost and at the very least highlights some of Frost's own aims. This is particularly so for the fact that for both Santayana and Frost the craft of art-making itself was an ethical issue. Exploration of this issue brings one beyond the circumstantial and closer to the evidentiary claims for Frost's place in modernism.

Frost's art-making at several stages of the craft shares similarities with Santayana's aesthetics. Santayana assumes the aesthetic premise that art strives for the beautiful, but he questions where that beauty lies. He puts his answer like this: "The stuff of language is words, and the sensuous material of words is sound; if language therefore is to be made perfect, its materials must be made beautiful by being themselves subjected to a measure, and endowed with a form."[11] One who has read carefully in Frost's letters and essays will find many echoes of this fundamental tenet, for Frost repeatedly emphasized that his was a craft of "sound-sense."

That sound-sense and euphony in its poetic casting, according to Santayana, are shaped like this:

> The elementary sounds are prescribed by the language we use, and the selection we make among these sounds is limited; but the arrangement

of words is still undetermined, and by casting our speech into the moulds of metre and rhyme we can give it a heightened power, apart from its significance. A tolerable definition of poetry, on its formal side, might be found in this: that poetry is speech in which the instrument counts as well as its meaning—poetry is speech for its own sake and for its own sweetness.[12]

A definition like this Frost could adopt; in fact, he would—and did—model his craft upon such a premise. His aim, as he often stated, was to capture the living speech of living people and to craft that into the poetics of sound-sense. Here too Frost sought the living speech heightened by rhythm and metrics that granted a power superseding the words themselves.

In a 1913 letter to John Bartlett, in which Frost complained about the slavish fidelity of some of his British contemporaries to rhyme patterns alone for melody, Frost asserts that "I alone of English writers have consciously set myself to make music out of what I may call the sound of sense" (*Selected Letters* 79). Further in the letter Frost distinguishes his sound-sense from what he saw as mere "versification," or a language of artifice:

> An ear and an appetite for these sounds of sense is the first qualification of a writer, be it of prose or verse. But if one is to be a poet he must learn to get cadences by skillfully breaking the sounds of sense with all their irregularity of accent across the regular beat of the metre. Verse in which there is nothing but the beat of the metre furnished by the accents of the polysyllabic words we call doggerel. (*Selected Letters* 80–81)

Evidence of Frost's stated beliefs may also be discovered in his earliest poems. Here one sees that he did not master the craft of sound-sense immediately, but slowly grew into it. *A Boy's Will* (published by Nutt in England in 1913, but mostly written previously in the U.S.) is striking for its power and beauty. At a technical level, however, one observes a tentative exploration of the ways in which sound-sense and euphony work in one poem.

In *A Boy's Will*, "Ghost House" and "My November Guest" stand as companion poems both in theme and content. Frost's "Contents" notes in the 1913 edition indicate that in "Ghost House," "He [the boy] is happy in the society of his own choosing." With the boy having so chosen, however, the poem throbs with a painful loneliness, perfectly conveyed by the tetrameter lines:

I dwell with a strangely aching heart
In that vanished abode there far apart
    On that disused and forgotten road
    That has no dust-bath now for the toad.
Night comes; the black bats tumble and dart. . . .

                                            (11–15)

While the AABBA rhyme is entirely masculine, clipped and
abrupt, the rhyme is countered by long and heavy vowels clustered
in the center of the lines: *dwell, abode, disused, no, now, comes, tumble.*
Furthermore, the internal *abode* of line 12 is picked up by the end
rhymes *road* and *toad* of lines 13 and 14. It is an exquisite bit of
versifying, incarnating well Frost's early belief in euphony. The
form sustains and illustrates the boy's sense of loneliness (the masculine rhymes) by the internal vowels that weigh heavily upon the
movement of the line.

  "My November Guest" is similar in form—iambic tetrameter in
five-line stanzas—and also in its development in the boy's life in
the text. Here Frost stated in the 1913 "Contents" notes: "He is in
love with being misunderstood." But is he? Here in the early stage
of his career, is Frost already setting one of his infamous traps for
the reader? The poem is relatively brief and should be considered
closely, primarily to observe the working of "sound-sense" and euphony, but secondarily to examine Frost's revelation of the boy's
character through natural images:

My Sorrow, when she's here with me,
    Thinks these dark days of autumn rain
Are beautiful as days can be;
She loves the bare, the withered tree;
    She walks the sodden pasture lane.

Her pleasure will not let me stay.
    She talks and I am fain to list:
She's glad the birds are gone away,
She's glad her simple worsted gray
    Is silver now with clinging mist.

The desolate, deserted trees,
    The faded earth, the heavy sky,
The beauties she so truly sees,
She thinks I have no eye for these,
    And vexes me for reason why.

> Not yesterday I learned to know
>   The love of bare November days
> Before the coming of the snow,
> But it were vain to tell her so,
>   And they are better for her praise.

The formal features relating this poem to "Ghost House" are quickly apparent. Both are iambic tetrameter and five-line stanzas (two of only three poems in the volume to use the format). The rhyme scheme in "My November Guest" uses nearly exclusively masculine end rhymes. Both poems thematically address feelings of separation and loneliness. The first-person narrator in each poem puzzles through the feelings, trying at once to accommodate and to understand them. Yet, "Ghost House," written in 1901 and based on a burned-out house near Derry Farm, appears to be a superior poem and provides us more clues to the shape of Frost's career. Why?

Ghost House opens with the narrator on a thoroughly concrete scene:

> I dwell in a lonely house I know
> That vanished many a summer ago,
>   And left no trace but the cellar walls,
>   And a cellar in which the daylight falls,
> And the purple-stemmed wild raspberries grow.

The metaphor is perfectly set up in the first line, with its teasingly ambiguous last phrase, "I know." Know what? The lonely house, or the fact that he inhabits it? The tantalizing indirection is partly solved by the following four lines detailing the house he knows. The cellar image, which will resurface in later poems, is, in a few deft strokes, brought to perfect clarity. But the second line, where the physical description begins, actually draws out the ambiguity. We add a third thing, then, to the "I know"—that the house "vanished many a summer ago." Knowing that, the reader also knows the title. This may indeed be a ghost house, but spirits, like the loneliness within the boy, still inhabit its vacant spaces. All the following descriptions of the deserted homestead powerfully and singularly abet the initial image and feeling of the poem. There is not a stray note in it, and such writing is clearly a precursor to Frost's later tight meldings of form to content.

While "My November Guest" shares the same kind of narrator—explorative, wondering, examining—the challenge of engaging these traits is quite different. The notable difference here, beside being far less sophisticated and complex in rhyming than "Ghost House" (although in a 1913 letter to John Bartlett, Frost declared the poem "a success in this assonant vein"), is that the poem begins with the personification of an abstraction rather than a narrator engaging a concrete but highly metaphorical setting. It is arguable that "My Sorrow" is in fact a physical lover. If so, she is provided no specifiable detail and no physical placement. She remains mere idea, less real even than the apostrophe. "My Sorrow" almost immediately evokes a sense of Romantic excess, and it was the sort of poem he would never use again (although he grew very fond of apostrophe). In a pattern similar to that used in "The Oven Bird," the poem uses sorrow as the personified voice of the poem, to which the young man listens and construes the meaning. It is, however, My Sorrow, and the voice is in many ways similar to one of Browning's interior monologues.

The poem is set in the "dark days of autumn rain." Sorrow teaches him the beauty of the season, which the poet in turn conveys by physical description and imagery. Yet, as we learn in the last stanza, the narrator has known these things all along, but simply enjoys hearing Sorrow praise them.

An ironic jest appears in the final stanza. What Sorrow has been singing the narrator has in fact known all along (16–17). She simply sings the praise of the season more sweetly. Could it be possible, then, to read the entire poem as a romantic jest at Romanticism? Is Frost tweaking the young man's wallowing in emotion? If so, that might explain the infelicitous language and constructions that do not appear in the graceful "Ghost House." Such a statement as "I am fain to list" not only presents a tense discord to euphony, but it seems a line plucked from the worst of the Romantics. Similarly the odd usage in line 15 seems forced to the meter, and the subjunctive in line 19 seems forced to the context. Perhaps, then, it is possible that the poem actually performs as a parody of Romanticism. It is possible, but improbable. Neither the interior elements of the poem nor the volume as a whole lend support. Rather, it may be seen as a lesser poem in a poet's first volume in which he didn't entirely fulfill his aims of "sound-sense" and euphony.

Even though variations of his belief in sound-sense and euphony arising from the tones and rhythms of human speech would appear in Frost's public and private statements throughout his life, from his earliest years he also added one significant caveat—that words signify deeds. In a 1915 letter to Louis Untermeyer, Frost distinguishes truth as something one lives by, rather than argues for. Immediately he departs from language as an aesthetic tool, then, to language as an ethical matter. Here he writes, "Sometimes I have my doubts of words altogether and I ask myself what is the place of them. They are worse than nothing unless they do something, unless they amount to deeds as in ultimatums and war crys [sic]. . . . My definition of literature would be just this, words that have become deeds" (Untermeyer 10). The implications of these views are seen in fairly similar form in Santayana's *The Sense of Beauty*: first, in order to capture the language of living people, Frost adopts a language of sound-sense rather than standard versification; second, that sound-sense enables him to capture characters in their living reality; third, what the poem says about those characters and that reality and the way in which it is said bear ethical significance. The word is the deed; that is, values that determine actions are manifested in the words, and also the arrangement of the words themselves bestow ethical values upon the actions committed.

In one crucial way, then, this poetics distinguishes Frost from his poetic ancestors. The art swayed from a cultivated, "classroom" speech to the rhythms and melodics of human speaking. It was an art that Frost would perfect, and which, in fact, also separates him from fellow modernists by his lifelong insistence upon it.

If the reliance upon sound-sense found in the patterns of human speech is one poetic device encouraged by Santayana and one that Frost apparently embraced, the second and more famous one—that one affecting the course of modernism generally—is objectification through the image. Contemporarily, we have taken our cue from Eliot and Pound to understand imagism as a flattening of human experience by correlating it with or incarnating it in artistic images. As Eliot said of his objective correlative, it is the correlation of being, mood, or spirit with some physical, concrete object.[13] Frost shares the general pattern, but never with the subversive, revolutionary quality of Eliot or Pound.[14] He remained more closely allied with Santayana's concept of Idealization—the birthing room of modernist imagism.

Santayana's premise is that "the poet's art is to a great extent the art of intensifying emotions by assembling the scattered objects that naturally arouse them. He sees the affinities of things by seeing their common affinities with passion."[15] Nonetheless, a danger lies in such a view, he observes. In a sense, it suggests a Romantic view of the poet, perhaps the very last thing Santayana would tolerate: "If the function of poetry, however, did not go beyond this recovery of sensuous and imaginative freedom, at the expense of disrupting our useful habits of thought, we might be grateful to it for occasionally relieving our numbness, but we should have to admit that it was nothing but a relaxation. . . ."[16] Poetry is not mere recreation, some amusing sensual sport. Therefore, Santayana pushes the issue further. And here, in effect, his aesthetic again acquires an ethics, for he questions to what end or goal is this poetics.

Interestingly, he starts with the characters of the poem, but with a significant caution. It is not the character him or herself, nor the success of the poet's creation of character that is most important in poetry. Important, yes. But the character's "effects and causes . . . is the truly interesting thing."[17] The ethical issues we face with such characters are these: What motivates a character to action or, in some of Frost's poems, inaction? What actions does the character then commit? What are the effects of such actions upon the character or others? These, of course, are ethical issues, but, as Santayana points out, they are also aesthetic properties (or virtues) when "the characters, although well drawn, are subordinate to the total movement and meaning of the scene."[18] The task of the poet, Santayana concludes, is to create scenes or occasions that, through characters at those scenes or occasions, manifest feelings and deeds we have actually had or experienced. In such a way, then, Santayana's appeal to Idealization recalls the more vigorous model of the classical hero, where the poetic-dramatic character incarnates human conflicts and vicariously for the audience works his way through to ameliorative or cathartic ends.

The theory of Idealization for Santayana began in his distaste for Romantic excess and his admiration for classical formalism. Thus, he spoke of "objectified pleasure"; that is, pleasure as a principle of the object in and of itself. But that pleasure becomes an aesthetic virtue when the artist modifies or manipulates the reality of the object toward the Ideal. Perhaps we can gain a fair sense of his meaning here by an analogy. In a photographic session, for example, the photographer is working with a nude model. Essentially, the *body* is the reality. Not the person or personality. Our reactions to that body, seen on a 9×12 black and white print probably, may be indiscriminate. For some viewers it may hold no more beauty or pleasure than a side of beef in the butcher's shop. But now, as the photographer structures the position of the body, adjusts light and shadow, teases facial expressions to reveal personality, the 9×12 print may, in the hands of a skillful artist, acquire aesthetic beauty and provide "objectified pleasure." So too, Santayana's image arrives at Idealization by the skillful artist.

The difficulty with Santayana's theory of Idealization, as some modern readers would be quick to point out, is his insufficient accounting for evil. For the early modernists, evil had insinuated its slitted eyes and forked tongue into every nook and cranny (and human heart) of early twentieth-century culture. And it affected their art. Yeats had his vision of gyres imploding under the weight of social and ethical conflict. Joyce declared in his *Portrait of an Artist as a Young Man* that art was religion and that art, in fact, was all the meaning there really was. Eliot used Santayana's idea of objectification and turned it on its head, not to find the ideality but to expose the emptiness of reality. And Pound, Frost's early champion and one whom Frost largely ignored until late in his life (1958) when he helped secure Pound's release from the asylum, used imagery like a bulldozer, flattening humanity and human experience out of recognizable shape as if defying the reader to put the pieces together again in any meaningful way. So the modernists beat on, faces toward the wasteland, finding little ahead, nothing behind.

Frost was keenly aware of the evil life had to offer; sometimes it seemed to him an overwhelming tide in which he bobbed like a wayward piece of driftwood. But he also had an ardent sense of life's goodness, even if, at times, he had to look hard to find it. In poetic artistry, moreover, we also find him toeing a middle line. The ambiguity he finds in the conflict between good and evil—his experience of and wish to prevent suffering and his restless search for enduring values in good and proper living—is also shaped in the verse he wrote. Frost's poetry is almost inevitably an "ethical" poetry in the sense that Santayana uses the term. Frequently the ethical issues he raises, however, dissolve in a tense ambiguity. Why and how this happens constitutes the primary search of this text.

While many studies have been devoted to Frost's religious beliefs, and to a lesser extent his ethical premises, very little work has been done to examine the way in which Frost's ethical beliefs affect the form as well as the themes of his poetry. To date, studies have generally taken one of two directions. First, they have relied heav-

ily upon biographical criticism, examining in addition to the life
his letters and essays, then using these as a matrix for reading the
texts. Or, second, studies have focused upon common thematic
patterns in the poems and have drawn conclusions or assumptions
from them—not only about the poems themselves but also about
beliefs Frost may have held while writing them. Perhaps an alternative lies in Santayana's aesthetics: art is a communication between artist and perceiver in which values are that which is
communicated. Values implies judgments—whether a character,
event, or concept is good or evil. Thus it is a work of ethics. One
of the most important of such ethical tasks, Santayana argues, is
confronting, understanding, and preventing suffering. Such, however, is a nearly impossible task of the human condition and inevitably runs into ambiguity. We still fall prostrate before the almighty
why of human suffering.

To search out possible answers, Frost exercises several important
poetic beliefs beyond his foundational notion of sound-sense, the
effort to capture the living rhythms of speech of living people.
Such beliefs enable him to set ethical issues in life, where, he believed, they originate and belong, rather than in the rationalism of
the Enlightenment or the abstraction of Romanticism.

Furthermore, like his fellow modernists Frost relied upon his
variation of imagism as a means for objectifying attitudes and beliefs. Imagism granted powerful freedom to modernist poets, since
it permitted them to suggest rather than declare. Frost's "The Sub-
verted Flower," for example, might be a poem *about* a flower, but
the poem itself provides an image that suggests a sexual act. By
using imagery, then, Frost can also suggest certain ethical implications of the poem. But also, by virtue of being couched in the
image those ethical implications are indeterminate. They are not
obscurantist—the reader has a sense of alternatives—but they are
ambiguous in the sense that two or more interpretations or values
are held in tension. In another pattern, evidenced in "Mending
Wall" for example, Frost may seem to suggest one view, but subtly
undercut it with irony. By so doing, Frost is the consummate ethical poet, forcing the reader to think through not only the words of
the poem, but also the sound-sense, imagery, and form in order to
shape his or her own conclusions.

An example of Frost's teasingly deliberate ambiguity appears in
the familiar "Design," first published in 1922 in *American Miscellany*
but drafted under the title "In White" in 1912.

I found a dimpled spider, fat and white,
On a white heal-all, holding up a moth
Like a white piece of rigid satin cloth—
Assorted characters of death and blight
Mixed ready to begin the morning right,
Like the ingredients of a witches' broth—
A snow-drop spider, a flower like a froth,
And dead wings carried like a paper kite.

What had that flower to do with being white,
The wayside blue and innocent heal-all?
What brought the kindred spider to that height,
Then steered the white moth thither in the night?
What but design of darkness to appall?—
If design govern in a thing so small.

The larger form of the poem is a Petrarchan sonnet, generally typified by setting forth a problem or tension in the octave, then resolving that problem or relieving the tension in the sestet. The octave may be further complicated by setting forth contradictory statements that complicate the problem in its two quatrains, or by intensifying the tension (as did Shakespeare in his sonnets) in the second quatrain. Frost chooses the latter pattern here.

At a superficial level the poem simply ponders an anomaly in nature. The normally blue heal-all flower is, in this case, white. Perhaps that is what attracted the white spider, as Frost suggests in the sestet. Whatever the case, a moth has been caught in the spider's web and hangs dead, with limp wings, in the morning light. Here Frost employs the tension already located in the Petrarchan form and intensifies it through imagery.

The sound-sense of the words and the resulting imagery of the objects contrast sharply with actual events. For example, in the first line we find the adjectives "dimpled," "fat," and "white," which evoke an altogether pleasant image, perhaps of a chubby baby, until the adjectives collide into the noun, "spider," an object that most people react to with a fair degree of scorn, if not abhorrence. The juxtaposition among objects continues: the white "heal-all" ironically holds up a "dead" moth, held rigidly like the satin cloth of a casket. Even the rhymes force together the juxtaposed meanings. The first quatrain ends with "blight," the second begins, oddly enough, with "right." What can be right in the midst of blight? It is the Job-like question of all humanity. It is also one

Frost worked through from the first draft in 1912 to publication. In "In White," as the poem was called in its early stages, none of the "baby" images are present. Attention focuses exclusively on the trick of nature, the singular aberration. But the added imagery makes the aberration abhorrent. The juxtaposition jars the reader precisely for the reason that the human imagery draws the reader into the uncertainty. The poem is to the reader as the web to the moth.

The second quatrain of the octave sharpens the opposing images, intensifying them with each line. Those things set to begin the morning right are now called a "witches' broth." Again, the spider bears the positive adjective "snow-drop"; the heal-all is like a "froth," bright and airy; the dead wings of the moth are like a "paper kite." Apart from the reality of events, the descriptions all bear a holiday quality—snow-drops, froth, a paper kite. The reality, however, is of a flower aberrantly changed, a spider weaving an unseen net of destruction, a moth rigidly dead.

The anomalies drive the poet to his own set of questions about the event. Three questions appear in the sestet that shape his pondering. Why the aberration in the flower? What led spider and moth to it? And, if there were a design behind this act, what could it be but a design of darkness?

Right there many traditional readings of the poem leave off— with the poet's bewilderment voiced in the questions. But two important parts are then missing. First, the third question asks whether it is a design of darkness to *appall*. Frost selects a powerful word here, as he moves from simple (but beautifully effective) images to ethical issues. If a design is revealed in this event, is it only a design of darkness to appall or horrify us? The consequence then is that life is completely random, and we too are thrown at the mercy of freakish events—life's sufferings and cruel trials—that horrify us with their pure randomness. That question of fear and trembling, however, is not the end of the poem, for the second important part is the last line, which is not a question at all but a reflective statement on the whole poem.

The statement, "If design govern in a thing so small," follows not only the question of the penultimate line but a dash, a punctuation device Frost used not so much to add additional information, but to issue a reflective comment on the foregoing matter. This also occurs in line 4 of the poem. The implied question in the final line, therefore, is reflective of the poem as a whole. Ethically, of course, it is an important question. If design inheres in these apparently minor events, then it lies also in both human and cosmic events (Frost's many poems on stars also have something to say about this). Conversely, however, if we are to claim that such an event as Frost just witnessed is mere happenstance, then that claim also has to extend to human and cosmic events. Ethical positions have to be woven whole; it is a fallacy in ethics to say that such and such is right and good in a certain place at a given time and nowhere else.

Not a few readers have seen in the poem an "argument from design"; that is, by observing design in creation one assumes a designer who creates. If one does so, however, the effects are similar—there is a designer of diabolical cunning who twists his design for his own unknown satisfaction, or there is a designer whose creation itself, for whatever reason, evidences its own aberrations apart from his design; or yet there is a designer who remains either unaware or unconcerned about events in his design. Because of such implications, David Perkins has argued that Frost himself is merely playing with the often bewildering possibilities, rather than working toward some definitive answer. The poem, for Perkins, is actually a parody of all such questions and attempted answers.[19]

But it is possible that Frost himself suggests something of an answer. Ironically, the reader has just observed how powerfully design can govern in a thing so small as a sonnet. The careful precision of this poet-designer, imposing order upon words and images, in itself displays a response to apparent disorder and an aesthetics of poetry. Poetry uncovers things, brings them forth to the reflective imagination, and prompts the reader in the sorts of issues implied in the poetic event. Such is not to say that the poet structures only one response for the reader. Indeed, for Frost with his belief in an ethics of ambiguity such would be an aesthetic flaw. Rather, his task is to uncover and order events for the reader in such a way that the reader must grapple with significations.

"Design" is far from the only poem of this order in Frost's canon. In fact, several of them, like "Mowing," for example, expressly signify the poetic craft, at once implying certain beliefs about poetic making and at once embodying those beliefs in the poem itself. It is here that Frost diverges from modernist traits in the early part of the century, and it is here also that we must return full circle to the initial premises of this chapter. Having seen a kinship between Frost's poetics and Santayana's aesthetics, and having established several initial ethical assumptions structured within that poetics, we are left with the question of Frost's own perception of his poetics in relation to the modernists. As it turns out, he was very much aware of a series of close distinctions.

FROST AND MODERNIST POETICS

The transition into modernism is most frequently linked to changes in formal technique, of which Frost was particularly well aware. But it was also an effort that sought a center of value and meaning in life and through art. In an age that seemed bereft of any normative, traditional guides to value, the task demanded a new spirit of artistic innovation. Even when, or especially when, those techniques became most abrasive and raw, the point was to jar the audience into questioning their present norms.

The task proved a formidable affair. As modernist authors soon realized, society is too immured in its own ease to listen. It may be fairly stated that, in an ironic sense, many modernist poets simply ascended the throne from which Reason once held sway. Their language was not that of common humanity; in fact, to penetrate their art at all often required enormous erudition. It was not altogether unlike a new poetic demagoguery, where the elite spoke with each other and the commoners just might overhear some truth in their utterances. Frost, on the other hand, wrote a far more democratic poetry. In effect, he took Whitman's ideals of a poetry for "the people"—an ideal Whitman seldom fulfilled—and made practical application of them.

Perhaps Frost's fullest statement about his contemporary modernist poets in this regard appears in a letter to his daughter Lesley, dated 1934, from *Family Letters* (pp. 160–64). Insisting that "Ezra Pound was the Prime Mover in the Movement and must always have the credit for what's in it," he then sets himself to defining several traits of modernism, each of which he finds personally distasteful.[20] Taken together, these traits set Frost's own poetics in opposition to modernist trends.

Not surprisingly, the first such indictment that Frost makes is that modernism forsakes rhyme and meter under the belief that these make the poet use too many words and subsidiary ideas. According to modernism, everything must be stripped back to the essential skeleton of the idea/image, necessitating a concomitant

linguistic stripping action. The premise violated Frost's own notion of sound-sense and his effort to grasp meaning in the patterns
of human speech. According to Robert Francis, for example, Frost
expressed disappointment with Marianne Moore because "She
gives nothing for the ear."[21] For Frost, the euphony of rhyme and
meter conveyed meaning "for the ear."

The second, and close corollary, trait that Frost observes in modernism is the sacrifice of outer form for "Inner Form." By outer
form, Frost points to the singular integrity of the individual poem,
that it focus upon one poetic event and develop that event as far as
possible within the formal and aesthetic limits of the poem. The
poem must be an organic whole. On the contrary, modernism deliberately undercut the organic wholeness of the work by fractur-
ing it into sharp splinters of idea and language.

In a fascinating essay on Gertrude Stein, "The Mother of Confusion," Claudia Roth Pierpont addresses the more radical side of
modernism in which ideas and art are flung like a slap in the face
against conventional norms. One recalls Stein's famous comment,
"They needn't be so afraid of their damn culture. It'd take more
than a man like me to hurt it." But above all, Stein's work was subversive, set to topple the received aesthetic notions of her time.
When she set out to subvert something, moreover, it was like a de-
molition crew planting explosives in a Chicago housing project.
Pierpont assesses Stein: "Before James Joyce (as she volubly insisted all her life), before Dada or Surrealism, before Bloomsbury
or the roman-flueve, Gertrude Stein was writing books and stories
that were formally fractured, emotionally inscrutable, and, above
all, dauntingly unreadable."[22] Precisely such fractured form Frost
abhorred.

The third characteristic by which Frost indicts modernism in his
letter is that imagery takes on such prominence that the "connective tissue" among images is forsaken. In effect, Frost uncovers the
code of the Symbolist in which the symbol is sufficient meaning in
and of itself. In his *The Pastoral Art of Robert Frost*, John F. Lynen
finds some resemblances between Frost and the modernists in
their shared effort to confront concrete reality after the collapse of
the Enlightenment's intellectual abstraction. But so too the Romantics, as we observed, simply substituted an equally abstract, divine, moral agency in nature that couldn't hold its own against the
rising tide of scientism at the end of the nineteenth century. Sym-

bolism, then, seeks a representation that transcends time and thereby retains a self-inclusive meaning.

In modernism, however, symbolism often becomes an end in itself, unrelated to the past or to the present as anything beyond a moment, and impervious to thoughts of the future. Such a view of art was decidedly uncongenial to Frost, whose poems as much as anything demonstrated the enduring impact of the past upon the present. Moreover, as is the aim of this study to uncover, that impact, and the choices people make in relation to it, determines values that guide humanity on its course into the future. When Frost engages his regional stories, as Lynen has pointed out, it is not an effort to escape past or present but to settle conflicts of time periods, of urban versus rural cultures, and of choices that mark moral judgment. Consequently, imagism as an end in itself is merely inadequate for Frost. It needs the "connective tissue" of story, artistry, setting, and ethics to prove its worth.

Frost finds modernism, fourth, self-contained rather than communicative. The modernist poem becomes a work of "intimation, implication, insinuation, and innuendo as an object in itself." The text is, to play with a modernist critical term that would have had no meaning to Frost, self-deconstructive. It becomes obscurantist "as an object in itself." The most dramatic difference between Frost and the modernists may lie in that very phrase. Rather than letting ambiguity coil in upon itself, Frost wanted ambiguity in his poems to point somewhere—and designed them to do so. The *work* of ambiguity ties directly to his ethics, forcing the reader (and poet) to choices that determine ethical values.

The fifth item Frost dislikes in modernism may be described as a certain artifice in language and a maze of allusions—the latter something for which he had particularly little patience. It makes poetry a bit too much of an intellectual game: "They quote and you try to see if you can place the quotation." Although Frost appreciated the learning of such poets, he believed it appeared as something of an intellectual parlor game in their art, and he clearly rejected it in his own effort to speak the sound-sense of the common person.

In ethical thought, such traits that Frost ascribes to the modernists, not all of them fairly, represent a closed system. The work circles inward, both in idea and form. Imagery flattens experience rather than supplying liberating metaphors. Free verse denies human patterns of sound-sense. The formal and subjective inwardness of such work produces a self-confining ethics that shuts one off from both spiritual probing and human relationships. As we see in the following chapter, Frost's effort was to turn human seeking outward again, through structured ambiguity in the poem, to an exploration of ethical relationships with the divine and humanity.

2

Personal Ambiguities: Suspended Action

"CHOOSE SOMETHING LIKE A STAR," A POEM TO BE DISCUSSED IN detail later in this study, suggests a pattern for human action in the frenzy of this modern world. Its message of steadfastness provides a lesson in ethical character, particularly in such traits as love, compassion, and mercy. The ethical actions are complicated, however, when the narrator remains inherently uncertain of his or her own position relative to a given circumstance. In nearly all such works, Frost leaves the poem in a fairly tense ambiguity, relying upon the larger metaphor of the poem and its formal structure to suggest alternatives.

POETIC THEORY

In such works as we will examine in this chapter—those in which ethical choice is held in suspension, is ambiguous, or is simply avoided—Frost situates the I-speaker in the poem in such a way that it refers not just to the narrator, nor to Frost only, even if the settings are part of his concrete experience, but also to the reader. Thereby the reader—the adoptive I—engages the poem and is led to the tensions of the ambiguities. This can be traced in part to the modernist technique of objectifying experience for the reader to participate in it. The method also agrees with the modernist abhorrence of didacticism or the hortatory. For Frost, however, additional reasons apply. One part of Frost's reasoning may be seen in his "Letter to *The Amherst Student*," where he insists upon artistic form as a means for imposing order upon a chaotic world. "When in doubt there is always form for us to go on with," he asserts. Even that seemingly straightforward assertion opens a world of implications. In personal doubt form will see us through? In moments of doubt our artistry, our craftsmanship, and form will clarify? The answer is yes, because the artistic order we make out of the chaos about us is also an assertion of self against that chaos.

If we understand form in Frost's work functioning in those ways, we can also see the organicism of his poetry, noting the way form and content marry in the experience of the poem. Discussion of technical meter and verse form help us understand Frost here. He was, after all, an extremely deliberate and skilled craftsman. Yet, however helpful that is—especially as it allies with the ethical struggle to penetrate the chaos—there appears to be yet a broader pattern at work. Not just the artistic *components* of the poem, but the poem as metaphor itself, replaying an experience in the reader's mind, is the ethical action of the aesthetic work. Many pages discussing Frost's use of metaphor have been written; in this case, however, it might be most profitable to limit the discussion to two of Frost's works, one prose and the other poetic.

In "The Constant Symbol," part wry humor, part sly denigration, and for the most part simply wise, Frost emphasizes form as a whole in and of itself. The poem itself is a metaphor: "Every new poem is a metaphor inside or it is nothing" (*Selected Prose* 24). After an illuminating discussion of how the poet uses the tools of the discipline (metrics, rhythm, and rhyme) to shape that "form," Frost creates his own famous metaphor to summarize the poetic task: "The mind is a baby giant who, more provident in the cradle than he knows, has hurled his paths in life all round ahead of him like playthings given" (*Selected Prose* 28).

That sentence itself, like a well-crafted poem, calls for explication. The mind is indeed a giant; this is assumed. It is, however, like a baby giant, at once playful and willful. It hurls its own ways, ideas, paths in life out ahead of it like an infant hurling toys out of its playpen. But here this baby giant hurling paths in the world of poetry uses the playthings given, the tools of poetic craft. As the baby giant tosses these out into the world, finding its path, the course will necessarily be zigzag, what Frost calls a "straight crookedness." That is sufficient to find the "general direction." So too the poetic work of this baby giant, by metaphor and indirection, will lead a reader on zigzag paths of straight crookedness. It cannot, however, give the reader the precise route or the precise destination. That is not the task of poetry. The task is to give a general direction, and then to let the reader search it out as he or she will.

This fundamental theory of Frost, which can be amplified many times by consideration of other essays and the letters, also shapes the organic development of his art.

An example in which the poem itself is metaphor for its meaning appears in "The Silken Tent," a brilliantly executed work of poetics. In one fourteen-line sentence, shaped to the form of a Shakespearean sonnet, Frost develops his metaphor of the tent. The opening "She" is purposefully ambiguous, unnamed. A loved one? A spouse? The reader enters the poem with the first word, placing a name on the "She." But every word thereafter is specifically concrete, detailing the image of the tent linked to the "She" by virtue of the simile. At one specific point, line 7, the poet steps outside of the concrete description and points toward its abstract meaning. Of the "central cedar pole" he writes, "That is its pinnacle to heavenward / And signifies the sureness of the soul." The poem is so arranged that this is also a tent the reader may crawl into and live in.

In his essay "Robert Frost and the Motives of Poetry," Mark Richardson describes the beauty of the work:

> "The Silken Tent" strikingly illustrates its idea of freedom-in-bondage by the way Frost sets the single, finely modulated sentence that composes it so comfortably into the strictly answered form of a Shakespearian sonnet. Hardly a "bond" of meter, rhyme, or stanza goes unfulfilled, though in the sonnet form these "silken ties" are especially arresting. And yet in reading "The Silken Tent" we are never "of the slightest bondage made aware."[1]

Here the case is not just that the tent is a metaphor for a love relationship, but that the fluidity, melody, and delicate beauty of the poem shape a further metaphor for the tent itself. The objective correlation between tent and love is amplified—or canopied—by that between poem as artistic work and the tent.

POEM AS METAPHOR

Perhaps the best known work that exemplifies this forceful metaphorical power is "Mowing" from *A Boy's Will*. Certainly it was a poem for which Frost himself had a particular appreciation. In a 17 July 1913 letter to Thomas Mosher, Frost wrote, "In Mowing, for instance, I come so near what I long to get that I almost despair of coming nearer" (*Selected Letters* 83). Later in the letter, in a discussion of Pound's increasing possessiveness of Frost's reputation, Frost makes clearer what constitutes that goal that he longs to get: "At least I am sure I can count on you to give me credit for knowing what I am about. You are not going to make the mistake that Pound makes of assuming that my simplicity is that of the untutored child. I am not undesigning" (*Selected Letters* 84). Indeed not, for with careful study "Mowing" reveals intricate design and carefully structured suggestiveness through an apparently simple event. We see here how early in Frost's career he was already charting a course for the poem that moved in several zigzag directions, each course amplifying the metaphor:

> There was never a sound beside the wood but one,
> And that was my long scythe whispering to the ground.
> What was it it whispered? I know not well myself;
> Perhaps it was something about the heat of the sun,
> Something, perhaps, about the lack of sound—
> And what was why it whispered and did not speak.
> It was no dream of the gift of idle hours,
> Or easy gold at the hand of fay or elf:
> Anything more than the truth would have seemed too weak
> To the earnest love that laid the swail in rows,
> Not without feeble-pointed spikes of flowers
> (Pale orchises), and scared a bright green snake.
> The fact is the sweetest dream that labor knows.
> My long scythe whispered and left the hay to make.

"Mowing" has been read with many sublevel layers of meaning. Jay Parini observes that "Frost would have been aware that "mowing" was also a traditional euphemism for lovemaking, thus giving a distinctly erotic echo to the last phrase: "and left the hay to make."[2] Katherine Kearns has discussed the poem in sexual terms, observing that "it cannot be entirely accidental that Frost chose the spiked orchis (*órchis* is the Greek word for 'testicle'). . . ."[3] Robert Faggen contrasts the reproductive power of the orchids with the solitary nature of the mower.[4]

The poem itself, as in "After Apple-Picking," is a reflection of a laborer on a hard day's work. Yet, the message given in the octave belongs entirely to the scythe. The laborer ponders in the first two lines what the scythe might be saying as it whispers in its swing over the ground. When he asks, "What was it it whispered?" the laborer is opening the poem to the reader's speculation as well. As in

"Mending Wall," where the narrator playfully suggests that elves knocked the stones loose, Frost invites the reader to see elves at play in this poem. Admitting that he doesn't know the language of the scythe, the narrator here can only speculate on some of the things it might be saying.

To understand those things, we have to understand something of the location of the poem. The laborer has been working a patch of swale, a low-lying, almost marshy stretch of ground that would bog down farm machinery. Because of its dampness, however, it grows sweet hay, far too good to let rot. The laborer goes at it with a scythe, the familiar implement with a long, curved, one-edged blade and a long handle with a handgrip about midway down. The scythe can be a difficult instrument to use. One can't hack or jab with it. It has to be swung in a long, smooth movement using the shoulders and upper arms rather than the wrists and hands. Moreover, it is physically punishing labor. If the laborer here is going into the swale, then, it is not as some lark to appreciate all the beauty nature holds.

Therefore, the scythe first whispers about the heat of the sun. The laborer sweats hard, working with this implement. More mysteriously, it whispers about the absence of sound. A profound quiet that lets the mower hear the scythe at all settles over the swale. The swale itself could generally be found in those odd, out-of-the-way places in the pasture, and if he can't use any farm machinery here, he is far from any other sound. The third suggestion is the intensity of the labor. The "easy gold" figuratively evokes the treasure left by "fay or elf," but literally evokes the dried hay after curing. Only by hard effort is the product achieved.

Formally, it may be argued that "Mowing" is cast in the form of a Shakespearean sonnet, typified by three quatrains of a steadily intensifying image or occasion, with an end couplet providing resolution. One does indeed find this pattern of transitional imagery and event through each quatrain. More properly, however, the sonnet is Petrarchan in form, embodying a conflict or event in the octave and then responding to or resolving it in the sestet. The colon following line eight divides the poem between event and reflection. It is not improbable, however, that Frost deliberately fused elements of each form in the poem.

Read as a Shakespearean sonnet, lines 9–12 do indeed intensify the foregoing passage. Opposed to the "easy gold," the narrator insists upon the truth of his hard labor. Nonetheless, two qualifications appear here. First, he engages the work with an "earnest love." He is not one to shirk the grueling labor; he wants to do the job right. Second, that labor is not without its own serendipitous rewards. As the scythe swings down almost level with the ground (of course he doesn't want to hit the ground), the laborer is startled by two surprises that seem to reward his earnest love. He uncovers a low-growing patch of pale orchises (a favorite flower of Frost). Their spikes are "feeble-pointed" for having grown in the shade of the taller swale grass, but arresting nonetheless. Similarly, the swish of the scythe startles a brightly colored snake (contrasted to the "pale orchises") that darts away. These constitute nature's bestowal of surprise and reward upon the laborer's earnest love.

Read as a Petrarchan sonnet, these same lines shape the transition to the sestet. The "truth" is the important issue in the sestet, responding to the questioning uncertainty of the octave. However, the last two lines—although clearly in the rhyme scheme of a Petrarchan sonnet—close off the poem in two sentences that circle back through the poem in Shakespearean fashion. The claim that the "fact is the sweetest dream that labor knows" refers to the concrete account of his labor in the preceding quatrain. The fact for the laborer is getting the work done, an act that supersedes reflection and speculation. Without the "sweet dream" of a finished product, all he would have is idle speculation. In a sense, this line also redirects us to the intense labor of the worker in the heat. But that portrait marries to the more imaginative one, for the last line of the poem returns us to the suggestive whispering of the scythe that started the entire speculation. The closing lines intertwine the hard labor and the suggestiveness that play throughout the poem.

Such details of the larger architecture of the poem are abetted by many subtle internal patterns. In *Toward Robert Frost*, Judith Oster has provided a comprehensive and thoroughly convincing analysis of these patterns (see pp. 64–66), but one of them might bear emphasis here. The poem doesn't merely evoke the scythe's whispering by evocative description, it also mimics its action by the alliteration of "s" sounds in the six lines. The lines themselves, in the epitome of sound-sense, whisper to the reader. The reader is listening carefully, hardly aware of being drawn into the conversation. The most dramatic changes in sound occur in lines 7–8, where the tone shifts to the declarative statement, "It was no. . . ." In line 9, however, where the sestet is initiated in the Petrarchan form, the tone reverts to wistful, reflective tones, as the "s" sounds once again whisper in the poem. There is in such patterns (and also the intensive use of "w" sounds) what Oster calls "something loving and private between this scythe and this field."[5]

But one might also suggest that "something loving and private" occurs between the poet and the work; indeed, that scythe and field are very much a metaphor of such. The intricate design of the stanza form also hints at the fact that the poem itself functions as metaphor. In that metaphor lies the deliberate ambiguity that snares the reader, for the metaphor itself is about poetry. In an exquisite twist, Frost supplies a metacommentary on poetics in the poem.

The clues accumulate in rapid succession. In the first two lines Frost adroitly furnishes the image of the solitary writer with the pen (scythe) whispering over the page. He himself seems lost in the act of writing, unable to say exactly what the pen whispers. That is precisely the point: different readers will hear differing messages. The task of the poet is to suggest, to whisper, rather than to overtly—and didactically—declaim. Nonetheless, a part of that whispering will arise from and be shaped by the concrete experience of this laborer-poet. Here too Frost announces that the work of poetry is neither dream nor gift. The poet doesn't wait for the gift of the poem to drop into his or her lap while in idle reflection—that is easy gold. Here again Frost disabuses us of the romantic notion of poetry. The labor is consuming.

Earnest love of the poetic task lays the "swale in rows." Concretely, the figure applies to the cut hay being raked into windrows for drying. Left unraked on the swale it would merely rot. It has to be given over to some other power. Metaphorically, the figure suggests the poem itself, concrete experience and figurative suggestiveness laid out in the rows of the poem.

Lest the process seem too mechanical (he is, after all, working with the whispering scythe and not farm machinery), Frost quickly appends a qualification on the labor of laying the poem in rows. Even in the act of writing, demanding immense concentration, surprises may suddenly appear out of the deeper places of the poet's mind and make their appearance on the page. It may be the glimpse of glory in a pale orchid; it may be the startled sprint of a green snake. When such surprises come, the poet hails them, allowing those too to become a part of the work.

Yet, as we turn to the last two lines, the poet acknowledges once again that the "sweetest dream" that his poetic labor knows is the fact. Here fact does not refer to the concrete experience that gave rise to the poem. The "fact" is the finished artistic work. The task of the laborer is to cut the hay; that of the poet to lay straight the rows in which experience and metaphor conjoin in the "truth." If the poet is done with the work in line 13, however, the work itself is not done. The last line deftly combines the concrete and metaphorical. The laborer finishes his labor and leaves "the hay to make." This is an intriguing phrase. Concretely, it suggests the fact that hay has to be raked into loose windrows for three days while the wind and sun dry it prior to baling. Commonly, the farmer would speak of this as "curing," or "drying" the hay. It may be that there was a colloquialism indigenous to New England at the turn of the century that used "left the hay to make." Nonetheless, it seems a very odd term, one almost executed to draw attention to itself. But consider it from the metaphorical stance of the poem. The Greek root (poietes) of our modern English word *poetry* literally means *maker*, or in its verb form *to make*. Reading the colloquialism with this in mind, the conclusion of this poem, as much about writing poetry as about mowing hay, points several ways. If the whole poem works together as metaphor, we see that the poet emphatically denies overt declaration. The poet's task is to whisper and suggest. This stance inevitably calls for a certain dangerous relinquishment of the poem to the reader. The reader "makes" the poem as he or she enters into it and appropriates from it. Indeed, "The Last Mowing" from *West-Running Brook* suggests that whole meadows should be given up to flowers in what Sheldon Liebman calls "occasions for communions with those who are either present to share in the tumultuousness of flowers, or, though absent, nevertheless able to send 'a message from the dawn' and induce a feeling of brotherhood" (419).[6] On such occasions, the poem becomes the reader's poem, to make of as he or she likes. If the poem is successful, the reader stores the hay the poet has cut.

In the same volume, *A Boy's Will*, "The Tuft of Flowers" appears as a companion piece to "Mowing" (one might also include "A Late Walk"). In "The Tuft of Flowers" the narrator wanders across a field that another laborer has already cut. In a way, he is like the reader of "Mowing," wondering what to make of it all. The mower has moved to another field; the narrator stands alone. The formal pattern of the poem abets the action. Each rhymed couplet in the forty-line poem provides a glimpse of the field or the narrator's reflection upon it. The predominant foot (although as elsewhere

Frost will deviate for sound-sense) is iambic, providing also a reflective, quiet tone to the poem. The third stanza positions the narrator: "I looked for him behind an isle of trees; / I listened for his
whetstone on the breezes." The narrator has opened his own
senses, looking and listening, in a reflective moment on the action
of "Mowing." Doing so, he is led to the "tall tuft of flowers beside
a brook." The narrator stands in this poem much as the reader
does in "Mowing," letting his own sensory imagination enter into
and participate in the scene. The narrator perceives a message
from the flowers of how the mower carefully avoided them, and by
so doing he feels a greater kinship with the laborer who is nowhere
near. The narrator claims that he can "hear his long scythe whispering to the ground," the nearly identical line from "Mowing."
Most importantly, however, the narrator begins to feel a kinship of
spirit. He has begun "to make" the poem.

"Mowing" and "The Tuft of Flowers" reveal much about Frost's
poetics. He crafts the poem in such a way that the concrete work
can also be a metaphorical work. But, ever wary of didacticism, he
gives the poem over to the reader "to make." Inevitably, the
method will evoke a sense of ambiguity. Instead of merely inquir-
ing "What does the poet mean here?" Frost places us in the position of asking "What do the poet and I mean here?" That
combined experience—both that meeting between poet and
reader and also that of concrete event and the poem as metaphor—is also exemplified well in "The Oven Bird."

The concrete setting of the poem is intensely specific, emphasizing auditory and visual experience.

> There is a singer everyone has heard,
> Loud, a mid-summer and a mid-wood bird,
> Who makes the solid tree trunks sound again.
> He says that leaves are old and that for flowers
> Mid-summer is to spring as one to ten.
> He says the early petal-fall is past
> When pear and cherry bloom went down in showers
> On sunny days a moment overcast;
> And comes that other fall we name the fall.
> He says the highway dust is over all.
> The bird would cease and be as other birds
> But that he knows in singing not to sing.
> The question that he frames in all but words
> Is what to make of a diminished thing.

The setting is mid-summer, poised between the fullness of spring and the dying down of autumn. In this forest setting the central character is the oven bird, so named because it builds a small, dome-shaped nest resembling an oven. The oven bird itself is a rather small (sparrow size) warbler, which, because it lives deep in the forest, is seldom seen. Its powerful song, however, can carry for a remarkable distance. The distinguishing characteristic of the song is a rapid repetition of teach'er, teach'er rising to a crescendo. In some areas the call appears as a monosyllable variant: TEACH, TEACH, TEACH.[7]

On the level of concrete experience, Frost makes several straightforward claims for the bird. It is, first, a common sound, not some mysterious or exotic entry in New England. Furthermore, it is very loud. By some estimates the song of the oven bird can be heard as much as a quarter mile away—a small bird with a powerful call. Third, the bird is most active during this mid-summer session, but, wary of humans, remains reclusively hidden in the woods. As if to trip the reader's imagination, Frost reiterates the power of the call echoing against the forest tree trunks.

The tripping action is appropriate, for a dramatic shift occurs in line 4. Lines 4, 6, and 10 open with "He says," the "he" referring to the bird. But the bird doesn't say anything at all; his call remains simply "Teacher." Lines 4 to the end of the poem occur wholly in the mind of the perceiver, as he creates metaphor from the concrete setting.

These speculations are his. The perceiver is aware of time passing in a reflective way of which the bird is not capable. The perceiver sees that the leaves are, at this mid-summer season, turning old, and that summer flowers pale compared to the fresh beauty of Spring. The second speculation follows tightly upon the memory of spring flowers, for they recall the showers of cherry and pear blossoms. They fell quickly, a brief shower of petals on a day incongruously bright and sunny. Indeed, the reflection on time's passing leads to reflection on all things passing. Thinking of the fall (Autumn) he thinks also of the Edenic fall, where creation first knew death. For a moment the poem nearly suggests the devolution of "I Will Sing You One-O," but the third "He says" redirects the perceiver to the immediate concrete scene. What could be more physical than highway dust over everything? I do not see this as a symbol of decay, necessarily, but merely a sign of the physicality the narrator perceives as he leaves his own reflections to a parting reflection on the bird itself. He has been instructed by this "Teacher" to be sure, but it has not been by anything the bird has said. The bird's singing has sparked the lessons this pupil has learned on his own.

It might be said that every poem is ultimately a poem about writing poetry. The manifestation of idea in a form is itself a new and never repeated enterprise each time. This is no less true for Frost. While it would be a violation of his artistry to force a poetics reading on every poem, one need not read long in his work to find those points where form, metaphor, and idea coalesce in such a way as to suggest certain things about the act of writing poetry. As is the case with "Mowing," "The Oven Bird" also is such a poem. The concluding four lines in particular suggest this, but from the outset there are clues similar to those given in "Mowing." The bird, for example, is the creator of the song; the listener, however, perceives his or her own meaning in that song. The hints are indeed given by the physical setting in which the song occurs—both in the natural setting and the way the poem is "set."

The last four lines, moreover, create a more specific metaphor. The oven bird would simply be one more bird—among all other birds—except that "he knows in singing not to sing." That is to say, the oven bird's "Teacher" is suggestive rather than overt or merely ordinary. The suggestiveness of its singing ("in all but words") is "what to make of a diminished thing." The diminished thing provides the tantalizing ambiguity of the poem. To what does *thing* refer? Is it the passage of the seasons, as the perceiver has heard it? Is it the diminishment of humanity since the Edenic fall, as some have argued? Or, indeed, could it be the diminished thing of this small, sharply crafted sonnet? The last option bears special attention when we consider that the oven bird's "singing not to sing" of line 12 parallels the poet's task also as Frost sees it. For him the challenge in the metaphor that is the poem is to sing in such a way that others participate. Metaphor shapes the words or lessons in exactly the same way that the perceiver of this poem does upon hearing the bird's song. Whether by listening to the whisper of the scythe or the song of the bird, the poet engages the perceiver in such a way—through suggestive metaphor and subtle ambiguity rather than overt declaration—that the reader participates in the making and meaning of the work.

Numerous other poems in Frost's canon function in this way. The poet deliberately crafts the poem with metaphorical ambiguity and sufficient openings in form to allow the reader access to the meaning and significance of the work. It may be called a gracious artistry, and as Frost developed it over the early part of his career it stood starkly at odds with those parts of modernist art (the use of foreign languages, the cryptic line, the obscurantism) that Frost loathed. Indeed, it would not be difficult—and perhaps not wrong—to see this as an ethical act by the author. By allowing readers to make choices, he gives much of the poem up to them. So many of his best known poems participate in the pattern, that only a brief reference to several of them is necessary to confirm the nature of the pattern in Frost's work.

In the same way that "Mowing" and "The Oven Bird" may metaphorically be seen as poems about poetry, so too the well-known "Birches," written in 1913–14 while Frost was living in England, bears a degree of this pattern. The sixty-line poem divides into three equal parts, each commenting on or responding to the others. The first twenty lines of the poem detail the physical, natural scene as the narrator perceives it after the ice storm. The description is rich in imagery, bringing the fact of the ice storm to an uncanny degree of life. The familiar images—ice glittering under the sun like the fallen dome of heaven, the bowed ferns like girls with their hair flung forward—place the reader on the scene with a powerful immediacy. We aren't just told *about* the storm; we are placed in its aftermath.

Line 21 breaks in with a jolting transition, however: "But I was going to say when Truth broke in." What was he going to say? And what is Truth? And why is it capitalized here? The Truth is where the poem starts, in the actual, concrete reality (one thinks again of "Mowing"). The bent trees evoke another fanciful world in the poet's mind, but his responsibility as poet is to place the reader on the scene that evoked the fancy. Then the reader may participate as he or she wishes. But for the poet to simply jump into the fantasy world—that is, the metaphor of the poem—without establishing the concrete reality would be, in Frost's view, self-interested. The Truth is the necessary "matter of fact" that roots the poem in reality.

The transition into the evocative fantasy continues the rich imagery in the pattern of an isolated country boy entertaining himself by swinging birches. Even though it is a seemingly carefree evocation, the boy climbs carefully, like filling a cup to its brim. The freedom lies in the great leap back to earth. So it is in the third section, the reflection upon the fantasy world, that we discover the intensely personal side to the poem. The poet himself, we learn, was once such a swinger of birches. Lessons from that time still prevail. At certain times, when he is weary of "considerations"—not the major disruptions in life but the accumulation of endless detail—he wishes he could still be a swinger of birches, to simply get away from it all for a while. At such times when life is like a "pathless wood," and one has taken a few blows trying to find one's way back home, to recapture the freedom of swinging seems a pure delight. But this is precisely what poetry can do. Poetry allows one "to get away from earth awhile / And then come back to it and start over." The key thought here is not the escape but the return. In the following line the poet affirms that "Earth's the right place for love"; he wants to go *toward* heaven but return to earth.

The poem, therefore, provides not a rhythm of escape but of engagement. That too is precisely one of the aims of Frost's poetics. As in "Mowing" and "The Oven Bird," we see in "Birches" the pattern where Frost creates the concrete setting, trips the reader by metaphor, and thereby engenders personal reflection. Perhaps the notable difference in "Birches" is that the narrator claims the reflection personally, but the loaded phrases about earth being the right place for love, about climbing toward heaven, and such others clearly call the reader into the reflection also. They are sufficiently ambiguous—Why return to earth? Why not escape?—that the reader participates in locating answers.[8]

PERSONAL AMBIGUITY

The foregoing poems demonstrate the way in which Frost uses ambiguity through metaphor as a poetic device to engage the reader and to invite him or her to participate in the poem's making and meaning. Thereby he achieves an aesthetic virtue of suggestiveness rather than didacticism. But what do we make of those poems in which the ambiguity is not triggered by the physical reality and narrator's reflection upon it, but is inherent in the scene and narrator themselves? It is the difference between proposing alternative choices for the reader or pondering whether there are any choices at all. For example, the grimly ironic "Fire and Ice" appears superficially a light-hearted reflection with its repetition of what "Some say." For some the fire of desire is sufficient to crisp the world; for some the bitter hatred of ice serves to shut it down. The almost flippant line that ice (hate) "Is also great," bears down like the stroke of an ax. The final line that either fire or ice would suffice bears a forlorn tone, not one giving options but one lamenting the inevitable. The same tone appears in "Nothing Gold Can Stay," also from the *New Hampshire* volume. Like the first green of nature itself, all nature sinks resolutely to an ending. The final grim tone of the poem allies it more closely with "I Will Sing You One-O" than does the open speculation of humanity's demise in "The Oven Bird." In the latter poem, the message is one deduced from the setting by narrator and reader working in concert. In "Nothing Gold Can Stay" it is an essential ambiguity of setting itself, abetted by the narrator's commentary on what he sees there.

This pattern of internal ambiguity occurs most intensely in several of those poems that are most personal. In these poems, the narrator is in the scene, a part of it, to such an extent that we might term these occasions as the ambiguity of anxiety. No answers seem clear; in fact, no choices seem apparent. Those stimulating alternatives that appear in the foregoing poems as suggestions buried in scene and speech now seem simply hidden. In his study "Civility and Madness in Robert Frost's 'Snow,' " Walter Jost employs some premises from Ludwig Wittgenstein's philosophy of speech in order to engage "Snow" in a sustained and careful analysis. The following from Wittgenstein, Jost argues, applies particularly well to the "paradox" of Frost's rhetorical hiddenness: " 'The aspect of things that are most important for us are hidden because of their simplicity and familiarity. (One is unable to notice something— because it is always before one's eyes.)' "[9] Such a "hiddenness" Frost employs, for example, in "Mowing." He reveals something that has always been right under our eyes. In such works, as Jost points out, "We know in general that . . . Frost playfully winks at us on a good deal."[10] The wink is not playful, however, when the narrator peers hard into the uncertainty and finds little or nothing to go by.

Perhaps the clearest evidence of this darker view appears in "Acquainted With the Night," first published in *The Virginia Quarterly* in 1928 and collected in *West-Running Brook*, certainly one of Frost's most troubling and puzzling volumes. In its initial printing the volume was divided into six sections. The second section, which includes "Acquainted With the Night," bears the title *Fiat Nox*—"Let there be night," an ironic twist on the Vulgate *Fiat Lux*,

"Let there be light." The tenor of the poems in this section is indeed night-like, the poems themselves filled with rage, terror, and loneliness. The lead poem in the section, "Once by the Pacific," envisions a "night of dark intent" coming. The violence of the Pacific storm becomes metaphoric in the concluding couplet as the narrator thinks of God's rage unleashed in the command: "Put out the light." Darkness and terror mingle throughout the poems. The harsh little poem "Lodged" personifies rain and wind deliberately smashing a flower bed, to which the narrator observes, "I know how the flowers felt." A storm of pessimism rages in him also. "Bereft," similarly, is a dark, storm poem. The narrator stands on a sagging porch, the autumn wind pummeling him, his eyes watching a bank of storm clouds moving in from the west. The imagery turns sinister. Coiled leaves hiss at him; the porch sags as if to suggest the unsteadiness of his support. He imagines that the threat has turned directly at him because the secret of his abject loneliness is out. The last line, "I had no one left but God," is so indeterminate that it simply exacerbates the loneliness. While some may understand the line as the overt proclamation of God as his last bulwark against darkness, it seems better understood as a bitter curse flung, Lear-like, at the stormy heavens. Those heavens are vacant of all but rage and darkness.

In "Acquainted With the Night," the darkness shutters down with impenetrable thickness. Here the narrator confesses that he can't understand the experience of sorrow and loneliness; he can only acknowledge it. He does so by utilizing four primary images in the mode of T. S. Eliot's "objective correlative." More keenly than in any other poem of Frost, the image correlates to the mood or state of being of the speaker. The first of these is the unrelenting rain. The previous poems capture an impending storm. Here the rain is steady, as flat and unrelenting as the narrator's spirit. Moreover, he has not been able to outwalk it. Out past the city, back into it—he can't escape the mood that leaves him desolately lonely in this night hour.

The second image is the sad lane, identified as the saddest of the city. The lane is vacant as he traipses along it, except for one other solitary figure—the watchman. Literally the figure is simply a patrol officer walking his beat, ironically as circular and lonely as that of the narrator. The watchman, however, "watches over" the people on his beat. He ensures their safety and well-being. As the narrator passes by him, he drops his eyes. How can he explain this disturbing inner malady, and what could the watchman do about it should he try?

In the context of the third image—the cry—the narrator stands still and stops "the sound of feet." The sound of feet are his own, but what arrests him is this momentary, disembodied sense of human contact. It is only one cry, short and interrupted, but then the narrator understands how distant it actually is. It originates from some entirely different street, lifting momentarily over the housetops. If anything, the cry accentuates his own isolation from humanity.

The poem moves from the cry to the final image—the clock—in the fourth stanza. Realizing that the cry was not for him, the narrator keeps his gaze directed toward the sky. There, at an "unearthly height," he spots an illuminated clock against the dark sky.[11] This clock, however, provides no satisfaction, direction, or renewal for the narrator. Indeed, he announces in the penultimate line that the clock "Proclaimed the time was neither wrong nor right." The clock, the only image of light in the poem, is wholly ambivalent in its connection to the narrator. The feeling of dark terror resides within himself, seemingly ineradicable, but also in the age. In his *Robert Frost: A Life*, Jay Parini convincingly argues that the descent into darkness is shaped by the form as much as the metaphor: "Although a sonnet by form, with a closing couplet, the poem has the fluid, repetitive aspect of a villanelle, with the three-line stanzas mimicking the terza rima of Dante—appropriate for a poem about the descent into darkness."[12]

The narrator's conclusion in the last line is about his own state of being, the recognition of which the images have only startled to awareness. What he is aware of is a haunting uncertainty, mirrored by the couplet falling tensely after the tercets. The narrator admits, "I have been one acquainted with the night." What a reader finds peculiar in that structure is the use of the past perfect tense. Does it imply that he is not now? Or does it imply that this darkness, just now firmly discovered, has always been within him? If one recalls Frost's enduring fondness for Emerson, one may well find a link here to Emerson's comment in *Fate*: " 'Tis the best use of Fate to teach a fatal courage." The fatal courage here admits to the reality of the narrator's state of being. The poem ends in a withholding of commitment because no clear course can be seen. The state of the narrator is presented as unalterable fact.

This pattern of intense inwardness, a sense of being trapped in a desolate self, occurs again in Frost's subsequent volume, *A Further Range* (1936). The volume is also divided into six sections. In the second of these, "Taken Singly," appears a trio of poems amplifying the narrative loneliness and the consequent inability to make choices. Here the Emersonian Fate seems to blot out human intellect and freedom. Indeed, the time during which the poems of this volume were first published was a troubled one for Frost, a time when he might well have felt Fate's hand like a blind assault upon him. His daughter Marjorie died in childbirth on 2 May 1934. In that same year, Elinor, never well to begin with, suffered a major heart attack. There is little question that the bleakness of these poems incarnates the poet's bleakness.

Yet, the first of this triad of poems, "Lost in Heaven," presents an odd narrative ambivalence, part of which is incarnated in the very form of the poem. The poem consists of three quatrains, each of which poses a situation in the first two lines and responds to it in the second. The rhyme scheme—ABAB CDCD EFEF—threads the dialectical alternatives of the two-line sections together into a whole. Encountering dialectic in nature and in human nature interweaves.

In the first stanza, the opening two lines set the scene of a stormy, rainy night—so familiar in these poems of disconsolation. Suddenly, however, the clouds part momentarily. The narrator immediately looks upward, attempting to locate "old sky-marks." He describes his looking as "impatient," conveying the sense that he has both waited long and also that without the sky-marks he has felt loss and disquietude.

When he searches this rift in the clouds, however, the narrator discovers that he can locate nothing with certainty. The stars are random, not oriented to their larger constellations. In the second section of stanza 2, the narrator discovers that not one was "bright enough to identify." The heavenly signs remain veiled, and the narrator's probing gaze seems to reflect off the random stars back upon himself with "consternation." But here the peculiar twist of this poem appears. The narrator says that this consternation is "not ungrateful." Something in him welcomes the obscurity. It may be simply the pleasure of the storm; it may be the sense of abandonment.

The third stanza gives us some clues, but also more perplexity. Opening once again with an affirmation of his lostness (physical and metaphysical without the heavenly signs), he sighs a question.

But even that verb—*sighed* in the text—is ambivalent. Is it the sigh of resignation or acceptance? The same ambivalence, of course, appears in "The Road Not Taken," "I shall be telling this with a sigh. . . ." The narrator asks where "in Heaven" he is, then immediately states that he really doesn't want an answer. It is as if the indecisive nature of the heavens' response has rendered the narrator indecisive as well. The final pair of lines psychologically fuse the narrator with the clouds. As they open, so too he opens to speculation. Even if the speculation consists of the nature of paradoxes and leads to no firm conclusions, it does occur. Therefore, the narrator is content to beseech the clouds in the imprecatory last line to let his "heavenly lostness overwhelm" him. Although the poem maintains a strained ambivalence for the most part, it finishes in a tone of psychological abandonment. The difference in this poem from others is the casual, accepting tone the narrator adopts toward the fact. In other poems manifesting his ambiguity of anxiety and estrangement, the storm and darkness are something to be raged against; here they are accepted with an unnerving calm.

Not so in "Desert Places," where the objective correlative of the desolate winter landscape nearly matches the narrator's inner landscape. "Nearly matches" is the key point for the poem. However desolate the landscape, the narrator asserts that he does not fear it because his own "desert places" are more powerful. It is almost like villainy flung at villainy. But what is it that might frighten him in the poem? In the first two stanzas we have the familiar landscape of snow coming down so fast the narrator is disoriented by it. Realizing that nature's creatures have their own snug harbors in the snow, he is caught by loneliness "unawares." In the final two stanzas, the narrator compares that loneliness to the snow. With the snow falling ever faster, he observes that the loneliness of the landscape will only deepen. The blank whiteness of snow is the perfect embodiment of silence. It has nothing to express other than itself. Similarly, in the final stanza, the narrator has nothing other to express than what he is. The silence lives in him, not in the remote spaces of the universe but in the desert places of his own being.

The well-established link between "Desert Places" and Hawthorne's *The Scarlet Letter* emphasizes this internal, or "existential" if one wills, loneliness.[13] At the beginning of chapter 18 of *The Scarlet Letter*, the reader finds Hester "outlawed from society" to a "moral wilderness." Hawthorne describes that wilderness like this:

"Her intellect and heart had their home, as it were, in desert places, where she roamed as freely as the wild Indian in his woods." The close affinity of Hester's heart to the wilderness shapes her desert place. So too in Frost's poem, as the white blankness of snow snuffs old landmarks and leaves the narrator wandering in desert places.

The action of "Desert Places" with its glance at a vacant sky is echoed in "Afterflakes" of the same volume. Once again the narrator appears in a "teeming snowfall" when he sees the odd occurrence of his shadow on the ground. Immediately he looks skyward, "Where we still look to ask the why / Of everything below." Even as he turns, however, he is convinced that the dark shadow emanates from within him, as if the darkness of his own character had leaked out and lain on the ground. Looking skyward, however, he discovers that the sky has turned full blue, and the flakes now are simply gauzy crystals floating on air. The crux of the poem lies in what the narrator does *not* say. He does not say that the sun has illumined him or lifted his spirit. Rather, it has revealed him, like some startled prey, for what he is. As with "Desert Places," no illuminating sign directs the narrator; in fact, he prefers the lostness of storm and cloud.

The pattern, while most intense perhaps in "Taken Singly" of *A Further Range*, whispers throughout the volume. In "Leaves Compared with Flowers" the narrator discovers that the nighttime darkness of leaves is better suited than flowers to his "darker mood." "Not All There" from the "Ten Mills" sequence presents itself as an apparently whimsical little lyric. Again, however, the emptiness the narrator finds by looking above for answers (to God this time) mirrors his own emptiness. In such poems, the choices that Frost elsewhere proffers to the reader by metaphor and form redound to an overwhelming personal ambiguity.

Ethical decisions always bear the weight of distinguishing between or among options. In these more intensely personal poems, either options do not clearly appear, or the narrator is frozen by anxiety or ambiguity to the point where he cannot distinguish them at all. Therefore, one can locate two kinds of ethical ambiguity in Frost. Of the first order are those poems that offer alternatives to the reader, particularly through formal openings. The aesthetic excellence of such poems is often clear, as Frost shapes the poem in such a way that the reader participates in the making of it. In the second order the narrator himself bears the weight of unknowing. The reader observes the anxiety or fear of the narrator, and may discover some replication of that in his or her own life experience. The reader, however, is provided no means intrinsic to the poem for relieving the anxiety or resolving the ambiguity.

THE ETHICS OF POETRY

To a limited degree, Frost's interest in theology may be evidenced in his personal library. The vast majority of those holdings were volumes of poetry, mostly modern, but he also held copies of works particularly important to him. In this latter category we find works ranging from his beloved Emerson to such humorists as Josh Billings that Frost had read since boyhood. But he also held five different versions of the Old and New Testament, including a French translation of the New. At Frost's memorial service, the Reverend Hobson reflected that Frost "knew the Bible as few—even professionally trained ministers do," and added that Frost loved the book.[14] In a piece for the *Chicago Sunday Tribune* in 1958, under the title "My Favorite Books," Frost included the Old Testament. Moreover, related texts, ranging from a work like *The Bible in Art* to John Bunyan's *The Pilgrim's Progress*, a work much loved by the entire Frost household, are represented.

Such discoveries, however, are ultimately accidental rather than causal. One finds it hard to claim that personal religious beliefs provided any causal effect upon Frost's poetry or ethics.[15] They lie more like an undeniable background tone against the rhythms of the work. He feared being overt. Ambiguity suffuses poetic speculation. That ambiguity is intentional and strategic. Frost's introduction to Robinson's *King Jasper* provides an interesting example. In a letter to Louis Untermeyer (21 August 1935), Frost included a copy of the introduction. Even though, by Frost's account, he had sent a copy to Macmillan on the same day, the published introduction is notably different. In the several pages Frost added appear brief mention of some of Robinson's well-known poems, but also a concluding paragraph that contains the appropriate memorial tone after Robinson had died. He closed by quoting the last two lines of Robinson's poem "The Dark Hills." After great woe, Frost writes, playing with lines from *Hamlet*,

And then to play. The play's the thing. Play's the
thing. All virtue in "as if."
                    As if the last of days
                 Were fading and all wars were done.
              As if they were. As if, as if!

(Selected Prose 67)

For Frost, the great "as if" was the source for virtue. What one
doesn't know on this earth, yet pursues with courage and faith,
constitutes one's fundamental ethical position. For Frost, few embodied this better than Robinson.

The kinship Frost felt with Robinson, beyond their regional similarities and shared preference for metrical verse, also appears to
some degree in their similar methods of taking a common, even
pastoral, scene, and then through careful use of imagery and language opening it to implication and ambiguity. (Richard Cory—
was he a good man or a bad man? The people hated him for being
rich; he was so lonely he put a bullet in his head.) Apart from his
lengthy "Man Against the Sky," however, Robinson seldom tried
to place humanity in the context of a divine presence. His ethical
world was distinctly human-centered. Frost's, however, was not.
That is where his ethical views grow complicated.

In her landmark study *Robert Frost: Contours of Belief*, Dorothy
Judd Hall cites a letter written to her by Lawrance Thompson on
22 September 1970, a few years before the biographer's death: "I
really think that Frost's religious belief provides more problems
than any other part of his art—and it happens to be inseparable
from his art."[16] Recognizing the difficulty, Hall proposes that

> The "God Question"—as Frost himself called it—cannot, then, be set
> aside in considering his work, notwithstanding the difficulties involved
> in posing it, let alone answering it. An independent Yankee, he es-
> chewed both orthodox theology and doctrinaire thinking. But he was
> deeply religious. . . . / I think the directive is clear: we must search for
> his belief in his poetic metaphors. The search is not an easy one, for
> Frost deliberately sets up verbal and stylistic barriers to over-facile
> thinking. In the end, an *approximation* of his belief may be all we can
> hope to attain.[17]

Hall's argument, however, that we can search out those beliefs in
Frost's poetic metaphors, a view shared by George Nitchie in
Human Values in the Poetry of Robert Frost, is only partial and not en-

tirely reliable. To metaphor we must add other elements of the poet's craft—sound, form, irony, and linguistic devices among them—that were explored earlier in this chapter.

Although following chapters will examine Frost's position within several traditional ethical theories and their relationship with literature, it is possible at this point to admit several foundational claims, shaped largely as conclusions from foregoing analysis. Our concern is with how those claims shape the ethics of his art.[18]

The primary requirement is the recognition that Frost's work, by being narrative in the general sense of creating story (even in image-pictures), is also teleological. The tendency of modernism is to deny any work of art a teleology; it is replaced by immediacy. On the contrary, narrative initiates progression toward certain ends. Yet, we know well enough of Frost that he would not confuse teleology with either the didacticism nor the frequent Idealism common to the Romantics. How then do we reconcile the use of the term?

In a particularly helpful study of this issue, "The End of Literature: Reflections on Literature and Ethics," Clarence Walhout works out a careful synthesis between teleology and ethics in literature. Walhout defines *teleology* in terms altogether applicable to Frost: "Teleology does not require an Aristotelian conception of an ideal or universal *telos* or end or goal. It does not even require that the *telos* be a certain or determinate good. It does imply, however, that living in time entails some sense of purposeful movement toward desired goals."[19] Such a view circumvents the common understanding of teleology as a fixed goal, and thereby outside of human endeavor. We might say that that is the fundamental misconception of Job and Jonah from the two *Masques*. Since humanity lives within the chronos flow of time, the *fixed* goal in its *kairos* state cannot be apprehended. The telos, as we are defining it, however, is achievable.[20]

Assuming then that teleology is the pursuit of ends or goals enacted in one's life—and consequently also in one's art—how does this belief affect what we make of ethics in literature? Again, Walhout expands his view in a way that also might apply directly to Frost:

> Though universal truths and values may be important for the study of literature, the primary purpose of literature is not to convey or represent such truths or values but to explore the possibilities and consequences of specific human actions and thoughts in a narrative

situation. Whatever we may mean by universal truths and values in literature, they are qualities that serve the end of literature and are not
themselves the end. The end is the narration of actions that have ethical significance. . . . Actions that are narrated in literature are often
taken as illustrations of universal truths and values rather than as what
they are—the uncertain and often stumbling efforts of characters to
find a way to act in a confusing world.[21]

Thereby, Walhout points out, literature dramatizes for the
reader the conflicts and choices universal to the human condition.
Literature may be described as a searching out, rather than a positing of apodictic and universal truths or values.

Frost's literature falls into a similar pattern. Eschewing the didactic, uncertain about universal values, Frost's poetry is marked
nonetheless by a persistent searching out of ethical value. His
method of doing so is to place the search in settings and characters
and then to probe the value of their teleological goals. While the
narrative often (almost inevitably, one might say) ends in ambiguity, the process of the searching itself leads to alternatives or possibilities one would not have known had one not engaged the
search. Thus, ambiguity becomes the essential dynamics of the literary ethics. Ethical humans need stories to explore the issues of
life in narrative form.[22]

In the current of modernism, with its steadfast emphasis upon
imagism, Frost swam against the flow on precisely this issue. On
the value of the narrative, Walhout reflects that, "We are drawn to
stories because they enable us to reflect on possibilities of action,
and we respond to them favorably when they open up for us new
ways of imagining and thinking about human action. The value of
stories (literature) in the final analysis is that they help us to reflect
on possible directions for our own actions in our own historical stories."[23] He adds, moreover, that "The teleology implicit in stories
helps us to deal with the teleology in our own lives, not in a pre-
scriptive way and perhaps not in ways that are characterized by
immediate application and finality."[24] Seen in this way, teleology is
a process one engages in everyday life, arising from everyday experiences, and requiring everyday responses.

How, then, do these two foundational points—teleology as an
ongoing process of discovering goals in this life, and the power of
literature through story to incarnate possibilities for the reader—
conjoin in our early understanding of Frost's literary ethics? They

direct our understanding of the literary works, first, by how we engage them as readers. In the reader-response theory a similar ethics also prevails, what we might call the ethics of responsible engagement of the text. Instead of bringing to the text preconceptions, or prejudices, the reader engages the text first of all for what it is—a work shaped by narrative, character, setting, and formal technique. Similarly, then, we do not approach Frost's poetry expecting an Aristotelian argument of truthful ends and right actions. Frost's poems do not adequately yield to the desire of some readers to have a poetic work resolve itself in a neat allegorical puzzle, where line A of symbols and structure are always totally fulfilled in line B of meaning. After shifting the pieces of the puzzle, as it were, one can say with some satisfaction, "Here it is—the aim and meaning of the work." That very reductionism, however, also kindles dissatisfaction. Such poems tend to die in the reader's memory. They are seldom true to life; they lack the ability to engage the reader as person and live on in that personhood.

Conversely, then, we may claim here at the outset, and hold it up for future reference, that a sense of teleology that is ongoing draws a reader into possibilities the author holds forth. Into a narrative, the author provides conflicts and choices that the reader works through, thereby placing his or her own personhood into the possible resolutions or effects of those conflicts or choices. The reader participates in the story. While symbolism may guide possible choices, it is not structured in an exclusively determinative way to admit one choice only. In arriving at an ethical position, then, both artist and reader necessarily work through the ambiguity that grants freedom of choice. To be sure, often the work ends in a tension of ambiguous and unresolved options. This is precisely the point to which Frost often leads the reader. Nonetheless, that very act of pondering conflicting values, of weighing alternatives, and of abandoning untenable responses constitutes an ethical act.

By declaring that Frost's position is an ethics of ambiguity, however, certainly does not imply that it was either unpatterned or made no sense whatsoever. The opposite is true. His ethics of ambiguity, while often couched in uncertainty as an epistemology, nonetheless is deliberative. This becomes clear in the following chapters that examine which major ethical theories Frost diverges from, which he seems to accept, and which seem to apply to him personally as an artist. In each case, the particular ethical theory will receive a brief historical introduction and selected works of Frost will be examined in relation to it.

3

Rationalist Ethics

W HILE SANTAYANA MAY HAVE FURNISHED FROST SOMETHING OF A modernist matrix that shaped his early poetic beliefs, the challenges Santayana held forth implicitly called into question ethical issues of the previous century. The two enthroned guides of Rationalism and Romanticism seemed to have collapsed in moral authority and normative values. It may be argued, although it requires the support of his later writings, that Santayana's aesthetics signaled an effort to extricate the artist from the crumbling debris of those twin towers and to harbor the artist once again in the security of classicism. To a large degree also, Robert Frost shared that longing.

By the turn of the century Rationalism had annealed into a rigid codification of ethical proprieties. Once valuing social well-being in its multiple ethical expressions, rationalist ethics at the end of the nineteenth century seemed to many little more than a book of etiquette that carried no liberating power for society. Romanticism, on the other hand, had expired on its own bed of ashes, consumed by its inward fires of the imagination. Once valuing the intuited initiative of the individual to rise above the strictures of any social contract and to make wise and just actions based upon individual experience, Romanticism vaporized into a fleecy world of incongruent emotions.

If the longing of both Santayana and Frost was for discovery of ethical values through the power of art, it was also for an extrication from worn ethical guides and for the formulation of new ones. Necessarily, however, the process of extrication had to come first. Part of that process for Frost may be seen in his own positioning in the American and European literary and philosophical traditions at the close of the nineteenth century.

RATIONALIST ETHICS IN HISTORICAL CONTEXT

Although seventeenth-century American literature consisted largely of letters, diaries, and journals intended for the Old World, it was during the eighteenth century, as the young nation fought to free itself from the old, that its literature fell most heavily under the sway of European Enlightenment. That is not surprising. A government had to be founded, a constitution written, people persuaded to a just cause, a war had to be fought. Consequently, the orators and literary spokespersons of the time dredged their heritage of European Enlightenment for all they could.

While those Enlightenment thinkers, and their American counterparts such as Paine and Franklin, assumed certain apodictic values, these values were held in trust by the thinkers themselves. The select few, not unlike Huxley's world leaders in *Brave New World*, had the task of imparting to the common classes which values were ethically acceptable. Not that they expected the commoners to follow necessarily, but they erected their own pedestal of perfectibility anyway and spoke to the masses from it. Since the time of Aristotle, that has been the general task of the rationalist ethics. The philosophical elite analyzes what is truly beautiful and just, discriminating according to logical analysis, and then modeling and positing their conclusions for society to live by. Thereby, reason supersedes any emotional or fanciful qualities of the mind, a point made clear by Samuel Johnson in a letter to Boswell dated approximately 15 March 1774: "Fancy is always to act in subordination to Reason. We may take fancy as a companion, but must follow reason as our guide. We may allow fancy to suggest certain ideas in certain places; but Reason must always be heard, when she tells us, that those ideas and those places have no natural or necessary relation."[1]

The American Enlightenment, although often riddled with egocentric excess, shared the same fervid reliance upon reason to lead one aright. We might be amused today reading in Franklin's *Autobiography* (1771) these words, "It was about this time I conceived the bold and arduous project of arriving at moral perfection. I wished to live without committing any fault at any time. . . . As I knew, or thought I knew, what was right and wrong, I did not see why I might not always do the one and avoid the other."[2] We look

askance at such an ethics as an eccentric wishfulness, until we realize that Franklin meant every word he said. The Man of Reason
was the hero of the age.

The difficulty perceived by Frost and other young modernists at
the turn of the century was that under the aegis of pure reason,
meaning in life had been reduced to schemata, a program. The
successors to the Enlightenment not only had to create new forms
of meaning, but also radically new approaches to discover that
meaning. They had witnessed the most devastating effects of rationalist schemata, a mechanized universe which threatened to enslave humanity as one more category in an iron-clad system. A
radical reorientation was necessary. Even if humanity proved ultimately to be an irrational being, this fact had to be discovered by
unique, personal methods to convince the individual mind. The
universal law of reason was no longer the way, but became a barrier that prevented meaning.

The primary sources of difficulty that Frost and the young modernists were to face with the rationalist ethics, then, were the nearly
exclusive reliance upon formal, logical analysis over intuition, reason over imagination, the hierarchical and didactic nature of the
logically derived ethics, and the imprisoning order of right actions
into a system of codified rules. In consort with the idealization of
human thinking, moreover, rationalists obliterated any sense of
the mysterious presence of the divine, an issue that some modernists, Frost and Eliot and Robinson among them, struggled with
powerfully. Perhaps the key Enlightenment thinker on this issue,
and surely one of the most influential internationally, was David
Hume. Several times in his life Hume met with Franklin (and, for
a time, believed that Franklin was going to publish an American
edition of the *Philosophical Essays*). Hume's place in philosophy actually wasn't confirmed until shortly after his death, when Immanuel Kant recognized and advocated his genius. Hume's ideas on
the divine, however, were seminal on both shores of the Atlantic
for many years after his death.

To the point of our comparison of the rationalist ethics and
Frost's positioning toward that, consider briefly several of Hume's
points in what is perhaps the most challenging chapter of *Human
Understanding*, his essay on miracles. The essay might be read as a
near proof text for Paine's *Age of Reason* and Emerson's "Divinity
School Address." Hume attempts more than a modern-day remythologization of miracles—the explanation of all purportedly su

pernatural events by natural law. Instead he attempts to discredit the validity of miracles altogether by a lack of primary evidence and objective accounting. That is to say, he finds no rational accountability for miracles. As a man of reason, then, Hume finds himself compelled to provide an argument that will "be an everlasting check to all kinds of superstitious delusions."[3] The argument itself is familiar to anyone in the twentieth century; that is, the arguments to evidence versus testimony, to proof versus probability, to the laws of nature versus violation of laws, to reason versus emotion. Each of these, explicitly or implicitly, seems to impugn the person who might believe in the miraculous, or even the supernatural. Here too we witness the intellectual elitism of the rationalist. Hume puts it thus: "The knavery and folly of men are such common phenomenon that I should rather believe the most extraordinary events to occur from their concurrence [i.e., the folly of men] than admit of so signal a violation of the laws of nature."[4]

Having denied proof for miracles on the basis of natural law, Hume and his fellow rationalists find little need for a divine power to work within natural law. The traditionally received notions of a God who was omniscient and omnipresent were erased to a vaporous Deism. Again, Hume writes on what would become a central dogma of rationalist thought: "It is impossible for us to know the attributes or actions of such a Being otherwise than from the experience which we have of his productions in the usual course of nature."[5] Having denied any special revelation (Scripture or miracles), and limiting the divine to signs of order in natural law, the rationalist effectively drew a veil over God. At the same moment, Rationalism effectively placed the entire groundwork for ethical decision making in the human mind.

The influence of rationalist thinking upon twentieth-century ethical thought arises from the lack of internal order in what seems at first glance to be a tight system. Rationalist ethics may indeed appear orderly and reasonable, but its order was inherently exclusionary. For example, as suggested in the discussion above, it may be observed that for the rationalists, the natural world is assumed to be orderly. Frost is the polar opposite of Hume here, for while natural order often sings with a sweet beauty in his poems, it also raises that Pacific storm that is metaphor for his chaotic spirit, or that New England blizzard that reminds him of desert places, or that Midwestern rain on sad streets—but the streets are only streets; the sadness lies in him. For Frost a vital current links humanity and nature.

At the same time, however, Frost searches nature for signs of the divine. One would be mistaken to call Frost a Pantheist. Rather, it may be said, as will be explored in the chapter on Theological Ethics, that nature provides signals to the alert and heedful mind. Nature leads one outside of oneself, enabling the probing of divine possibilities that do not occur in the closed formality of the rationalist.

In his exhaustive study *Robert Frost and the Challenge of Darwin*, Robert Faggen demonstrates the transitions from Emerson, Thoreau, and James, authors generally considered influential upon Frost, and Frost's own conception of nature. The unity assumed between humanity and nature became fractured by Frost's greater skepticism. Frost's poetry seduces one by the appearance of order, both in form and setting, only to jar one into awareness of disorder. Faggen argues that, "Frost is often diabolical, seducing his readers into a world that promises clarity, order, and beauty only to show increasing complexity, irony, and dysteleology. And the style reflects the irony of his view of nature; it appears lovely but, as Darwin himself envisioned, hides competition and destruction."[6] Faggen adds that "Frost's poetry aims at those who claim human superiority to nature as well as those of romantic sentiment who regarded nature's beauty as an example of its moral purity and fail to recognize the more subtle examples of the way other creatures suffer and compete."[7] Frost portrays the dialectic; seldom does he attempt resolution. All too often, the presumption of order wrenched by apparent disorder closes a Frostian work in tense ambiguity.

Probably most significant to the case here is Frost's early and lasting interests in astronomy coupled with Darwinian thought. One of his lifelong favorite books, by his own accounting, was Richard Proctor's *Our Place Among Infinities*. In his *Paris Review* interview, collected in *Interviews with Robert Frost*, Frost recalled that "One of the earliest books I hovered over, hung around, was called *Our Place Among the Infinities* [sic], by an astronomer in England named Proctor. . . . I mention that in one of the poems: I use that expression 'our place among the infinities' from that book that I must have read as soon as I read any book, thirteen or fourteen" (*Interviews* 231). The poem Frost refers to here is "The Star-Splitter," where Brad McLaughlin buys a telescope to probe the mysteries of "our place among the infinities."

Proctor's book, however, is not a mere guide to astronomy or a chart to the heavens. Appearing as it does in the full bloom of the debate over evolution, Proctor's aim was nothing less than an effort to trace the origins of solar bodies. Equipped only with the rudimentary astrophysical tools of the late nineteenth century, Proctor's effort was severely handicapped, relying more upon speculation than science. Nonetheless, he held adamantly to the evolutionary infinitude of the universe. Robert Faggen points out the conclusions of such thinking: "He justified his own claims of the infinite evolution of the solar system and the infinitude of space and time, in part, on the ground that they do not comfort those who want to see a purposeful God's design in everything."[8] As with Darwinism at the turn of the century, it is not the case with Proctor that there is no design, but rather that design is indeterminate from the evidence given. The proposition, while directly threatening Rationalism, was a common sensibility of early modernism.

Furthermore, Frost is keenly aware of the surprises nature holds. Perhaps nature itself is the miracle, for often in Frost's poems nature adopts the metaphorical voice speaking both to narrator and also to reader. Nature constantly discloses, and most often what it discloses is something of what we ourselves are. Frost himself is ever alert for "what just might be"—the miracle of a sudden insight that can either change the contours of a poem or the course of one's life.

Frost also departs significantly from the rationalist ethic by paying close heed to a common people's voice, both their intense secrets and their superstitions. He brings them a degree of credibility by featuring them as characters in his works. Moreover, the narrative tone held toward such people, through Frost's use of soundsense whereby he enters their lives through the currents of their speech, either dignifies the struggles of such people to find the right actions in their settings, or, at the very least, withholds denigration by the objectivity of a closely listening ear.

With this transition from rational dogmatism to a greater focus on individual experience and searching, it is not inaccurate to describe modernist literature as romantic. In fact, Nathan Scott has done exactly that in *The Broken Center* by claiming that, "It is precisely the extreme self-reliance in the quest for first principles that I have been positing as the inescapable necessity facing the modernist writer—it is precisely this that makes evident his descendance from the great Romantics of the nineteenth century and also makes evident the fact that the literature of the age of Joyce and Kafka is essentially a late development of the Romantic movement."[9] Scott points out that to compensate for the disintegration of traditional guides, of those primordial images that objectify a people's beliefs, the romantic tendency seeks a mythos, a corporate story that also holds true individually. Myth, not objective data, incarnates our mystery. Frost's poetry may well be understood as such—stories embodying the mysteries of humankind.

Robert Langbaum makes a claim similar to Scott's in *The Poetry of Experience* by arguing that the "change of direction" in Romanticism begins when the artist "discovers his own feelings and his own will as a source of value in an otherwise meaningless universe."[10] Langbaum argues that it is the matter of choosing value in the absence of traditional guides to value that marks the romantic tendency, and which marks the modern age as romantic, for we are still caught in the quest for personal value and meaning. This quest must be validated by experience, by acting on individual choice rather than rational justification, hence his title "The Poetry of Experience."

Rationalist ethics celebrated the analytic powers of the individual human to discern matters of truth and right action and set them forth in a form congruent to the ideas themselves. While the prose format suited many rationalist thinkers, poetry too was governed by rigidity of formal patterns to achieve the decorous balance between form and thought. For the modernist, rationalist ethics was altogether too hierarchical. Since ethics for them was indeterminate, the form of the work similarly became more indeterminate. While cautious of the romantic celebration of ethical individualism and sprawling poetic forms, nonetheless many of them participated in what Langbaum called the Poetry of Experience.

FROST IN THE CONTEXT OF RATIONALIST ETHICS

While he turned against the romantic excess in poetic form under the influence of Santayana, Frost nonetheless retained the unsettled, questing spirit of the romantic legacy. On a quest for personal value, or a validation of self, his poetic characters must choose and

act to make that validation. The choices held open for the character, and the ambiguities of choices that prevent clear and decisive
actions, are also those that confront the reader. One of Frost's best-
known examples of this ambiguity appears in "The Road Not
Taken."

> Two roads diverged in a yellow wood,
> And sorry I could not travel both
> And be one traveler, long I stood
> And looked down one as far as I could
> To where it bent in the undergrowth;
>
> Then took the other, as just as fair
> And having perhaps the better claim,
> Because it was grassy and wanted wear;
> Though as for that the passing there
> Had worn them really about the same,
> And both that morning equally lay
> In leaves no step had trodden black.
> Oh, I kept the first for another day!
> Yet knowing how way leads on to way,
> I doubted if I should ever come back.
>
> I shall be telling this with a sigh
> Somewhere ages and ages hence:
> Two roads diverged in a wood, and I—
> I took the one less traveled by,
> And that has made all the difference.

The poem may seem to many to be the great pastoral symphony of
his works; upon closer probing, however, one uncovers discordant
notes and tense ambiguities. To fully appreciate the achievement,
the poem should be situated in several different contexts, each of
which provides differing angles of vision on the work.

After selling his farm in Derry, New Hampshire, Frost moved in
1912 with Elinor and their children to England. There two of the
most important events of his life occurred: the publication of his
first volume of poetry, *A Boy's Will* (1913), and his deep friendship
with the English poet, Edward Thomas. The friendship would be
all too brief. Thomas died in 1917 in World War I, but the friendship left a profound and lasting impact upon Frost.

According to Lawrance Thompson's *Robert Frost* (vol. 2, 88–89,

544–48), "The Road Not Taken" was originally written in a piece of correspondence to Thomas, and, Thompson speculates, it was intended to satirize the indecisive Thomas. Indeed, it isn't difficult to detect a tone of jesting, but friendly, conversation in the poem. Regardless of the difficulty of Thompson's reading the author's intentions into the work, the poem itself nicely captures the frequent walks of Frost and Thomas across the English countryside.[11]

Substantial evidence, however, suggests that the idea of the poem antedates Frost's acquaintance with Thomas. In a 1912 letter to Susan Hayes Ward, Frost writes of "two lonely cross-roads" that he walked frequently during the winter. After a snowfall, he would observe the road lying trackless for days, showing that "neither is much traveled." Frost goes on to describe how one evening he was surprised to see a figure in the distance walking toward him. Oddly, he felt he was approaching his own image in "a slanted mirror," or as if two images were about to "float together." In the end, Frost writes, "I stood still in wonderment and let him pass by" (*Selected Letters* 45). That experience sheds substantial light upon the ambiguities that have perplexed readers of the poem, for certainly "The Road Not Taken" dramatizes the narrator's encounter with his own self.

The poem was first published in *The Atlantic Monthly* (August 1915), and was collected as the opening poem in Frost's third volume, *Mountain Interval* (1916). As he had done in his previous volume, *North of Boston*, Frost set the opening poem and the concluding poem, "The Sound of Trees," in italic, rather than roman type. A comparison of the two poems brings forth many striking similarities beyond the function of introducing and concluding the volume. Both poems pose the narrator in a moment of ambiguity, where a choice may be made but no certain responses to that choice appear. While "The Road Not Taken" locates the narrator "in a yellow wood," "The Sound of Trees" locates the narrator in his lodging listening to the sound of trees. In fact, as the trees sway and bend, so too his whole body sways and bends to their pull. To what end, however? As in "The Road Not Taken," the narrator of "The Sound of Trees" is not certain. He announces that "I shall set forth for somewhere / I shall make the reckless choice." But not now. Now he feels the tug of action, but leaves it in the tense ambiguity of "someday." Whereas in "The Road Not Taken" the narrator actually does step out on a "leap of faith," the action of the narrator of "The Sound Trees" is indeterminate.

Thus, the two poems frame conflicting actions when forced with ambiguous choices and ends.

As seen previously in his essay "The Constant Symbol," Frost declared that the "mind is a baby giant," hurling its toys ahead of itself. So too it is with the poet, flinging out words, prosody, and other playthings of the craft ahead of him. But they land in zigzag paths; thus, the "straight crookedness" of the poem. We should not misunderstand so careful a poet as Frost as abdicating method and design, but rather as using them seductively to bring the reader into the poem and thereby to unveil shades of meaning to the reader. Such is one fundamental trait of his poetic ethics. Rather than shouting the truth, as his poem "Mowing" has it, the poet would prefer to whisper along the zigzag path that is the poem.

The point is important to "The Road Not Taken" for it is indeed one of his superb pastoral poems, perfectly capturing as if by camera one momentary scene in nature. The autumn setting, nearly always a nostalgic and sometimes melancholy season in Frost's poetry, evokes a tone of sweet wistfulness here. Nature's life is passing; if "Nature's first green is gold," its last green is yellow. But nature in this poem also acts upon the narrator, further than a mere evocation of wistfulness. As Johannes Kjorven has argued in *Robert Frost's Emergent Design*, the poem's focus centers primarily upon the choice/action of the narrator. In this case, nature, at one unexpected point, presents him with two leaf-fallen paths—divergent, branching off into the unseen distance. So it is in nature; one reaches such a point, one makes a decision, one travels on. But it is not that way for the narrator, and herein the poem itself branches off into complexities as we observe the narrator's reaction to the choice that nature presents him.

While the pastoral scene may seem simple, the form of the poem itself propels the zigzag paths. In fact, the form belies the pastoral quality for, unlike "Mowing," it is far more intense, suggesting uncertainty and vacillation against the compelling need to make a decision. The stanzaic rhyme scheme appears in perfect regularity: ABAAB CDCCD EFEEF GHGGH. The rhymes are all masculine, with a curious twist in lines five and twenty where the penultimate syllable rhymes, pairing the "undergrowth" and the "difference." Within this tightly clad system, however, rhythm and word patterns shift and strain, reflecting the narrator's own mind. With his reliance upon sound-sense, as many scholars have pointed out, Frost should not—perhaps cannot—be placed tightly within a reg-

ular line prosody. Even his sweetly flowing "Mowing" is broken by
irregular accents since he speaks as a laborer, not as a poet writing
about a laborer. So too in "The Road Not Taken" accents shift
spontaneously, trochees mixing freely with iambs. Frost captures
the mind of the woods-walker in such a way, eliciting discovery,
uncertainty, and sadness by the varied structures.

The linguistic deployment of the poem abets this fluctuation.
The first thing one notices is a shift in the wood itself. Line 1 discovers two roads in a "yellow wood." The opening trochee manifests the surprise of the walker stumbling across those roads. His
relationship with and decision according to those roads constitute
the bulk of the "telling" of the poem until the last stanza where the
decision is made. In line 18, however, the reader finds an echo of
line 1. Something is missing. It reads simply, "Two roads diverged
in a wood." The "yellow" wood, with its beauty and surprise, has
been suspended, held in thrall by a decision between two roads
that has to be made. It is possible, in fact, that if one follows this
transition one could read the poem as expressing a wholly negative
attitude toward decision making. The beauty of the world around
us slips away under the weight of the need for pragmatic decisions.
Whether read this way or not, the formal techniques of the poem
nicely evidence the baby giant using its toys to set a zigzag course.
In this case, it most powerfully lures the reader into that course for
deeper probing. What further evidence in the poem's setting can
be determined to guide that course?

After the objective description in stanza 1—what in fact lay before him—the narrator engages the why of his choice. The evidence in stanzas 2 and 3 is inconclusive. Yet, in the third stanza the
imposition of the context of time on the poem again subtly shifts
the meaning. At the present moment, the yellow leaves have not
been "trodden black." Something of the narrator's passage will in-
delibly change that, but so too he will be changed. Although he
claims to keep the first path for another day, he knows full well
that with one step it disappears forever into the past. The "sigh"
of the fourth stanza is anticipated in the third as the narrator
makes his choice, "Oh, I kept the first for another day!" But there
will be no other day, no other precise moment such as this.

Even as he stands in the present, then, at this seemingly harm-
less juncture in the woods, the poet feels the dramatic moment of
the future. The fourth stanza shifts to the future, which, of course,
he can't know. All he has is the present moment. The indecision of

the narrator here contrasts sharply with the fierce energy of the narrator of "A Leaf Treader," something of a parallel poem. There the narrator, by his own admission, has trod the leaves to stamp out fear. Not so with the narrator here. He steps out at last on the path that he chooses to call less traveled, but it is only his choosing to call it that that makes all the difference for his sense of the future. In his essay, "Whistling in the Dark: Robert Frost's Modernist Quest for Meaning," William Doxey emphasizes that the choice/act determines meaning since "each choice excludes its alternative." Doxey adds, "What is done cannot be undone, so the meaning here seems to be that one must live as though his judgment were correct, regardless."[12] In this context also, it is not difficult to see the implications for Frost's personal commitment to be a poet. His choice during the England years was fretted by unusually heavy financial concerns, a lack of a reading public, and a commitment to a poetic form unlike that practiced in the modernist trend. The risk of the future weighs like a sigh in the poem.

"The Road Not Taken" does indeed, then, follow several zigzag contours. It may be an ironic jest with his friend Thomas. It is indeed a pastoral scene. Its formal qualities expertly snare and lead the reader. It reveals nature working upon the narrator by offering the complexity of seemingly identical choices. Finally, it holds forth the tension—unresolved in spite of the last line—between the present moment and the unknown future, and the need to shape some ethical stance toward present and future through human action rather than received tradition. In these ways it also manifests what Langbaum calls "The Poetry of Experience." The choice to be made is not grounded in some rationalist scheme; rather, it is an existential product of the immediate moment.

RATIONALIST ETHICS: BEHIND THE MASQUE

Frost insisted that *A Masque of Reason* and *A Masque of Mercy* be placed at the end of his *Complete Poems*, a fact that has in itself raised considerable speculation among scholars. Mordecai Marcus, for example, is of the opinion that by Frost's placing them at the end he was "surely viewing them as summary comment on his life and work."[13] Similarly, Reuben A. Brower, who reads the poems as "the final experiment in his search for a 'form of outrage' in which he could push to the limit the stress of opposites," believes they are Frost's "culminating" poems.[14] Here, Brower argues, the poet "refashions forms he had used earlier and . . . sums up concerns persistent throughout his poetry."[15] Also, working from evidence in Frost's unpublished *Notebooks*, Dorothy Judd Hall asserts that "Frost regarded [the Masques] as the culmination of his poetic achievement."[16]

It may also well be that Frost set the poems apart from other works because of the generic distinction. He had written many works with dramatic qualities, including several attempts at plays, but none with the starkness of a masque. Moreover, if these poems are seen as "culminations," one has to ask culminations of what? In language, tone, and setting they are different from anything written before. Furthermore, they differ in subject, for while certain poems foreshadow the Masques, none of them treats the subject matter of the encounter with suffering with quite the same stark, confrontational drama. In other poems, the subject is muted by images and settings; here it is shouted. Finally, one may account for the placement by the fact of the altogether different publishing avenues of the two poems. *A Masque of Reason* was published in 1945 (during the irrational carnage of WWII) in a limited edition of only 800 copies signed by the author. *A Masque of Mercy*, although first published in *The Atlantic Monthly* (November 1947), was also published in a signed edition of 751 numbered copies. The limited and distinctly more private (by this time Frost was one of the best-selling poets in the world) distribution of the poems suggests that Frost might have wanted them individualized in the collection not necessarily because they were any sort of culmination—he did, after all, publish many more poems after 1947—but simply because they constituted a different sort of writing and thinking than his other works. That point may seem trivial. If we isolate this sense of artistic and thematic individuality in the Masques, however, we are also in a better position to understand the full range of Frost's effort in them, from the wit to the wondering, from reason to outrage, from mockery to meaningfulness.

The dramatic form of the masque developed particularly during the Renaissance with its appetite for courtly processionals and elevated speech and song. The speakers wore masks, thus becoming more allegorical types in the drama than actors. The "idea" was the thing of importance. Since it was a courtly production for celebration and entertainment, however, even the allegorical idea was subservient to the sheer spectacle of the procession and songs. Perhaps the most famous masque is Milton's *Comus*, presented at Ludlow Castle on 29 September 1634, to celebrate the inauguration of the Earl of Bridgewater as Lord President of Wales. Milton accepted the assignment as an interlude from his private studies at home, but he practically reinvented the whole genre from those masques with which Ben Jonson had been lining his pockets. Milton followed standard conventions—spectacle, song, dancing; he even included the grotesque of the "antimask" to conflict with the order of the whole. However, the breadth of intellectual seriousness set the play apart from others of its time. Influenced by Homer's story of Odysseus and Circe, Milton made Comus the son of Circe and took the story from there into a probing examination of the conflict between good and evil. Comus, appearing as the perfect gentleman of reasonable and cultivated order, is revealed as a corrupted vessel of moral disorder. Thus he contains in himself the conflicting good and evil, the appearance and the reality, the reasonable and irrational, the ethical and the corrupt. In "Robert Frost's Masques and the Classic American Tradition," Peter J. Stanlis accurately points out that, "Frost's two plays depend more on poetry than on spectacle, and like Milton his main purpose is to state a serious theological and moral principle about an important religious or philosophical problem."[17] If there is a model for Frost's masques, it does not lie in the sunnier works of Jonson, Thomas Campion, Thomas Carew, and James Shirley. Clearly it lies in the at once more agonizing and difficult, and therefore altogether at once more human, *Comus*.

Some of the ambiguity and conflict that Frost struggles with in the two masques appear in earlier works. Although the forms may vary, the sense of searching for some clear sign is an oft-repeated theme. "Neither Out Far Nor In Deep," first published in *The Yale Review* (spring 1934), exemplifies this perfectly. In the first of four quatrains, Frost depicts people standing on a beach. They have all turned their backs on the land to stare at the sea. The land behind them is the familiar, what is known; the sea before them the unfamiliar and unknown. What is it that so fascinates them as to stand watching all the day?

The second stanza seems to supply an answer—a ship passes by. Nearby a gull stands upon the wet shoreline. Both of these, however, are simply demarcations between the people and the sea itself, as if they were some signs in a foreign tongue of the secrets the sea might hold. Thus in the third stanza, Frost thrusts the reader into the world of ambiguity with the line, "Wherever the truth may be." Where is it? In the familiar landscapes of our lives, or in the unfamiliar sea, so unyielding of its mysteries.

The closing stanza is a fascinating one, quite unlike many of Frost's deliberately ambiguous poems that he leaves in final suspension. Here he recognizes the limitations upon the human condition to search out such mysteries: "They cannot look out far / They cannot look in deep." Rarely does he make so overt a comment on the human condition. In "Frost's 'Neither Out Far Nor In Deep,' " Peter Poland understands this commentary as explicitly negative. The people stand like gulls, "Symbolically turning their backs on their domain, the land, to stare incessantly seaward." Thus, they are "unnatural," and "Their efforts are life-denying in the extreme."[18] It seems possible, and perhaps more likely, however, to see the people straining at their limitations, seeking to know what is presently unknowable. The final two lines, although posed in the form of a question, celebrate the human tendency to try to look far and deep. Human limitations are never a final bar "To any watch they keep."

The two Masques, however, are more than an effort to probe the mysteries of God; in fact, one goes seriously astray by limiting the poems to such. The poems are also very much about the mysteries of humanity in two areas especially: the nature of epistemology and the problem of human suffering. Philosophically the two issues always intertwine.[19] Poetically, the issue for Frost was a lifelong wrestling with the problem of suffering. One finds it starkly present already in "Trial by Existence" from *A Boy's Will*:

> 'Tis of the essence of life here,
>   Though we choose greatly, still to lack
> The lasting memory at all clear,
>   That life has for us on the wrack
> Nothing but what we somehow choose;
>   Thus are we wholly stripped of pride
> In the pain that has but one close,
>   Bearing it crushed and mystified.

Not only is that a tightly packed final stanza in and of itself (are we only victims of our own pride? Are we able to transcend pride and thus suffering?), it could well serve as an epigraph to the two Masques.

The ideas of these "Neither Out Far Nor In Deep" and "Trial by Existence" tie neatly into the two Masques, for in each the characters look far and deep into the nature of God and his actions, but also into the nature of the human condition. The human characters are thoroughly human, but they are also watchkeepers, searching for some sign of revelation while they stand at their dry little shorelines.

THE EXPERIENCE OF UNREASON

In *A Masque of Reason*, the searching of Job and Thyatira[20] in many ways represents someone looking out far and in deep. Indeed, Robert Faggen sees a significant trace of all Frost's poetry embodied in the poem: "Frost's *Masque of Reason* encompasses a tension that runs throughout his poetry, a tension between a human desire for ultimate causes and designs and a natural world that always refuses to satisfy that desire."[21] Such appears to be the case as we enter the poem. In this instance, instead of an ocean shore, Job and Thyatira rest under a palm tree at an oasis in the midst of a desert. Entangled in a tree that they alternately call the Burning Bush or the Christmas Tree, a figure of light attempts to extricate itself. The Burning Bush refers to the Theophany to Moses at Mount Horeb, recorded in Exodus 3. There God identifies himself to Moses as "I Am That I Am," the one who is all being and who does not need to be identified by any referent beyond himself. For the Old Testamental Job, this is the God Yahweh that figures prominently in the story. But Frost takes license with time. The fact that this "forty-third" chapter of Job is set approximately a thousand years after biblical events is irrelevant, for the second tree, "The Christmas Tree," evokes not the authoritative Father but the sacrificial Son. Ironically, however, Job and Thyatira recognize the figure from neither of these references, but from Blake's masterful painting of God. It's a subtle point, not to be missed. The recognition comes by means of human perception rather than divine revelation. Indeed, this will be the essential issue of the poem. Do we contain God by our reason, as rationalist thought would have it, or do we accept that God has reasons for events that we can't possibly understand?

Such, of course, is the issue also of the biblical Book of Job, but with some important differences that serve as backdrop to this "forty-third" chapter. The first two chapters of Job, recounting the wager in heaven and the awful affliction upon Job, serve as a brief preface to the larger issues of the book. The second chapter closes with his wife's imprecation to "curse God and die"—an appeal to blank nihilism—and the arrival of Job's three friends—Eliphaz, Bildad, and Zophar. The dramatic quality of the book, then, is whether any of the three can argue a position more tenable than nihilism.

Each of the three captures some facet of Deuteronomic tradition. Eliphaz praises Job for his good deeds and piety, but is quite certain (through a vision he had) that Job has committed some unknown or secret sin. Therefore, his advice is to appeal to God. Frost's *Masque* affords that opportunity. Eliphaz, however, simply relies upon his own variation of Deuteronomy 8:5, "Blessed is the man whom God corrects." The difficulty with Eliphaz's advice is that it is cast entirely in human inability. He isolates portions of Deuteronomic tradition to depict humanity as the subject of impulsive errancy and God as a master of divine caprice:

> As I have observed, those who plow evil
>   and those who sow trouble reap it.
> At the breath of God they are destroyed;
>   at the blast of his anger they perish.
>
> (Job 4:8–9, NIV)

Recall "Neither Out Far Nor In Deep." There the watchers at least had the sea itself to search out. The biblical Job's response to Eliphaz touches on that same point, "If only my anguish could be weighed and all my misery be placed on the scales" (6:2). Job wants to understand his suffering in concrete, practical terms rather than in abstractions. Few of Frost's poems have elicited so widely varied and often contradictory views as this one, but John Doyle penetrates to the heart of it in his observation that "Because Frost's approach to life has always been essentially empirical and nonconformist and his poems based upon observation and experience, Job was the perfect character for his poem on Reason, for Job was an empiricist and the great nonconformist of the Old Testament."[22] Unlike Eliphaz, Job seeks experiential evidence.

Nor does the situation change much as Zophar and Bildad enter with their admonitions and advice. Zophar essentially urges Job to be a kind of mindless statue, face turned toward God but expecting nothing really. To their words, Job responds, first, that he would have answers from God rather than from mortals; second, that his friends should comfort him rather than try to convince him by their sophistries; and third, that he adamantly believes there is a God who can deliver him. Those assertions lead Job to his famous proclamation that inspired Handel's *Messiah* and has inspired countless others: "I know that my Redeemer lives, and that in the end he will stand upon the earth. And after my skin has been destroyed, yet in my flesh I will see God" (19:25–26). This is a choice of the human spirit, not at all the consequence of rational pursuit.

With Job's final insistence that he will speak only with God, his three philosopher-friends fall silent. But standing in the wings is a young man named Elihu, who thus far has deferred to his elders. He now wants a chance to show that all four of them are wrong. His aim, as he announces it, is that God does speak to humanity in many different ways. Although Elihu treats Job as a person rather than a subject of theological discourse, one of these ways of God's speaking, he argues, is through human suffering. His message is that God has supplied a lesson for Job. Now Job has to figure it out. According to Elihu, God speaks in such various ways as natural revelation, metaphor, human mediators, and personal experience. This is necessarily so because "The Almighty is beyond our reach and exalted in power" (37:23). Thus any revelation of God is veiled and indirect. Ironically, precisely at that moment God himself speaks.

The pattern of the divine discourses in Job is fascinating. God does not say a word directly about Job's suffering or divine judgment—the subjects of *A Masque of Reason*. But neither does God condemn nor chastise Job, a fact that disclaims the earthly philosophies of Job's accusers. The implication instead is that Job is vindicated. In some of the most memorable poetry in the Bible, God discloses the ways in which he has revealed himself to humanity, and they are all evidentiary rather than rational proofs. Having heard God, Job now repents of his presumption to "accuse" God (42:4–6). Accepting the repentance, God restores Job's fortunes multiple times, and grants him, once at the point of death, an additional 140 years to enjoy his blessing.

As Frost introduces us to his Job, however, the man is not "old and full of years." Rather he is of some indeterminate age in some limbo-like region where time seems suspended. Yet the subject matter is much the same as the biblical Job. When human reason simply cannot account for the actions of God, what possible *reasons* can God have for acting the way he does? The issue bore paramount importance for Frost himself, who in the face of certain sufferings in his own life found reason itself vain and reasons for events absent. In April, 1934, as his daughter Marjorie lay dying, Frost wrote to his son Carol, "But I try not to give way to either hope or fear. I am simply determined in my soul, my bones, or somewhere, that our side shall win. Reason is no help" (*Family Letters* 164). Again, after Elinor died, Frost wrote his daughter Lesley that "No matter how humorous I am [,] I am sad. I am a jester about sorrow" (*Family Letters* 210).

Something of both of those letters echo in *A Masque of Reason*. Reason is abandoned, but what do we have left in its place? If there are only reasons that God hides from us, then we have the inscrutable, unknowable God of whom Elihu spoke. But both the biblical Job and Frost's Job are situated in God's presence, bringing their grievance before him. Similarly both characters are trying to account for the suffering in their lives, with the notable exception that Frost uses, as was his custom, his slicing wit to be a "jester about sorrow."

In Frost's *Masque*, God's effort to disentangle himself from the Burning Bush/Christmas Tree may be understood two ways. If from the Bush, then God extricates himself from the years of Hebraic commentary and tradition that evolved from his first stunning theophany to Moses. The option is fascinating because in the book *Job* the three friends/accusers address Job solidly from within that tradition, appealing repeatedly to Deuteronomic law and custom. Job, however, longs for an unveiled God. In effect, he would like to be like Moses, standing at the burning bush.[23] The Christmas Tree, on the other hand, represents the modern mythology of godhood from which the actual God disentangles himself. Lines 11–16 detail a tree chock-full of Yeatsian artifice, its very self a kind of gaudy present.

After extricating himself, God pitches his plywood porta-throne, so flimsy a contraption that he has to hold it upright rather than the other way around. Again, Frost may be exercising some sly wit here in his love for contrarieties. The rickety, prefab throne God totes around with him, like divinity in a briefcase, may suggest that God himself is as empty of significance as the battered plywood. Or, it may suggest precisely the converse—that God has no need of real thrones or props, that the person inhabiting the prop is king whether the throne is made of plywood or gold, and that Job is now getting to see the unveiled God precisely as he wishes.

Job starts the discussion with his questioning (37–45), but God quickly turns the tables on him, thanking Job for his help in establishing the principle "There's no connection man can reason out / Between his just deserts and what he gets" (49–50). There is no reasonable congruence between action and results, virtue and rewards. Is life then all whimsy, relative to God's caprice? Or is there some divine, ethical standard? God points out that this ambiguity was in itself the very essence of Job's trial (61–61). God adds that, "It had to seem unmeaning to have meaning" (63).

In a sense, Job places us on the cusp of an old philosophical conundrum: can God make a stone so heavy he cannot lift it? The answer appears to be yes. If God is infinite, he can make something infinitely heavy. But if God is omnipotent, then there is nothing that God cannot do, including lifting the infinitely heavy stone. In philosophy we point out that if the conclusions are contradictory, the fault lies in the premises. That is to say, it's a bad question, for God himself cannot be God if he is self-contradictory. Some answers to some questions, then, lie beyond the scope of human reason. Such is the lesson God imparts to Job.[24]

Job is ready to grant this. His concern is not really with his reasoning capacity at all. What he is looking for is not some propositional Truth, but rather some understanding of reasons for events. In this way, Frost's Job resembles the biblical Job, intent upon evidentiary and experiential understanding. The genuine suffering lies in "not knowing."

God picks up this thread of the argument by saying that Job liberated him. Since the fall of humanity in Eden (71–72), God himself has been in bondage to the Mosaic laws he imposed. The forfeits and rewards, curses and blessings of that law, although biblically understood as covenantal, are revealed here as a sort of police state ethics. Such is the danger of any covenant. By the wager in heaven, and Job's enduring it, God is returned to his throne. But he is also freed from having to give reasons (105–6).

Thyatira is not so easily persuaded. Indeed, she shouldn't be. It's a pretty impoverished argument that Frost's God advances here. Thyatira recounts how she cared for Job while he suffered (there is no biblical record of that), and that it was only reasonable that God should care for his made creature also. She accuses God of a petty tyranny, "All You can seem to do is lose Your temper /

When reason-hungry mortals ask for reasons" (135–36). She
makes it clear that she is not asking for some wide-ranging system
of philosophical proofs, as Plato would have it (137–40), but rather
"scraps of palliative reason."

At that point Job, saying that Thyatira always manages to get in
ahead of him, picks up his argument. What was it all about? he
wonders. What was the point? God asserts that his only claim is
Truth, but that Job helped him demonstrate where truth lay. It is
a matter of a spiritual discipline where humanity learns its "submission to unreason." Peter Stanlis is one of the few critics to have
perceived this fundamental crux of the Masque. In "Robert Frost's
Masques," Stanlis pinpoints Frost's conflict with national certitude
in the modern age:

> Perhaps nothing could be more antithetical than the philosophy of
> modern secular man, with his faith in reason, and Frost's satire on rea-
> son based upon a theology which derives from Old Testament religious
> orthodoxy. Where the modern rationalist makes man's reason su-
> preme and simply eliminates God as irrelevant to his temporal or spiri-
> tual salvation, Frost exalts the omnipotence of God's arbitrary justice
> and makes man's reason appear peevish and impotent by compar-
> ison.[25]

One hesitates, perhaps, at Stanlis's use of the word *exalts*, simply
because it is something implied behind the scenes of this Masque.
At this point, Frost's Job is busy untangling a confusing webwork
of suffering and power, justice and omnipotence, skepticism and
purpose.

We do see at this point that truth is not so much categorical as it
is existential; that is to say, we apprehend it not through categories
of reason but through experience. The problem for Job, and for
Frost we should add, is why those experiences so often have to be
ones of suffering. Cued by God's "submission to unreason," Job
engages his longest speech in the poem in which he begs for God's
"beforehand" reason. He longs for the purpose of the design—
"the artist in me cries out for design" (261)—and not what theologians concoct *ex post facto*. What satisfaction, Job wonders, can a
God get in laughing at how badly humans "fumble at the possibilities" (275). Not until Job's cynical wife joins in with taunts and
jeers, does God reveal something of the great wager with Satan in
heaven—something the biblical Job knew nothing about.

In lines 331–33, Job thrusts one of his satirical barbs, targeting the chief irony of the poem:

> 'Twas human of You. I expected more
> Than I could understand and what I get
> Is almost less than I can understand.

As human creation, it is impossible for him to understand the mind of divine Creator. It is like studying one individual index finger and concluding that I now understand all of humanity. Conversely, to try to place the divine wager in terms that a Job could understand is to reduce it to the merely trivial. In his article "Robert Frost's Masques Reconsidered," Heyward Brook has argued that this is the essential point of the whole poem. The play is an elaborate satire of humanity's effort to capture God, and if the play makes God appear ludicrous it is simply to reveal the ludicrousness of finite efforts to probe the infinite. Such a view, though, does not fully account for the entrance of Satan—at God's beckoning. Here is an agent for evil, and the appearance of Satan introduces a separation between agency and permission that Job had not been fully aware of before.

With Satan's entrance Thyatira is jarred fully awake. This is more to her liking. Enough with the boring theology, as she searches for her Kodak camera to capture the three luminaries on film. It is, of course, the supreme absurdity—the great cosmic trio captured by technology. Thyatira badgers Satan mercilessly as she tries to get him to pose as *she* wishes—"No—no, that's not a smile there. That's a grin" (404). After Thyatira's pestering of Satan (she even asks for one of his prime apples), God feels compelled to explain Satan's diaphanous appearance—like a wasp here—and his lack of speech. Just as God himself has been stripped of personality and his divine godhood in the use of rational categories about him, Satan has been stripped of personhood by "church neglect / and figurative use" (424–25). Like the technology of Thyatira's little Kodak, the modern church flattens the reality and divinity of God and the reality and power of Satan. The necessary consequence is a portrait of humanity standing alone and bereft of any significant meaning beyond its own being. Abandoned to the confines of its own rational scrutiny, humanity continues to search "out far and in deep," but sees only the surfaces below which the ultimate mysteries lie.

Which is precisely where this Masque ends. Human reason is altogether insufficient to understand God; indeed, to understand humanity itself. Satan is reduced to figurative use, a metaphor for a sort of indwelling evil inherent in the human condition. The tensions are self-consuming, ending in a final futility as the cynical Thyatira poses her three characters for her photograph and says, "Now if you three have settled anything / You'd as well smile as frown on the occasion" (464–65). The Masque ends in nearly perfect ambiguity and inconclusiveness. If you three have settled anything? It doesn't appear so—unless what has been settled is the insufficiency of human reason. Whatever the case, we may as well smile as frown. We can't do much of anything one way or the other.

FROM REASON TO MERCY: HEAD TO HEART

While *A Masque of Reason* grows out of one of the longer, and certainly the theologically most complex, books of the Old Testament, *A Masque of Mercy* grows out of one of the shortest biblical books, *Jonah*, with a very straightforward, explicit theme. Both books share similarities, of course, which undoubtedly drew Frost's attention. Neither is properly a history, although each is situated at an indeterminate moment in Jewish history. Nor is either one properly a prophecy, although prophetic elements, such as Jonah's three days in the belly of the fish resembling Christ's crucifixion and resurrection, have been extrapolated. Both books are highly parabolic, and serve as rich ground for remythologizing theologians. Perhaps the most powerful similarity between both books is the revelatory quality. But in each case, unlike other revelatory books in the Old Testament, such as Daniel among the prophetic works or Deuteronomy among the legal books, Job and Jonah share revelation about a theme on human living, on the ethical values humanity requires to live at peace in this world.

While dates for the life of Job are indeterminate, placed virtually anywhere in the second millennium before Christ, Jonah may be fairly accurately dated as the first half of the eighth century B.C. His contemporaries included Amos and Hosea. The historical situation for Israel was dominated by the threat of Assyria. The book narrates a single prophetic mission, that of Jonah to Nineveh. Its theme is the prophet's human desire to prophesy bitter destruction upon "that wicked city," and his growing understanding of the ethics of mercy that must be extended to those very people. Thereby, Jonah sets a pattern for Israel (and humanity) itself: that God is concerned with all of creation, not just with a select few.

The story is familiar. When God tells Jonah to go to Nineveh and "preach against it," Jonah flees from the task aboard a ship. During a tempest at sea, the crewmen cast lots to see who the troublemaker is. When the lot falls on Jonah, and he agrees with the placement, he is cast overboard and swallowed by "a great fish," where he remains three days and three nights. From inside the fish, Jonah prays a prayer of deliverance, after which the fish vomits him up on dry land. When God reiterates his command, Jonah marches off to Nineveh, preaching destruction against it if the people don't repent. By this point, he would rather enjoy seeing fire and brimstone wash down in heavenly torrents to destroy the city. But an odd and unexpected thing happens. The people do repent. The peevish Jonah walks back into the desert to seethe for a while. He wanted justice. The Ninevites were wicked; they deserved a cosmic blast of vengeance. This is no place for the tenderness of mercy. That is, until Jonah needs it himself. In the searing heat, God causes a vine to grow up to shade Jonah. Then he permits a worm to attack it. Jonah is left shelterless in the scorching sun and wind. The parable is insufficient for the angry Jonah. God explains it pointedly, telling Jonah that his mercy in shading Jonah with the vine differs not at all in quality from his mercy in delivering the 120,000 inhabitants of Nineveh. Quantitative assessment of mercy is always secondary to the ethical quality of the act itself.

In structure and theme *A Masque of Mercy* may be considered of one piece with *A Masque of Reason*. In her careful study of relationships between the two, "A Man in Front of His God," Paola Loreto traces Frost's pattern in comparison to Ben Jonson's "spectacle of strangenesse," or the *antimasque*. In each the problems and turmoil of the antimasque are resolved in the *masque*, disorder achieves harmony, discord is supplanted by a ruler. Loreto observes that:

> The two masques can be taken together as one dramatic piece. *A Masque of Reason* can be interpreted as an antimasque representing the disquieting doubt that there is no motivation for the heap of misfortunes God sent to Job, a man who had always been exemplary for his integrity. *A Masque of Mercy*, then, should be seen as the masque proper, whose function is to dispel the impression that the world is dominated by chaos and to restore man's faith in divine justice. In the

masque, though, man's idea of God's justice is corrected. Man's merchant mentality is done away with and replaced with God's freely given mercy.[26]

Loreto isn't the first to suggest the antimasque/masque configuration. Heyward Brook made similar claims in "Robert Frost's Masques Reconsidered," but Loreto takes us to the point where rational order dissolves in a chaos that calls for a desperate corrective. The issue here, then, is what ethical guidelines Frost can forge out of the chaos to lead humanity into order.

Frost's *A Masque of Mercy* translates us to a modern day spiritual desert of the city of New York. Instead of seeking refuge aboard ship or under the vine, Jonah Dove (the Hebrew "Jonah" is translated as *dove*) seeks refuge in a bookstore kept by the odd couple, Jesse Bel[27] and the Keeper, presumably a pun on both the shopkeeper and also Cain's cynical response to God after murdering Abel, "Am I my brother's keeper?" (Gen. 4:9). Jesse Bel, however, tells us that the name came about from Keeper's mother's time in the Brook Farm community, Transcendentalism's idealistic experiment in socialism. The fourth character, Paul, represents of course the principal New Testament theologian, and he speculates that the book of Jonah may be the first instance in literature prior to his own to be specifically about mercy (375–77). Frost's *Masque*, however, moves at least at two levels—the conflict between divine justice and mercy but also the conflict between human justice and mercy at the political and social levels. The first conflict is carried between Paul and Jonah primarily; the second between Paul and the social liberal Keeper. Throughout the play, even when he is simply lurking in the dusty background of the bookstore shelves, Paul seems to be a central figure.

The play opens with Jonah, yet once again, fleeing God. He had been scheduled for a prophecy performance in New York, but at the last moment his courage failed him and he fled. Thus he is introduced as The Fugitive. Once he introduces himself by his right name, however, he also introduces the vexing problems that caused him to flee. He no longer trusts God to carry out his threats against an evil city. In fact, he "can't trust God to be unmerciful" (115). The difficulty for Jonah lies in the illogical fact of God's mercy. Jonah fears that mercy absolves the consequences of human sin. The redemptive acts of God don't make sense because they counteract "Anything we once thought we had to be" (315).

A large degree of what "we once thought we had to be" to Jonah's mind lay in the Mosaic Law, and represents also the modern misunderstanding of that law as a rigid accord of laws and punishment for violation. In fact, such was never the case in the covenantal form of the Suzerain treaty which God gave them. God reveals himself as a Lord of love, desiring the well-being of his people, and giving them the laws so that they could live in a loving relationship with him. This understanding clearly prevails in modern Judaism also, but seems to be missed or ignored by many other traditions. Jonah, in this case, represents those many others. Thus, when Paul asks him how he would want God to be other than merciful, Jonah responds, "Just, I would have Him just before all else" (363). But this is an impossibility already shown as such in *A Masque of Reason*. "Just" according to what and whose standards?

Dallas Willard, professor of philosophy at the University of Southern California, has in his book *The Divine Conspiracy* made observations that indirectly throw considerable light upon Frost's ethics. Willard's argument comes to bear upon Frost's examination of the ethics of justice. The view that has dominated the twentieth century, Willard says, is that "our culture holds reality to be limited to what can be discovered by scientific observation and exploration."[28] The consequence is a belief that scientific laws make everything intelligible, including ethical propositions and moral values. But of course naturalistic or scientific laws cannot exercise force in these domains for the simple reason that "There must be certain 'initial conditions' before the laws of science can explain anything. In their 'explaining,' those laws have to have something from which to start. And they obviously do not explain the existence or nature of those very conditions that must be in place before they can explain *anything*."[29] Nor, we might add, can such laws explain justice or mercy, the issues of this poem.

Jonah's complaint sets up the compelling philosophical drama that will center to a large extent upon Jesus' Sermon on the Mount. Paul introduces it by stating that "Christ came to introduce a break with logic / That made all outrage seem as child's play" (475–76). The Sermon on the Mount, he says, "'Twas lovely and its origin was love" (479). Here is the radical departure from reason, and the spiritual counter to divine justice seen merely as laws.

Keeper argues, and one can imagine that he does so with a magnificent sneer, that the Sermon is a "frame-up," its high ideals assuring universal failure so that we will be "Thrown prostrate at the

Mercy Seat for Mercy" (485). The Sermon, he argues, is "a beautiful impossibility" (493), an "irresistible impossibility" (493), because it gives us such lovely ideals that no one can attain. For
Keeper, the Sermon is an impractical absurdity. Beauty without essence.

Precisely because of that, it is an absurdity and beauty apprehended only by faith, not by reason. Paul argues that "Mercy is
only to the undeserving" (500). Mercy is not earned, or it is not, by
definition, mercy. This is the simple truth that Jonah and Keeper
have failed to see. The argument, however, creates a slight shift in
Jonah's point of view. Instead of looking backward as the Fugitive,
he begins to look forward, "You ask if I see yonder shining gate, /
And I reply I almost think I do" (530–31). In his response, Paul
nicely defines this as a conversion, "Yes, Pilgrim now instead of
runaway, / Your fugitive escape becomes a quest" (534–35). The
key line of this passage occurs when Jonah exclaims "I'm all turned
round" (548). The Latin root for conversion, *conversio*, literally
translates as "to turn around."

But where does Jonah turn to? Not back through the outer door.
Rather, he has to find his way through the cellar door, into the
darkness, down a stairway he can't even see. The passage represents an existential leap of faith, daring the unknown. Paul points
out, however, that it is the only way Jonah can prostrate himself
before the cross. As Jonah admits that his need for justice has faded
before his need for mercy (625–26), he steps toward the door.

As he does so, the door slams before him and Jonah crumples on
the floor.[30] Aware that justice was all he ever had, all he ever pursued, he pleads for mercy while he too fades away like the justice
he had built his life upon. The death of Jonah may be understood
in two ways. Crumpled by justice, he is untouched by mercy. Or,
mercy has overcome the justice he had built his life upon. But the
inconclusiveness about Jonah is less important than the effect of his
passing upon the other characters. They now confront the essential ethical issue: How then shall we live?

Keeper, accepting Jesse's earlier stated belief, declares that we
have to live by courage, which, he points out, derives from the
heart. Fear emanates from the soul. In this sense, then, courage is
an act of fidelity, holding to beliefs even when fears attack those
beliefs. Courage is also, it should be pointed out, a cardinal virtue
in Frost's own code of ethics. Perhaps it is not surprising then that
the poem ends with a deeply personal tone from Keeper and Paul.

Both have been powerfully affected by the night's events. Kneeling by Jonah's body, Keeper confesses that

> I can see that the uncertainty
> In which we act is a severity,
> A cruelty, amounting to injustice
> That nothing but God's mercy can assuage.

(710–13)

Our very lives, in which we are forced by courage to make choices and act upon them, are injustice—simply because we have no certain knowledge of the outcome of those choices and acts. Hence the huge significance of courage. Courage not only acts *against* fear; it also acts *in* the fear of uncertainty.

Paul's final statement also bears a fascinating twist, particularly in the light of one of Frost's stated beliefs. Paul picks up Keeper's argument that we have to confront the fear deep in our souls that our courageous sacrifice is not the best we have to offer, and may not be acceptable in "Heaven's sight." But Paul has already established in his discourse about the Sermon on the Mount that such ambiguity inevitably comprises the human situation. We cannot attain mercy *or* perfection of our own right. Therefore, Paul insists that the only prayer worth offering is this: "May my sacrifice / Be found acceptable in Heaven's sight" (724–25). The sacrifice is one's life courageously lived; the acceptability of that sacrifice is an act of mercy on Heaven's part.

At about the time *A Masque of Mercy* was being written (although Anna K. Juhnke points out that the three early versions of "To Prayer I Think I Go" are also pieces of the poem),[31] Frost wrote G. R. Elliott that "My fear of God has settled down into a deep inward fear that my best offering may not prove acceptable in his sight" (*Selected Letters* 525). The concern similarly arose through Frost's friendship with Rabbi Victor Reichert. The Rabbi had written a scholarly study of Job, and their discussion frequently focused upon biblical issues. While visiting Reichert in Cincinnati on 10 October 1946, Frost agreed to give a few remarks at the Rockdale Avenue Temple. His remarks were based upon Psalm 19:14:

> May the words of my mouth and the
> meditation of my heart
> be pleasing in your sight,
> O Lord, my Rock and my Redeemer.

According to Lawrance Thompson, "RF later told Reichert that the service helped him find precisely the ending he wanted for *A Masque of Mercy*" (*Selected Letters* 555). In a 1953 letter to Reichert, the subject was still on Frost's mind, this time because he wasn't sure that his poetic idea had a biblical grounding: "Do you want to tell me where in the Bible if at all the idea occurs as a prayer that our sacrifice whether of ourselves or our property may be acceptable in His sight? Have I been making this up out of nothing? You know how I am about chapter and verse—somewhat irresponsible some would say" (*Selected Letters* 555).

If that concern helped Frost find the conclusion to his poem, however, the idea is also enacted in deed. Keeper has the final words. He reiterates his concept of courage of the heart battling against fear of the soul. Thereby he also affirms his kinship with Jonah. But he also concedes to Paul the necessity of laying Jonah's body before the cross in an act of mercy. The act responds to Keeper's earlier taunting of Paul about three crosses: star-crossed, mercy-crossed, or evil-crossed (440). The allusion works in several directions. The three crosses figure those on Golgotha at the crucifixion. Star-crossed love derives from *Romeo and Juliet*, a play where love breaks through all logic. The mercy-crossed derives from the act of Christ's crucifixion itself. Evil-crossed is the insistence upon justice, the fact that there had to be a crucifixion at all. It is fitting then, that as Keeper moves to take Jonah's feet to lay him before the cross, he says, "Nothing can make injustice just but mercy" (738). His very bending to Jonah in itself shapes an act of mercy.

Many readers see the mercy/justice conflict, which Frost calls "the pain of opposing goods exactly" (*Selected Letters* 466), unresolved in the poems. The change in Keeper, however, where he does in fact become My Brother's Keeper, suggests a resolution based upon love and mercy. In fact, one of the few other readers to consider this theme to be the fundamental continuity between the two *Masques* is Peter Stanlis. In "Robert Frost's Masques and the Classic American Tradition," Stanlis argues that human reason is insufficient to unravel life's moral mysteries, but that *Mercy* provides the alternative by affirming God's love as the basis for hope and faith.

The primary assumption of the poems is that reason has failed as a normative guide for right actions. Justice, however, is conceived by the characters of the poems as a rational category as opposed to an individual act or quality such as grace, forgiveness, love, or mercy. "Justice" is a legal term that attempts to be all-encompassing for the widest body of people possible. Else, of course, it is not justice but arbitrary whim. Indeed, all the characters' accusations of God's injustice fall precisely on that point: that it is arbitrary rather than absolute and normative. The problem is that when one's own reason cannot comprehend God's reasons, the human mind devises its own solutions to the conundrum of Justice/Injustice. We see several alternatives enacted in the *Masques*.

Job intemperately pleads for understanding from a God who insists that each person apprehends understanding existentially. Thyatira, whose role in the poem is too easily overlooked, represents the modern skeptic of all things supernatural. She often hides behind a thin, cynical sneer, ready to scoff at heaven and hell alike. She nicely shows how comfortable cynicism can be; she drifts off to sleep any time she wishes. But she also represents the modern age, cast in an ethical ennui.

In the case of Jonah we have the pleasure of watching a genuine transformation in character. Jonah enters as a frightened fugitive; he leaves like Bunyan's frightened Pilgrim, his eyes just glimpsing the Celestial City. Keeper too changes dramatically. Or, one might say, he finds the correct reasons for and proper understanding of his initial, cynical socialism. At first it is all anti-wealth and brittle railing against political injustice. At the end, as he bends to Jonah's body, he sees social justice as an act of love and mercy.

Although she has more lines than Thyatira, Jesse Bel is essentially a foil in this play. An alcoholic who preaches courage but can't practice it, Jesse drops into the background of the bookstore from where she makes her (often amusing) quips. Perhaps her most powerful line, however, occurs when she stands by the cellar door, which she has donated to Paul's use "To bring faith back" (566). One can almost imagine a plaintive wistfulness in her voice as she says, "Still what we need / Is something to believe in, don't we, Paul?" (567–68).

One finds change in Paul, too, and perhaps because of Jesse's plaintive question. He moves from titular Defender of the Word to an enactor of the Word. It is one thing to talk about Justice and Mercy; quite another to enact it. The fascinating thing is that the man seemingly without religion, the Brother's Keeper, New Deal Socialist, aides him in that transformation. It is very nearly, in fact, like a blending of two disparate sides into one, albeit slightly messy, whole.

Even though written relatively late in his career, the two *Masques* nonetheless represent a starting point for a consideration of Frost's ethics. The primary beliefs we glean from them are, first, that categorical rationalization is not a safe guide to ethical values, indeed may be inimical to them; second, that often confusing ethical values such as mercy, loving-kindness, and forgiveness are apprehended existentially, by an act of faith; and, third, that ethical values only become significant as they are acted upon. They are not merely abstract ideals, but concrete actions exemplified by Keeper moving to Jonah to carry him to the cross of mercy. If we find the Rationalist Ethic an unacceptable accounting for Frost's works, perhaps the Theological Ethic will provide clearer understanding.

4

Theological Ethics

THE VERY INDETERMINACY OF THE SO-CALLED GOD QUESTION FOR Frost surprisingly assists us on understanding his ethical beliefs. While some facets of the theological ethics might seem, upon first glance, to capture Frost perfectly, upon closer examination one discovers several radical departures. The Theological Ethics takes its name from the perspective of religion, which offers an interpretation of the nature of God and such God–human-nature relationships as sin, evil, goodness, and salvation. The defining nature of such relationships focuses upon some transcendent but always immanent source. The latter is the central issue of this ethical view, for it holds that God has not left humanity in spiritual isolation but has revealed to it certain revelations of divine will. Thereby it lies in direct contrast to the Rationalist Ethic.

THEOLOGICAL ETHICS IN HISTORICAL CONTEXT

The theological ethics requires an historical contextualizing for it is properly understood both as a revolution against prevailing philosophies of good and evil in the ancient world and also as a radical formulation of new philosophical structures. Perhaps the premier ethicist of the classical world was Plato, with his stated aim of understanding the correlation between the Ideal and the Real to further understand the just Republic. Confronting the skepticism of the Sophists, Plato grounded morality in the functions of the soul. Thereby he divests ethics from popular opinion, for example, or from tyrants, or from mere expediency. But to what end is Plato's morality of the soul?

The early twentieth-century philosopher George Patrick provides a helpful analogy to answer the question. The question of the analogy is whether ants or bees have "duties." Do they act rightly

or wrongly? Patrick's response: "They certainly exhibit in their in-
stinctive actions a very high degree of *cooperation* toward a certain
end; and that end is well-being of the swarm or colony; and this
well-being would seem to consist in the prosperous and continuous
life of the species."[1] In such a way also, the *telos* of human ethics for
Plato is Justice—the Ideal of his Republic. Justice is corporate, but
abetted by individual justice. In Plato's words, "We shall conclude
that a man is just in the same way that a state is just."[2] Herein lies
the trickier part of Plato's ethics, for the following question is what
constitutes justice in the individual.

Justice in the state consists of the harmonious working of three
distinct parties: Tradesmen, Auxiliaries, and Guardians or Rulers.
Injustice occurs through intemperance, when one class usurps the
privileges of another:

> Where there are three orders, then, any plurality of functions or shift-
> ing from one order to another is not merely utterly harmful to the
> community, but one might fairly call it the extreme of wrongdoing.
> And you will agree that to do the greatest of all wrongs to one's own
> community is injustice.[3]

Justice in the individual similarly consists of three parts: appetite,
reason, and spirit.[4] And, similarly, when any one of these usurps
the "privileges" of the other, injustice occurs. For example, when
appetite says, contrary to reason and spirit, drink to excess, disharmony or injustice occurs. But where does this sense of justice itself
come from? As always for Plato, it derives from the Ideal. The
Ideal is the perfect good, the truly just. When it enters the body,
however, it can become warped by the gross, earthly, *real* materials
of which the human body is formed. Thereby, evil in society is always an aberration of the Ideal.[5]

However neatly packaged in *The Republic*, Plato's ethics was less
than satisfying to his successors. The substantive issue was his failure to account adequately for the nature of evil. To say that evil—
"injustice" in Plato's thought—is synonymous with disharmony in
the state or the individual assumes the existence of ethical freaks,
like organisms with an aberrant gene, rather than a force to be
reckoned with in the world and in individual lives. The disharmony occurs in individuals when reason and spirit fail to overrule
appetite. Why they fail to do so is answered by a flawed argument
of circularity. That's the way the person *is*—the way an individual

body has corrupted its *soul*. Little in an ameliorative sense can be done for it. Therefore the necessity of the Guardian class to impose order.

In response to Plato's ethics, several radically juxtaposed and extremist ethics developed during subsequent years. The first steps toward a theological ethics in the philosophical, as distinguished from strictly religious, sense of the term, arose during the early church's battle with Gnosticism. One can find skirmishes of the battle in the letters of Saint Paul, but it took two giants of early church philosophy, Plotinus (204–70) and Augustine (354–430), to formulate a position that defined theological ethics for many centuries.

Plotinus's life spanned some of the most turbulent years of the Roman empire, but the political affairs of that time scarcely touched the surface of his philosophical thought. He still lived in Plato's legacy, now identified as "middle-Platonism." One telling testimony to this legacy lies in Porphyry's famous biography of his master, where he says, "Plotinus was ashamed to have been born into a body." Plotinus's philosophical quest was to identify the Ideal, but not, as Plato did, as some great cosmic mind. Rather, he sought some personality, which he deemed "The One" or "The Good" and which exercised a relational experience with humanity. (It should be noted, however, that Plotinus had rejected the Christianity of his youth and that he does not single out this being, even though he calls it "God," in any orthodox Christian sense.) For Plotinus, the One produces all creation and therefore, by necessity, must be other than all creation.[6] It "exists in Itself, a unique Form."[7] Furthermore, all things depend upon the One for their being and nurture.

If the One is beyond all thought (Reason) and all being, and if the One transcends all experience of which we have knowledge or are capable, then these hypotheses, refined from Plato, are used by Plotinus to attack the radical extremism of the Gnostics. In particular, Plotinus attacked the Gnostic "special knowledge" that certain rituals and ceremonies lead one to God. The Gnostics believed that hidden knowledge, kept in the hands of the few who knew the code-signs, was the key to salvation. Thus, they posited a radical dualism between this world and God's, deleted the immanence of God, and abandoned humanity to a somber darkness to which only they held the light of knowledge.

On the one hand, Plotinus confronts the remoteness and indeterminacy of Plato's Ideal; on the other he engaged, often vituperatively, Gnosticism's presumption of special keys to divine knowledge. The synthesis for Plotinus lay in the concept of "the Good," or in an ethical relationship with the divine. Absolute goodness may be attributed to the One only insofar as God is *The Good*, rather than "good." Where, then, is humanity situated in relationship to the Good?

Plotinus writes metaphorically of emanation of God. The emanation, however, is not an outpouring of God, since God is unchanging, but rather a diminution of him. The world issues from God by necessity (as Aquinas would later argue). It is necessary that the less perfect should originate from the more perfect, in the same way, perhaps, that a photograph originates from the object photographed but provides a diminished image of the reality. Nonetheless, emanations of God do appear in this world, the most important of which for Plotinus is the *Nous*.[8] The *Nous* is a kind of intuition or apprehension that operates in a two way but syncretic fashion—awareness of the One as being and awareness of oneself as person. Thereby Plotinus defines a relational experience between humanity and God.

Finally, this relationship in the human soul is manifested in several ways. The highest level is simply designated by Plotinus as *Nous*, rooted in the world of ideas. Such ideas might include, "What is God like?" "What is humanity?" "What ends does humanity strive for?" But they also include the ethical intuition of "What is right by God?" This Plotinus designates as the "ethical ascent," leading to a mystical union with the One. This life permits only brief moments of such union, when one thinks and acts accordingly with the One by the power of intuition or the *Nous*; it is necessarily momentary until one is freed from the hindrance of the body.

Properly understood, Plotinus's ethics are deontological—that is, one acts properly according to a sense of intuited oughtness— rather than theological. The significant change of direction he brought to western philosophy, however, lay in the relational aspect between human and divine. It was left to Augustine to formulate this fully into a theological ethics with his concept of living in the kingdom of God.

Augustine is best known in the western tradition for his concept of two kingdoms—the City of God and the City of the World, either of which an individual inhabits at the present moment. The distinctions between the two cities rest upon a series of principles;

for example, that God is all good and all being and that the worldly city is, therefore, a simultaneous privation both from good and being. The less good a person is, the less being a person is. In developing his argument, Augustine, like a heavyweight brawler, took on several schools of thought at once: the Skeptics with their sophistry and uncertainty of truth; the Pelagians with their view that grace is nonessential; the Manichaeans with their dualism of good and evil. But, surprisingly, in addition to Scripture he looks to Plato and Socrates for guidance in his battle. "To Socrates," he wrote in *The City of God*, "goes the credit of being the first one to channel the whole of philosophy into an ethical system for the reformation and regulation of morals."[9]

Augustine felt deeply indebted to Plato, even wanting to believe that he had been influenced by Hebraic thought in his concept of the Ideal and humanity.[10] The only difficulty for Augustine was Plato's insufficient accounting for evil. Nonetheless, the most striking contrast to Plato, indeed to all western philosophy to this point, is Augustine's epistemology, which also forms the basis for his ethics. Augustine's philosophy has faith for its foundation, and this faith involved the whole of a person—heart, soul, mind, and strength. Thus he formulated his famous statement of epistemology: *credo ut intelligam*—"I believe in order that I may understand." If there were a guide in the ancient world for Augustine's thinking, it had to be the Old Testament prophet Isaiah who said, "Unless you believe, you shall not understand."[11]

Augustine did not jettison reason in his epistemological configuration. He simply subordinated reason to revelation. Nonetheless, this would prove to be one of the revolutionary acts in western philosophy. To make a faith act the basis for an epistemology is also to make certain assumptions—or belief acts—about the One in whom one places faith. If, for example, this One, or God, reveals its will, then it is a relational being, concerned about the humanity to which it reveals its will.[12] Heretofore in the western tradition, "God" was a "Being" or "State-of-Being," one attained by mental action. Augustine posits a divine knowledge revealed by a divine being.

But why would such a being do this? It would do so if, and only if, that relational being went beyond revelation to some deeper, more personal, and individual relation with humanity. From his epistemology of revelation, Augustine arrives at an ethics of relation. On the one hand, God reveals his laws and directives for liv-

ing justly; on the other humanity reciprocates in a loving
relationship by living with God, humanity, and nature according
to those laws and directives. This reciprocation does not, of course,
occur naturally or easily. After all, Augustine did establish the two
kingdoms—that of the world or love of self and that of God or love
for God. The very reason it does not come easily is because God
left us at liberty to choose one or the other. We do not find in Augustine an ethics of enslavement; rather an ethics of free human
choice.

FROST AND THE THEOLOGICAL ETHICS

The theological ethics begins, we see, with a faith act. At that point,
we observed, *A Masque of Mercy* ends. The individual accepts the
divine reality as central, and therefore certain ethical obligations
follow upon this faith act. The primacy of obedience to God (rather
than to a human economic or political system—"the common
good"—central to philosophical ethics) may be seen in ethical admonitions such as "Love the Lord your God with all your heart
and with all your soul and with all your strength" (O. T. Deut. 6:5),
and "Love your neighbor as yourself" (N. T. Matt. 22:39). If one
loves God, one has a duty or obligation to love others (a cynic
might point out that Frost did neither very well).

The first step of a theological ethics, then, is a faith act in which
one places obedience to God rather than to rationalist constructs—
one such example being the principle of loving others even when
they are unlovely or unloving in return. The second step, however,
recognizes that human love is not the absolute, but is a means of
revealing the absolute that is in God. God alone, in the absolute
sense, may be called Love. Therefore, any act not based in love is
wrong. To steal your car is a criminal wrong. If found guilty, justice
will be served and I will be punished. But to steal your car is also
an ethical wrong in this belief system for it is not a loving act. The
theological ethics stresses the loving or unloving ways we hold fellow humans and the natural world. "Do I hate someone? Or do I
love and protect and help provide for the lonely and unprotected
and impoverished? Do I pollute the environment?" These are the
sorts of questions a theological ethics addresses. One finds them
nicely summarized in the words of the Old Testament prophet

Micah: "What does the Lord require of you? To act justly and to love mercy and to walk humbly with your God" (6.8).

Literally dozens of poems in Frost's lengthy canon address what Dorothy Judd Hall calls "the God question." In particular, the 1947 volume, *Steeple Bush*, ripples with such poems. "The Fear of God," for example, almost reads as a coda to *Masque of Mercy*. "A Steeple on the House" reflects upon eternal destinies. "Innate Helium," with its famous first line, "Religious faith is a most filling vapor," reflects upon the presence, or absence, of faith within one's life. The short poem is nicely structured with two tercets, rhyming ABC ABC that juxtapose the idea of faith to the image of "buoyant bird bones." Yet the last line, "Some gas like helium must be innate," twists the poem into ambiguity. Is religious faith that which lifts us up, or is it just another form of "gas"? While many such poems lead us into the teasing ambiguity so typical of Frost, several lead us to a starker confrontation with his ethics.

Many of Frost's poems edge toward theological ethics, but none of them embraces it fully. This may be seen in several ways. Nowhere does he purport to be a spokesperson for God. Indeed, just the opposite occurs. Most of the poems that explore the human relationship with God remain inconclusive with a strained tension of opposing views, or they end with an equally tense ambiguity. Furthermore, while the popular attraction to Frost's poetry has often rested upon the serenity of human lovers in nature (e.g., "Two Look at Two"), as one probes deeper into the poems one discovers they are often fraught with human tensions, hostilities, and sometimes overt hatred. Frost isn't denying the need to love; he emphasizes, however, how very hard it is to do so.

Frost's poems that deal with a form of theological ethics may be cast into two frameworks. The first of these would be explicit deliberation over the human response to the problem of good and evil; the second would be those poems that use metaphor to probe metaphysical issues. Consider as representative poems in that first category "Quandary," "The Lesson for Today," and "Directive." All are relatively late poems, published from 1940–60, a period during which Frost's own work had become increasingly reflective.

In this grouping, "Quandary" bears interest because the poem purports to address very directly the issue of good and evil. In a not unusual move, Frost adopts a light-hearted tone, highlighted by hexameter couplets, for addressing the serious topic. Clearly, he does not intend to be either pontifical or didactic. The tone of the poem is almost playful. Frost indicates from the outset that he remains, in fact, neutral about evil: "Never have I been sad or glad / that there was such a thing as bad." Good and evil necessarily exist as dualities in which one defines the other. Frost supplies us here with the modern equivalent of Manichaean dualism. For the Manichaean, the choices that humanity makes between good and evil ultimately determine the power of one or the other; therefore, the primacy of one or the other is relative to human discrimination. This was the heresy of the early church that Augustine attacked in *City of God*. Himself a former Manichaean, Augustine pointed out that one must distinguish, first, between a created order in which good and evil occur and the Creator, and, second, between a supreme God who is the creator and any lesser divine force. For Augustine, evil is always a lesser "deprivation" from "Good" and "Being."

While Frost sets up a dualism of a Manichaean sort in the first six lines, he does so for his own particular ends. If good and bad are dualistic, then humanity needs "a lot of brains" to distinguish.[13] The question whether humanity has those brains isn't answered right at this point, but Frost suggests one directive from Apollo's oracle in the ancient city of Delphi (II). Frost neatly bysteps the similar New Testament injunction to love one's neighbor as one's self to include the Delphic injunction to hate one's neighbor as one hates oneself. Is one simply the dualistic converse of the other, like good and evil? The key point is discrimination according to individual choices and values. Whether one loves or hates oneself determines one's ethical relationships. Thus, according to Frost, there is no substitute for brains (16). Divine directives are elided from the ethical equation.

Such choices, however, are often influenced not by rational discrimination but by emotions and sensations. Thus begins Frost's elaborate pun from line 17 to the end between "sweetbreads" and brains. "Sweetbreads" refer to either the pancreas or thymus of a young animal, usually a calf or a lamb. The two glands are associated with sexual potency, and are suggestive of an aphrodisiac ("innuendo I detest"). The "quandary," then, is not only the dialectic between good and evil itself, but also humanity's discrimination either by sexual and emotional desires or by rational distinction.

The poem, which first appeared in *The Massachusetts Review* (fall 1959) as "Somewhat Dietary," is one of Frost's most heavily revised in later versions. In fact, nine lines were cut from the initial version, which elaborated the pun and the "quandary," to larger degree. These lines suggested that by eating sweetbreads and by acquiring sexual potency, the narrator acquired his "high I.Q." The ending of the current poem is surely more ambivalent. Lines 20–21 point out his foolishness in ever confusing sexual desire and rationality with making ethical choices. The lines themselves bear a clever supporting wordplay: "fool to think," "brains and sweetbread the same." Yet, in the final line of the poem Frost still wants to hang on to his "high I.Q." In ethical choices between good and bad, human discrimination—not divine revelation—is the guide.

In "Quandary" Frost looks to the ancient past—the Delphic Oracle—for guidance in modern ethical choices. If one is to love or hate one's neighbor as one loves or hates oneself, the question remains whether emotional desire or rational scrutiny governs the discrimination. In "The Lesson for Today" Frost also turns to the past, this time in a dreamlike monologue to Alcuin (735–804), a tutor in the court of Charlemagne. Frost situates himself in the poem in an uncertain and dark age at the end of the millennium. Therefore he turns to the "undebatably dark ages" to see how a poet then dealt with issues at the threshold of our millennium.

The narrator is well aware of the gulf between the millennia. Alcuin's position was a decisively minor one, his time still overshadowed by the luminous legacy of Virgil. Alcuin simply didn't have the force of communications to tell him what was right or wrong. On the contrary, the narrator suffers under a blizzard of dogmatism. Echoing Hamlet's statement that "the time is out of joint," the narrator laments the pattern of modern poets to write poetry that matches the "disjointedness" of the age. Frost's own answer to the charge of living in a dark age appears in his "Letter to *The Amherst Student*."[14] There he states, "You will often hear it said that the age of the world we live in is particularly bad. I am impatient of such talk. We have no way of knowing that this age is one of the worst in the world's history. . . . It is immodest of a man to think of himself as going down before the worst forces ever mobilized by God" (*Selected Prose* 105). At all times, in any age, Frost adds, the work "to save your soul . . . Your decency, your integrity" is the battle in darkness toward Heaven (106).

The belief in the unmitigated darkness of an age, Frost argues in his *Letter*, necessarily affects the art of the age. In one of the most forceful lines he ever penned, Frost states of modern authors,

"They can write huge shapeless novels, huge gobs of raw sincerity bellowing with pain and that's all that they can write" (106). What then is our stay against the chaos? For Frost, it is form. Form in art is the assertion of self over darkness. It imposes order and channels meaning.

In "The Lesson for Today," Frost's conversation turns in line 43 to the same topic. Acknowledging that one cannot accurately appraise the state of one's own age (it passes too quickly to be seized whole), he plays a little game with Alcuin by surmising that the age is indeed dark. For the fun of it, the narrator says, let's examine which age was the worse, or the better for being dark. Thereby the narrator situates us in a Valley of Despair. In line 58 Frost strikes what has become a familiar note—again, one thinks of Santayana—suffering in this life leads us to faith. Faith in what, though?

Continuing his monologue with Alcuin, the narrator allows that both ages belittle humanity. The middle ages labored under a theology of a vindictive and remote God ruling a humanity of "violent worms." The modern age enacts its own belittlement by a reduction of humanity under science. The hugeness of space and advances in scientific knowledge diminish humanity like an ant farm. The narrator imagines Alcuin calling his "violent worms" of students to instruct them in the day's lessons. Perhaps he teaches them the Latin word for *alas*. Surely, this is one attitude to take toward a dark age—simply throw up one's hands with a stoic *alas* and succumb to it. Perhaps, second, Alcuin teaches them "how to be unhappy yet polite" (88). Here the student may learn to treat Despair with a life of manners, by living according to the medieval courtly code of *courtesie*. Third, however, perhaps Alcuin simply teaches them rhetoric, to impose form upon the chaos. In this case, Frost makes it clear that such art is teleological (94–95). It directs an age rather than fading to black in the darkness of an age. This, then, is the act of faith. The imposition of form through writing surmises that there are things in this life worth salvaging; it directs these things toward ends beyond this immediate life.

One could find easier solutions than listening to the poets and tutors, Frost admits. We could simply turn everything over to state control, which he calls automatic salvation. But he doesn't want it that easy, since that responds to humanity's destiny only in one time and place. It abdicates any individual sense of *telos*. Rather, "The universals" (104) refer to line 96, "*Memento mori* and obey the Lord." These are teleological issues that direct humanity's thinking—and necessarily humanity's actions—in this age. Therefore, all ages are also the same for the individual soul (113). Thinking of Alcuin's *Epitaph* (126)—a work that admonishes a passerby to think of how fleeting life is and to live for the spirit rather than the physical (*memento mori*)—sets the narrator off to a graveyard for reflection. There he reads other epitaphs, observes dates ranging across many years. The variation of life spans impresses him. One man lived one hundred and eight years. But the cemetery is proof that all things end—including by extension, governments, careers, perhaps the earth itself. Confronted by that realization, the narrator accepts his limitations also, and accepts Alcuin's *memento mori* in principle. Yet he insists that he will live his life teleologically, with purposes and aims that endure beyond this life. These he summarizes in his own epitaph: "I had a lover's quarrel with the world" (161). The terseness of the lines beautifully compacts the opposing tensions Frost himself held. If he quarreled with the world, it would not be with the "huge gobs of raw sincerity" he spoke of in *The Amherst Student*, nor would it be with the anger/despair of his contemporaries. If it is a "lover's quarrel," it is done in love, but also in expectation of some betterment and constant hope of reconciliation.

In its own way, "The Lesson for Today" tells us how to have a good, fair fight. Alcuin tells us that politeness and manners go a long way. The narrator tells us of a "lover's quarrel." These in themselves constitute ethical guidelines for practical "good" living. The primary ethical issues of the poem, however, probe much further. Even more decidedly than in "Quandary," in this poem God is an absent and non-decisive force. Rather, the emphasis is upon humanity's duty to itself and to its age. This emphasis translates into two specific tasks for the poet. The first task is to impose form upon the apparent chaos and to shape some order from the darkness. This thoroughly accords with Frost's own poetic beliefs, and also with his dismay with the flattening imagism and abdication of traditional forms by some modernists. Even though as poet Frost often leaves his own position ambiguous in the poem, he situates the reader in confrontation with alternatives that "trip the reader head foremost with the boundless" (*Selected Letters* 344). The second task, or belief in this case, is to direct the reader to some teleological goals beyond the immediate context of the poem that inform one of how to live this life. The "universals" Frost asserts in this poem (although he would accumulate others elsewhere) are *memento mori* and the existence of God. Remembering one's death and awareness of the divine provide directives for how one lives in any age, even one as dark as the present for the narrator or for the Dark Ages of Alcuin.

Other such directives arise in Frost's poem by that title, "Directive," one of the poet's most heralded and frequently discussed poems. Simply on the level of its intrinsic poetic beauty, Randall Jarrell in his "To the Laodiceans," an often negative assessment of Frost's work, declares it one of the "most dismaying and most gratifying poems any poet has ever written."[15] And George Nitchie, although not fully appreciative of the poem, nonetheless judges it to be "to my mind one of Frost's best."[16] Apart from the poem's widely-acclaimed merits (the tightness of plot, the evocation of the past, the tone of mystical recollection, the precision of natural placement), "Directive" is also a crucial work in understanding Frost's ethics, particularly as it relates to the ideas we have already located in "Quandary" and "The Lesson for Today." We discovered there an ethics of duty to make choices between good and evil, the necessity of a faith act in the midst of darkness, and the purposeful setting of one's life and work toward teleological ends. Through carefully assimilated metaphor (the poem itself) and symbolism (elements within the poem that shape the metaphor), "Directive" more clearly defines that human quest for a positioning before the divine.

As in "Mowing," "Directive" is one of Frost's powerful examples of a poetics that leads the reader inward to discovery. "Directive," Mark Richardson has pointed out, is marked by a deliberate invitation, but with a very real and personal guide: "This is no easy step over into a pasture, though. And I'm not being asked just to watch some 'I.' I am *being* watched, spoken to. The focus is on a 'you'— *me*."[17] This is the very heart of Frost's poetics—luring the reader into participation of the situation. At once it is also the heart of his poetic ethics—once having lured the reader into the situation he sets options into play for the reader. The title "Directive" may, in this case, also be understood as directive among possible options or ambiguities of choice. Always the narrative voice is one of opening. Richardson observes that "Like all directives, this one speaks in the imperative, but never down to me. It is gentle, seems to give directions to get to someplace I want to go, even if I hadn't realized it."[18] Indeed, the poetics exercised in the poem are precisely that of leading the reader—the fellow adventurer—to discoveries.

The metaphorical journey of the poem moves concurrently into the past and also toward a regenerative source. The poem starts with a stripping action, since this *now*, read as a noun, is too much with us. The line plays on Wordsworth's "The World Is too Much with Us," but for Frost the world cannot be escaped. Nor should it be. The individual embarking on this journey, by searching out the spring of renewal, also renews his understanding of the world. The present, therefore, must only be momentarily escaped. The motion here is analogous to those memorable lines in "Birches":

> I'd like to go by climbing a birch tree
> And climb black branches up a snow-white trunk
> *Toward* heaven, till the tree could bear me no more,
> But dipped its top and set me down again.
>
> (11.55–58)

Frost does not seek escape in the sense of fleeing imprisonment. His escape is necessary in order to move toward something. From the outset, then, the poem clearly does not situate the reader on a holiday nature tour. It places one on a quest, with a sense of searching toward initially indeterminate ends. As with the poem itself, those ends don't become clear until we give ourselves up wholly to the seeking.

The quest costs something. It is no mere casual adventure, where anything might happen and all will return safely home at night to tell stories around the firelight. The quest immediately places us in uncertainty. As we step into an earlier age, we let go the present and lose ourselves in a world of fuzzy details and blurred outlines. We don't "know" as we have known, having known heretofore by science, memory, and precision. We become vulnerable under the poem's course and as we submit to the quest. In fact, we set out on a road along which we are guided by one "who only has at heart your getting lost" (9).

This "getting lost" is the final step of moving from the *now* to the quest itself. We have to divest ourselves of our routine ways of seeing things, of valuing things, of seeking truth. Only then, with a complete and necessary innocence, can we begin to set out on the path of the quest. In effect, we start over again as mere infants. We give ourselves up to the quest, despite its riddling uncertainties at this initial stage. In this context, the biblical allusion in lines 8–9 directs our understanding and embarking upon the unknown and uncertain. Luke 9 tells of the miracle of Jesus feeding the five thousand at Bethsaida. After a long day Jesus and his disciples draw aside to pray. Here for the first time Jesus reveals to his disciples that he will be killed but will be resurrected on the third day. On that basis—losing a life to gain life—Jesus says, "Whoever wants to save his life will lose it, but whoever loses his life for me will save it. What good is it for a man to gain the whole world, and yet lose or forfeit his very self?" (Luke 24–25). At this stage in the poem, we are also at the point of gaining or losing. Deliberately losing the *now*, we set out with our strange guide who has at heart our getting lost. But in the process, perhaps we shall gain something.

At first the quest seems to go further backward from the *now*. We pass the ruined foundations of the town (10–13) as we leave behind ordered society and become yet more solitary. On the mountain ledges the guide points out the prehistoric work of a glacier that has left its imprint on the earth (14–19). As we enter the forest beyond the abandoned town, moreover, the journey grows ever more mysterious. Eyes seem to watch our passing. The woods send a slight rustling of excitement through their leaves as we go (20–25). It is almost as if we have left immediate and temporal concerns for a prehistoric consciousness, primitive in its connectedness to a spiritual world. We are, in fact, becoming lost.

Here Frost initiates a second major pattern of allusion. If the first is the biblical injunction that to gain one's life one first must lose it—turning from a present world to a spiritual world—the second arises from the Grail Quest of *Morte d'Arthur*. At the stage of the Grail Quest, Arthur's kingdom is beginning to crumble from interior evil. The king who had instituted civilized order in a dark land, who had driven the beast of disorder out of the country, and who had established Camelot as a shining symbol of civilized order, has now been attacked by the evil within through the lust of Lancelot and Guinevere. Seeking a force for renewal, several knights search out the Holy Grail, purportedly brought to Britain by Joseph of Arimathea as his symbol of renewal and power in his crusade to Christianize the land. In the intervening years, the sacred goblet, used by Christ at the Last Supper, was lost, but supposedly held in the Chapel Perilous.

When Galahad hears that the Grail has appeared once again, he vows to find it, crying out that "If I love myself, I save myself." Percival also sets out to see it. Percival enters a wasteland of illusions, including a grove of apple trees. When he tries to eat the apples, they turn to dust. In Frost's poem, the apple trees are few, old, and "pecker-fretted" (28). As Percival relates his story to the old monks—guardians of the way—he tells of meeting Sir Bors, who, also seeking the way, had searched out old religions, including the Stonehenge. The figurative language in lines 10–12 of "Directive," which, as Jay Parini points out, emanate in actuality from an abandoned quarry on a neighbor's farm, suggest Stonehenge. The road behind the ruined farm, Frost writes,

> May seem as if it should have been a quarry—
> Great monolithic knees the former town
> Long since gave up pretense of keeping covered.

The quarry cliffs evoke a distant past, chiseled out by a glacier eons ago. But where does one go from that past? In the Grail Quest, Percival's own way leads through a land of increasing decay, of ruined cities, and of preternatural phantoms watching his every move.

The guide of "Directive" routes us over similar terrain. His purpose is to bring us to the point where, he says,

> If you're lost enough to find yourself
> By now, pull in your ladder road behind you
> And put a sign up CLOSED to all but me.
>
> (36–38)

We have traversed the dangerous terrain, having lost ourselves to find ourselves. Consequently, it is time to turn in a new direction. That road is closed to all but *me* because it has been *my* journey— each person has to make his or her own. But also it is time to pull that ladder up and begin anew.

The Grail allusion still prevails here. When he approaches the Chapel Perilous, Lancelot, who wanted to find the Grail to redeem his sin, has to climb a thousand stairs with great pain. Climbing toward renewal, he too is pulling the ladder road up behind him. In the Arthurian story the climb may be viewed as existential, a stripping off of all things just as he nears the source of personal renewal.[19] Although he confesses that he was nearly mad with his quest by then, Lancelot claims that even he saw the Grail.

In "Directive" Frost begins in line 39 turning away from our "losing" and toward our "gaining." It begins with the innocent imagination of the child. Seeing the little playhouse with its scattered (and broken) remnants brings tears (44) for an irrecoverable innocence. Yet something of that willingness to believe, which the children so dearly and easily possess, continues into the adult life. At least it does on this quest of recovery and regaining. Next we pass the adult house, now in ruins. But the delicate use of key adjectives protects the house from appearing like a monstrous dereliction. The cellar hole is "belilaced," testifying to a life that can grow from the "lost" ruins. This, writes Frost, was an "earnest" house, an adjective he reserves throughout his poetry for a positive sense of determination, love, and hard labor. So passing, we arrive finally at our destination, which is also our "destiny"—the brook that sustained earlier inhabitants (and pilgrims).

This brook, perhaps an allusion to the "living water" of John 4:10–14, still flows pure and cold as it had in previous ages. It is water to be drawn and drunk from. For that purpose the narrator has secreted in an old, waterside cedar tree—nourished by the brook itself—"a broken drinking goblet like the Grail" (57). Two qualifications are placed upon that goblet, however, and they are very much like those placed upon the Grail itself. First, the Grail is placed under a spell so the "wrong ones can't find it, / So can't get saved . . ." (58–59). The narrator then follows this biblical allusion by attributing it to Mark. Specifically, the passage in Mark 8:34–38 is itself a command to a quest, and provides a certain spiritual parallel to the entire poem. Here Jesus turns to a crowd of people following him and provides his own summons for losing and gaining: "If anyone would come after me, he must deny himself and take up his cross and follow me. For whoever wants to save his life will lose it, but whoever loses his life for me and for the gospel will save it." The second qualification arises more subtly from the fact that the narrator had earlier stolen the goblet from the children's playhouse. The implication is that one must drink from the living water in innocence and faith. The final line of the poem affirms this, in a benediction based loosely upon the communion liturgy of the church: "Drink and be whole again beyond confusion" (62). The variation lies in the last words. This quest is restorative, not just of the individual, but of the individual back in the treacherous *now*. The combination is not merely a momentary stay against confusion; rather, a transcending of confusion itself.

For Dorothy Judd Hall, "Directive" is the central poem in what she deems "salvation by surrender." This may be so, but I don't believe "salvation" should be read in any orthodox sense. Hall cites a letter from Frost to Hyde Cox in which Frost once again veils his own intentions in ambiguity. Pointing out that the journey to the source is the key to the poem, Frost quickly qualifies—"whatever source it is."[20] Hall compares the metaphor of the poem to fundamental elements of Christian belief: "Salvation in 'Directive' rests on paradox. The guide's technique of getting the reader 'lost' in order to 'find' himself can be compared to the Christian idea of going through the gateway of death to reach eternal life. Attaining salvation by suffering was the way of the martyrs, and of Christ on the road to Calvary."[21] Frost uses Christian and biblical elements for his own poetic ends, just as he uses those of the Grail Quest. Such elements, however, cannot be locked into a narrow allegorical sense in the poem.

Viewed from a metaphorical position, "Directive" seems to set forth a tightly-woven quest of losing the self caught up in the confusing *now* to gaining the self that restores wholeness beyond confusion. The metaphor is abetted by a series of sustaining symbols—the road taken, the perilous journey, the renewal of innocence, the living water of the brook, the Holy Grail, among others. As such, the poem seems one with the more ambivalent and equivocal acts of human-centered faith in "Quandary" and "The Lesson for Today." Despite its biblical allusions, one would be mistaken to call it a theological poem or elucidating a theological ethics. It is ultimately a poem about human actions, although surely predicated upon a faith act. A God who directs or reciprocates that act doesn't appear in the poem. The ethical pattern of all three of these poems is that a person has to step out in a faith act in order to apprehend any lesson for today or any directive for the future. It might be more accurate to view the poems as the individual striving for an existential ethic. If we can't find full satisfaction in a theological ethic, then, perhaps we can do so in its polar opposite, the existential ethics.

5

Existential Ethics

THE INDETERMINACY OF FROST'S ETHICS WHEN CONSIDERED IN A theological context may strongly suggest a human-centered ethics where right and wrong, duty and obligation, good and evil are determined by individual choices and actions. This isolation of humanity became, in fact, one of the hallmarks of modernism. Modernist art focuses intently upon a character acting with little ulterior motivation for the actions, little framework for reflection upon them, and little weighing of the necessity for the actions or the consequences of them. Humanity is stripped of the divine altogether, and is simply "being there."

Nonetheless, every ethical system "leans upon" something; that is to say, ethics makes suppositions in order to relate the individual to the world and to fellow humanity. Similarly, existential ethics proceeds upon certain assumptions about humanity, the world, and the divine. It is also the case with ethics that changes occur most rapidly and explosively during critical periods in history. Stress and tension forge ethical concerns; peaceful days breed languid unconcern. So it is also that ethical issues have careened wildly throughout the twentieth century. Twentieth-century philosophers grew more intent upon examining one's duty to oneself. What indeed is this being called humanity? Does it have any worth? During Frost's lifetime the questioning simply grew more tense, more stressful, and as loud as the bombs thudding throughout two World Wars. The answers, however, remained indeterminate. While by no means presumptive of covering the wide range of existential ethics, consider several representative traits that developed during Frost's lifetime.

EXISTENTIAL ETHICS IN HISTORICAL CONTEXT

While dozens of minor skirmishes on the field of ethics intensified during the early part of the twentieth century, a few people achieved authoritative prominence. In some ways, one might say, they were building in the house that Nietzsche ruined and that Edmund Husserl tried to rearrange. But surely the most prominent of these ethical reshapers was Martin Heidegger, who laid the groundwork of Existentialism that Camus, Sartre, and de Beauvoir built upon.

In *Being and Time* (1927) Heidegger proposed to elucidate the meaning of being. Humanity had heretofore, he argued, labored under the error of identifying itself in natural categories (a possible influence from G. E. Moore's *Principia Ethica*, 1903, whose first three chapters take up this issue). The central issue for Heidegger becomes this—I am not an animal with reason. I am an independent being, but what is it that makes me such?

The answer, says Heidegger, lies in *dasein*, a term that he uses in lieu of *human*. The word designates existence; literally it means "being there" (*sein da*). The implication is that humanity comes to awareness of itself in a situation—a space and time for which the individual has no responsibility. Furthermore, the nature of one's existence in this space and time is ambiguous. We must come to know ourselves as the particular and personal in order to define our existence. While our existence is accidental and not determinative by others, then, it nonetheless appears in the world and among others. It is not pure I, as Nietzsche would have it. *To be* means to be *in* the world and *with* others. By this relational positioning, Heidegger also assumes an ethical premise.

Seemingly, then, as Heidegger observed in his *Introduction to Metaphysics*, it should be relatively easy to determine who oneself is, because oneself is who one is closest to. Yet, he says that nonetheless the essential I is often the one we are remotest from. Basically, we don't know who we are. Why? In answer, Heidegger introduces his famous triad—facticity, fallenness, and authenticity. Not only did this triad supply the groundwork for his own ethics, it held dominant sway over the ethical theories of later existentialists.

The familiar elements may be summarized rather quickly. Facticity is simply the premise that one exists, and exists in a particular world. Whether one is aware of it or not, one's being resides in a time and place; it is being-in-the-world. However, being is befuddled by "being-in-the-midst-of-the-world," or the state of fallenness. In such a state one is not aware of one's uniqueness of being, but is merely an objective entity in a worldly process. Authenticity is the recovery of one's individual being from the inauthenticity of fallenness. One becomes authentic by discovering possibilities for oneself and freely choosing from among them.

Thereby, Heidegger moves to his term Existenz: "The 'essence' of Dasein consists of its Existenz."[1] Existenz (literally, *ek-sistenz*: "standing out") projects possibilities for the individual. Facticity never allows that or attempts the act. And most people are content to allow system and society to rule their lives. Neither, however, will these ever be authentic people. Existenz permits the freedom for "the possibility of being or not being our own self."[2]

Heidegger develops his theory, of course, over many more stages. Two of the more important are that the nature of being in our age is characterized by mere chatter, and that confronting death as possibility forces one to see all life as the present moment. Confrontation with death wrenches one from facticity and turns to the individual being with resoluteness. Such a view is liberating. In fact, it liberates one from time itself, hence the title *Being and Time*.

It should also be noted that Heidegger himself refused to use the term "ethics" in relation to his theory; in fact, he believed ethics fell under some purview totally apart from philosophy. He can't have his way quite that easily. In a discussion about Heidegger's metaphysics and ethics in *From Rationalism to Existentialism*, Robert Solomon points out that "If there is no clear distinction between knowledge and practice, between what the world is and what we aspire to make of it, then these two traditionally very different philosophical enterprises, the search for truth and search for values, are indistinguishable."[3] Solomon goes on to elucidate several questions implicit in the very framework of Heidegger's premises. ("If it is the very nature of Dasein to 'question its own being,' why is it not some sort of obligation of Dasein to ask this question?") Fundamentally, that is the dilemma of existential ethics. Are there obligations, albeit to oneself, that arise from outside oneself? Conversely, do I have obligations to the world beyond myself and for the actions I commit?

Heidegger's thinking provided the groundwork for twentieth-century existentialism by defining a clearer relationship between being and place/time than had been seen before. Quickly, as was the case also in the arts (witness the Surrealists), the issues became central to twentieth-century philosophy. These issues of being and time received greater urgency yet with the psychological, spiritual, and physical devastation of World War II. It was a stage made to order for Jean-Paul Sartre.

Even though echoes of Heidegger roll through Sartre's work, Sartre himself made it clear that his teachings were based on the phenomenology of Edmund Husserl. Nonetheless, Sartre's fundamental premise—existence precedes essence—is uncannily close to Heidegger. The phrase, however revolutionary, simply means that you are before you discover who you are. One is simply placed in a situation where one exists. To discover who one is, however, requires a radical commitment. For the Theistic Existentialists (Kierkegaard, Dostoyevsky, Shestov, Berdaev) one discovers real essence by a radical commitment to God. From the outset, Sartre ruled God out of the picture. Precisely because there is no God with claims upon humanity, one is free to make of oneself whatever is freely chosen. In fact, a person acts in "bad faith" (de Beauvoir's central term) and is an "inauthentic" person whenever he or she allows influences other than self to determine the choices.

Sartre moves his argument several steps further in *Being and Nothingness* to arrive at some ethical position in the world. Although Heidegger claimed disinterest in ethics, for Sartre it was a compelling issue. Having dismissed God, however, Sartre sees humanity as abandoned by any divine claims—and values. We are given only facticity, a term culled from Heidegger. Facticity is simply a set of facts that define one's situation. We can, however, transcend facticity by "nothingness," an act simultaneously annihilating the past but also admitting possibilities. Envisioning alternatives permits the self to become a phenomenon making free choices.

Thus we arrive at Sartre's cardinal ethical value: freedom. Never to be understood simply as "a person can do anything he or she wants to do," freedom is the fundamental premise from which all human and human-nature relationships arise.[4] This insistence upon freedom is the central legacy of Sartre over the second half of the twentieth century. Indeed, the guide to right (good) ethical actions is to respect the freedom of others to choose freely; any bad ethical action is the imposition of one's own will upon the freedom of others. It should be noted that Sartre himself abided by such an ethics, providing a model in his underground work during World War II.

FROST AND THE EXISTENTIAL ETHICS

Parts of the existential ethics may seem particularly attractive to Frost and useful in understanding his work. Indeed, it is not unusual for some readers to find a complete moral neutrality in Frost's works. Thus, Arnold Bartini argues that "A careful examination of Frost's work reveals . . . an essential indifference to moral perspective."[5] Focusing upon such poems as "Design," "Range-Finding," and *A Masque of Reason*, Bartini believes that any moral perspective is left to the reader to supply. Several cautions have to be reiterated, then, in examining Frost's place in an existential ethics. First, the fact that mainstream existentialism in the twentieth century is decidedly atheistic is not an issue here. Even having worked our way through the contradictions and confusions that infuse Frost's public and private statements of belief, he unquestionably is not an atheist. The least that can be said about his religious beliefs is that he was understanding of and sympathetic to biblical teachings. Even so, however, we fail to see in his poems, despite all their crowded biblical allusion, a clear and undeniable divine voice directing human action. Rather, that action seems more often to arise from an individual faith act. The faith act of choosing defines the individual as much as the rightness or wrongness of the act itself. Intrinsically, then, it shares some of the ambiguity foundational to existentialism. Although the limitations of the existential ethic finally proved it unsatisfactory in Frost's work, it is tantalizingly depicted in several poems, especially those that depict an individual acting in a social context.

Although Frost's dramatic poems would seem the most likely and clear examples to demonstrate individual and social ethics, that concern marks his poetry from the earliest stages. The first edition of *A Boy's Will* divided the poems into three sections in the table of contents, and included a brief gloss on each poem linking it to the boy's will and his coming of age. Part 1 follows the boy on his individual journey of self-identification, during which he confronts several fears about himself and society.

In this context, the poem "Love and a Question" expressly confronts the individual will in conflict with social demands. Here a bridegroom is stirred by a knock at the door. Already he confronts a decision. The house is far from any other. He has no responsibility to answer the knock. Nonetheless he arises, leaving his bride by the fire. Opening the door, he finds the stranger, a plea for shelter evident in his eyes. All he carries is a walking stick ("green-white" as if half-alive and half-decayed). Attempting to shield his bride within from the stranger's intrusion, the groom leads him further out onto the porch. Doing so, the groom feels the winter on the wind and seems to have a momentary sympathy for the stranger.

More on his heart, however, is the picture of his new wife leaning toward the fire, and the knowledge of what burns in her heart for this night:

> Within, the bride in the dusk alone
>   Bent over the open fire,
> Her face rose-red with the glowing coal
>   And the thought of her heart's desire.
>
> (17–20)

The groom is caught between two immediate needs. Outside the cold whispers of winter; inside the glowing heat of desire. Outside the mysterious stranger whose mere presence claims a need; inside the bride and her needy expectations. It would be a slight thing for the groom to give the stranger something to eat, a few coins, maybe even a blessing in prayer or a curse upon the rich (25–28). All that is an outward action. Ethically, it would even be judged a good action. But the undeniable facts are that the night is cold and windy, that there is no other shelter along the road. Then is it the groom's ethical responsibility to abrogate his own pleasure for the sake of another's comfort? Would it be right to harbor woe in the bridal house?

Here Frost has set up one of the ethical problems that persistently appears throughout his work. Do I have obligations to others, even if they should interfere with my own happiness and freedom? In this poem the answer is not given. We are left with a picture of the groom, "who wished he knew," standing on the porch. Different readers have pointed out some suggestive passages here that may be read symbolically. For example, there is a possibility of an allusion to Jesus' parable of the wedding feast, and that those who arrive late will be cast out (a parable about the kingdom of God). Such doesn't apply here. It is long past the feast. The groom too clearly represents any individual human caught in a conflict between his desires and the needs of someone else. Similarly, some read the capitalized stranger himself as some kind of deity mutely begging entrance into the new home. It seems more reasonable in this very human-centered poem that the stranger is just a universal Anyone. Thus the ethical dilemma rests powerfully upon whether one will sacrifice human freedom to benefit another. In this poem it is left open-ended.

In the same volume, however, Frost forges something of an answer. Instead of the divisions in humanity and the anguish of choices in "Love and a Question," the brotherhood and unity of humanity is emphasized in "The Tuft of Flowers." The poem eerily echoes, even in phrases and word choice, the heightened solitariness of "Mowing," but in this case the narrator is keenly mindful of one who has gone before to mow this field, even before the dew was off the grass. Now the narrator enters the field to turn the grass to dry in the sun before it starts to rot. Both tasks—mowing and turning—are essential. Therefore, even though the narrator doesn't see the mower, he feels an intense community with him through the shared labor.

Following the sporadic flight of a butterfly, the narrator notices the tuft of flowers by a brook, carefully spared by the mower. Love for this bit of nature on the part of mower and narrator binds them—"sheer morning gladness at the brim." Having seen that, the narrator feels more sharply than ever that he is not working alone, but in the presence and with the aid of the absent mower. Their hearts have been drawn together in a shared moment of pleasure. It may be the act of mowing and turning the grass. It may be the act of sowing and ordering the poem. Two hearts move together. Like poetry itself, the narrator reflects that he "held brotherly speech / with one whose thoughts I had not hoped to reach."

The poem counters the indecisiveness of the groom. To be sure, the groom is caught in awful position, torn between the desires of his beloved and the needs of one unlovely. That is a major trait of his dramatic poems, however, where Frost limns the individual in confrontation with the unlovely in society.

Although written as a first person narrative, "Mending Wall" takes an interesting place here in its presentation of a meeting between two neighbors, of different dispositions and interests, in one common but necessary act. The communality of mending the wall cannot be avoided; there must be one on each side to balance the stones properly. Even though it is necessary to meet thus to rebuild the wall, the decidedly more playful narrator wonders why the *act* of rebuilding is necessary at all. The narrator, after all, works an apple orchard; the narrator has let his land go to pine trees. Voicing that fact to the neighbor, the narrator is met simply by the famous, and slightly notorious, slogan of the poem, "Good fences make good neighbors." But, as Mark Richardson has pointed out in *The Ordeal of Robert Frost* (142–44), the neighbor isn't the only one captive in aphorism, for the narrator twice repeats his own, "Something there is that doesn't love a wall." Yet, ironically, he has indeed come out to work the wall, merging with his neighbor in the task.

The underlying tension of the seemingly benign pastoral quality of the poem is heightened by the unfolding revelation of personality in the two characters. Although the narrator admits that "Spring is the mischief in me," it is surely more than that. The neighbor, after all, represents a long tradition, unchallenged and unchanged. One might almost say, here in this poem written early in Frost's career, that the neighbor also represents a poetic tradition, received and clung to as rigidly as a stone wall. Each new generation simply builds on that wall. The narrator brings to that wall an imaginative lightheartedness.

This is manifested in two ways. First, he dares question the tradition itself (30–36). He feels uneasy both with walls and with seeing things only one way. But, second, he also brings a new, imaginative way of seeing things. He lets the reality trip the imagination. Playfully, the narrator thinks of suggesting that elves knocked the wall askew. He carefully qualifies, however; "I'd rather / He said it for himself" (37–38). It is not difficult to see Frost's entire poetic theory wrapped up in these two loaded lines. He could be overt and didactic with his poetic discoveries. But he won't. He fashions the poem as metaphor, hoping to trip the reader's imagination into seeing the "elves" there. The basic question we ask whenever we read Frost's poetry is, what elves do I see here? The neighbor sees none. He simply has a job to do, walking a path from which he has never deviated. Thus he appears like an "old-stone savage," and mutters his slogan once more. Yet, we recall once again that the narrator has joined him at the wall. As in an act of poetics, where narrator and reader fuse in the process of the poem, here too narrator and neighbor meet in the mutual task of building. The ominous sign, in what appears to be upon first reading a thoroughly playful poem, appears in line 4, where we find "gaps even two can pass abreast." These will be filled in by the labor. Separation rather than joining constitutes the final action of the poem.

In this poem, humanity remains separated and, in fact, remote. Custom and tradition separate. If the hard choice isolates the groom in "Love and a Question," here the irascibility of individual human nature isolates the narrator. The two men in "Mending

Wall" are flung together by exigency and nothing more. They are merely players in Heidegger's game of *Dasein*. Ethically, the poem collides into an existential isolation. Nonetheless, the poem does suggest a means for bridging the wall held between human nature—the poetic imagination.

Frost's short poem "A Time to Talk" (1916) provides an interesting companion piece to "Mending Wall," and a near reversal in human relationships. The poem itself has not gathered nearly as much critical attention as the so-called major poems. It is, nonetheless, a nicely crafted and rather quiet little poem, and in the context of *Mountain Interval* with its studied reflections on human relationships with the earth and with each other it is, perhaps, more important than many readers have credited it.

Only ten lines, the poem captures in one photographic frame a rural event. It is nearly perfect incarnation of Frost's poetics of sound-sense. The first line, "When a friend calls to me from the road," carries the extra anapestic beat, like a call itself. Like the narrator, our attention is arrested. The same action occurs in line 5, where the narrator thinks of a responding shout (which he does not give). The line rhythms, with the basic tetrameter, vary throughout the poem to accommodate natural rhythms of speech. As the friend passing by on horseback calls to another working in the field, the photographic event turns epiphanic as Frost brings us inside the mind of the first person narrator.

Three things work on the narrator in this moment, all nicely isolated but harmonized in this brief poem. First, he loves the work he is doing in this field some distance from the wall where the friend calls. The ground, says the narrator, is "mellow." It is a good day for hoeing. The feeling accords well with other poems in the volume. For example, in the preceding poem, "Putting in the Seed," the narrator calls himself a "Slave to a springtime passion for earth. / How love burns through the Putting in the Seed." The sexual metaphor of the poem simply intensifies the unity of both human and human, and also human and nature.

If he enjoys the work, this narrator is nonetheless fully aware that the work must be done. As his friend hails him, there *are* hills to be hoed. Yet, the narrator insists that he will not "stand still and look around" upon them. That would be an affront to his friend. In his insistence lies the clear fact that he is mindful of that work, but also the call of his friend.

Then why, thirdly, does he turn? We notice that in line 2 the friend slows his horse "to a meaning walk." The phrase is ambiguous. What differentiates this walk from any other? What does the walk mean? Or is the walk simply meaningful because the friend hails him and slows down to chat? The narrator posits a possible response. Somewhat like the crotchety neighbor of "Mending Wall," he could stand where he is and shout, "What is it?" But this irritated, not-to-be-bothered voice is not that of this narrator. As he rejected this option of standing still and looking around, so too the narrator rejects this option. He tells us, "No, not as there is a time to talk." If we construe *as* here as the more common *since*, it clearly suggests that for the narrator human contact and conversation are more important than the work that can get done later.

It is possible, of course, to view all these interior protestations of the narrator as actual ones, to see him as fundamentally unfriendly, even resentful of the neighbor's intrusion. The concluding actions, however, suggest a different picture. The narrator thrusts his hoe blade-end up into the ground. It is a significant gesture. The hoe is set aside, although ready to be picked up again. And in this picture, the human end of the hoe, the handle, is rooted in the earth, suggesting that even though the work has been momentarily broken by the conversation, the contact remains. And then perhaps the most significant words in the poem follow: "I plod." His walk to the stone wall nicely matches the slowed "meaning walk" of the horse as the two friends meet to visit. It is not a meeting of huge consequence; simply a visit, after all. But here in this quiet little poem, Frost nicely demonstrates that friends need to set aside their labor for "A Time to Talk." A communal ethics surpasses individual demands.

Mountain Interval, in which "Mending Wall" is the lead poem, is perhaps Frost's most penetrating volume on interpersonal relationships, and the conflict between personal desires and community obligations. So it is, for example, that in "The Death of the Hired Man" Mary and Warren argue about their responsibility to Silas. The heart of the poem is often seen as Mary's comment, "It all depends on what you mean by home" (114), but an important background discussion plays on the issue of what Silas ever contributed to them. Truly, he could stack and tag the hay neatly, but that was as much for his own convenience as anything else. Silas's legacy is a trail of failed ambitions and half-completed tasks. Interestingly, Silas has a brother to whom he could go, but he is too ashamed to approach him. So he has returned to the farm to die.

It might be argued, as Richard Poirier does in *Robert Frost: The Work of Knowing*, that the poem itself is about poetics: "It could be said that the central subject of this poem is poetic form seen in the subject of domestic form."[6] In such a reading, for example, the subject of place or "belonging"—of word, metaphor, and expression—would be central to the analysis. The narrative positioning of the poem, however, suggests more clearly an ethical engagement—the place or belonging of one human to another.

The conflicting event of Silas's return also brings out the conflicting natures of Mary and Warren, seen especially in their differing definitions of home. Mary speaks with mercy and tenderness; Warren with a tone of formality and justice. One represents "what can I do for another"; the other represents "what has he done for me."

Frost's story of the wayward and shamed Silas and his forlorn return to the only place he has left to call home replays Jesus' parable about interpersonal relationships and the values we place upon others in the midst of our own hard decisions. The parable of the prodigal son (Luke 15:11–32) is the last in a series of three about lostness and grace. The interesting variation in this third one is that when the lost son returns—filthy, starving, and near death—he is met by two figures—the merciful, compassionate father showing grace and the irritated elder brother showing bitterness at the intrusion. In "The Death of the Hired Man," Mary clearly accords with the merciful father; Warren mirrors the elder son.

One of the most powerful artistic depictions of this homecoming parable appears in Rembrandt's *The Return of the Prodigal Son*, one of his final works at a point when his own life, unlike his rakish and wanton youth, was now steeped in suffering and bitterness. The majesty of the painting, as Henri J. M. Nouwen has pointed out in his book of the same title as the painting, lies in the compassion of the elderly father. The father spreads his hands across the back of his kneeling son. For Nouwen the image evokes feminine and masculine aspects of God—the authority to forgive and the tenderness and mercy to forgive. The elder son, however, stands rigidly erect to the side of the reunion, wearing a cloak identical to his father's as rightful heir, but a look of absolute disdain upon his face.

"The Death of the Hired Man" does not, however, need to be compared with the parable to achieve its own power. As it stands, it is one of Frost's most searching works on human relationships. About the lost Silas we find two conflicting patterns. Mary represents responsibility to society, bringing to it the ethical values of mercy and compassion. Hers would be the radical action of setting self aside for others. Warren, on the other hand, represents a justice-oriented ethics, but it is according to what *he* deems just. "Has he done anything for me" is the response to "Should I do anything for him." As a consequence, his moment for action passes by. Silas had died in his last desperate effort to redeem himself by ditching the meadow. Warren is left holding only the existential self.

In "The Death of the Hired Man" a means for human unity is suggested but not achieved. The reader is left in a disturbed world and wonders how it went so wrong. It is profitable to examine this conflicted and unresolved poem with one of Frost's most enchanting works. In "Two Look at Two" all things seem to fuse in perfect wonder. Human nature and earthly nature meet in one rhapsodic moment from which lessons ripple like tiny waves. Frank Lentricchia observes that

> "Two Look at Two" embodies one of the supreme moments of wonder in American literature and is, among Frost's major poems, the one that best confirms the more capacious sense of self given to us in the brook poems. We find in "Two Look at Two" that the poet is open, that he wants to put aside self and self-consciousness as the closed self revealed in the house poems cannot.[7]

The poem provides an opening of human consciousness that is restorative and directive. The story contained in this blank verse narrative is really quite simple; it is a beguiling simplicity, however. As in many of Frost's narrative poems, the simplicity gives way to a deepening profundity. The narrative focuses on a couple climbing a mountain trail. As evening comes they decide that they will have to turn back; the trail poses too many risks to travel in darkness. But it appears that the choice has already been made for them, for ahead lies a tumbled wall held together with barbed wire. The couple says good-night to the woods and is about to turn back down the mountainside. Then their movement is arrested. A doe steps out from behind a spruce on the other side of the wall. For a moment Frost holds the reader miraculously in the field of vision of each—the couple and the doe. The scene, as the doe slips past, seems over but oddly incomplete—until the buck steps from behind the same spruce and also turns to look at them. He is bolder, more challenging, as he tries to determine if these other two are even alive. Then he too passes by. Two had looked at two in one of those serendipities that nature provides, and in this case the looking affirms the human couple's love for each other. Implicitly, the gendered pairing in nature has affirmed their own union.

The depth of this pastoral love story may be appreciated by reading it in contrast to Frost's earlier "Mending Wall." While in that poem Frost declares that "something there is that doesn't love a wall," he is carefully nonspecific about what that "something" is. Yet, there, as in "Two Look at Two," that "something" should be quite clear. In "Mending Wall" it consists of the separation of imagination from pragmatism at a metaphorical level, and the separation of humanity from nature at a physical level. The first separation is figured in the narrator's playful, imaginative approach to the wall, as opposed to his neighbor's approach according to tradition and duty. But at another level the poem questions why it is that we need walls at all. They separate us from the land, confine us to a proprietary view of the land, and as such ultimately diminish our own nature. As "Mending Wall" has it, these physical barriers between humanity and nature cast us into some kind of stone age savagery.

"Two Look at Two" may be viewed as a healing of these rifts. Here the wall is "tumbled." It is not fully broken down for there will always be an essential distance between humanity and nature. The wall provides necessary separation. As there is a whisper of hope in "Mending Wall," however, by the very fact that the wall has brought the narrator and his neighbor together, that whisper is amplified many times here.

The deer come out of hiding, viewing the human couple (in natural terms—like a boulder "split in two") and the humans, so close, can see them as they are—doe and buck. Such a seeing of nature through the eyes of love, Frost asserts at the end of the poem, is rewarded by earth's favor upon the human couple's love.

But the other subtle relationships between humans and nature arise through Frost's careful diction. The "love" in the first line of the poem represents the love of the couple, but also their mutual love for nature. They would travel further uphill if they could forget that there are still dangerous barriers between them and nature; the path is rocky and steep; it is dark and unsafe. What is clearly affirmed, however, is their earnest love for nature.

The final stanza, like an envelope sealing the poem, reciprocates nature's love upon them. As the couple stands still after the encounter, they believe that earth has provided them a special favor. It has, at the very least, made them feel that their love for nature has been returned. Ironically, however, that reciprocation is *their* seeing, their perception of the scene before them. The deer are mute; they pause in some bewilderment before the human pair. Further, a rather subtle suspension occurs in the poem by the thrice-repeated "as if." In the first instance, the doe

> . . . Seemed to think that two thus they were safe.
> Then, as if they were something, though strange,
> She could not trouble her mind with too long,
> She sighed and passed unscared along the wall.
>
> (21–24)

By means of the "as if" the narrator maintains an ironic detachment from the romantic fallacies of the human viewers into nature. Similarly, the buck shakes his head, "As if to ask, 'Why don't you make some motion?' " (32). But he doesn't ask, no more so than the oven bird spoke, "He says." In the third "as if" we find the couple's response: "As if the earth in one unlooked-for favor / Had made them certain earth returned their love" (41–42). That, however, is their perception of the event.

Frost's use of the pathetic fallacy, however, here as elsewhere, is ironic. Earth is earth; the couple has seen in it something they wanted to see. Such is the ambiguity of the poem, moreover. As he does so often, Frost provides a trail-like opening in the poem for the reader to follow, permitting readers opportunities to draw their own conclusions. In *Toward Robert Frost*, Judith Oster emphasizes the different modes of seeing in the poem. The deer see the couple apart from each other and at different times. The human couple see the deer together and at the same time. Their perception of the event fuses. The effect, according to Oster, is that "The respectful communication so necessary to human love is present in the human lovers and totally absent in the deer. . . ."[8] Therefore, the lovers "found an unlooked-for favor because they had come with it." By extension, and following the parallel pattern in the poem where the poet holds out an invitation to the reader, they have fulfilled Frost's poetic aim of finding themselves in the concrete event—precisely what they wittingly or not came looking for.

The trail they followed was that of the poet's making; the steps and discovery were their own.

That reciprocating pattern is embellished internally by several small strokes. For example, in line 13 the couple "sighed" a good-night to the woods. In precisely the same manner the doe "sighed" as she passed them by. A strange spiritual spell (36) occurs, one too easily broken if they were to move past the wall between. In the case of "Two Look at Two," what separates, then, also unifies. The wall stands between human and animal, and so they stand in their distinct worlds. The narrator here is carefully objective in his telling, reporting events as they occur. Even the two-fold seeing beginning in line 17 is kept in perfect journalistic order. The objective rendering precludes the temptation to see a romantic interpretation between the two couples and nature. They inhabit separate worlds. Yet each set of twos has its own individual unity. The poem, then, seems to dance at the edge of an existential ethic. No clear communication, and certainly no didactic teaching occurs between the two couples. Nonetheless, the physical event worked upon the couple with such an extraordinary power—having opened themselves to it—that they come to realize a relational earth ethic. There is, in fact and contrary to existentialism, meaning apart from self, not in the sense of any pathetic fallacy but in the way one *responds* to stimuli of the earth. The couple does change; they escape the poem with wonder.

Frost's later poem "The Most of It" (1942) stands in dramatic contrast. Here the scene of a man who "thought he kept the universe alone" stands against the couple of "Two Look at Two." "The Most of It" ranks as one of Frost's most eerily lonely, and thoroughly existential, poems. Standing on a cliff jutting above a lake, the man shouts out into a vast and vacant distance. It's almost as if he were a man on a dark stage shouting "I am" toward the deserted seats. (As the irony has it, perhaps the janitor shouts back from a wing, "Who cares?") Finally the man's frantic cry is reciprocated by a noise, which he first mistakes for human. But it is only a "great buck," swimming powerfully through the water. It reaches the shore, disappears into the underbrush, "and that was all." Separation and disunity scissor humanity and nature in the poem. The tattered shreds precisely reverse the mellow wholeness of "Two Look at Two."

"Two Look at Two," then, provides a skillfully crafted story celebrating a loving unity between humanity and nature. Yet it is, and must be, love at a slight distance. The very thing that separates them—the wall—also unifies them. Respecting those independent worlds, however, one may feel love flow like a wave that washes over any walls. As such also, it encapsulates Frost's response to the locked-in consciousness of the existential ethic.

While it may be an attractive proposition to view the ethics manifested in Frost's poetry from an existentialist point of view, finally that view is too limited. One indeed does find, repeatedly, a character or narrator in a situation where, when faced with conflicting choices, the choice made (or left unmade) colors that person's nature. The reader too confronts these situations and is compelled to posit his or her own alternative. Time after time, Frost brings character, narrator, or reader to the fundamental question: Now what does one do about the situation? The choices determine the essence of the person who chooses.

Frost also claims certain existential individuality for humanity that is non-categorical. It may derive from the Emersonian influence upon his thought, particularly Emerson's idea of humanity as a self-transcending organism, groping for one's place in the cosmos. "A Cabin in the Clearing," first written as one of Frost's Christmas poems (1951), is a central work for investigating this sense of place. The fact that it appears in *In the Clearing* (1962) raises several other interesting qualities. First, this late volume itself represents a working toward clarity of human understanding of place and purpose. Second, as such, Frost grapples in several poems (i.e., "Kitty Hawk") with fundamental issues of faith and belief. But, third, it is also a volume of reflection on the past, seen most particularly in "For John F. Kennedy: His Inauguration," but evident elsewhere as well. An existential seeking, the response by faith, and the guidance from the past form the triumvirate themes of the volume. They are also focused in smaller scope in this one poem, "A Cabin in the Clearing."

Certain clues place the cabin in a much earlier historical era. A young couple (the bass and the soprano voices) have cleared a small area from the forest and settled in a cabin. They have begun domestication of the land—there is a path to their door and garden growing—but they still live far from equally "bewildered" neighbors. Their closest neighbors, in fact, are Native Americans, for Smoke observes that they must have lived here long enough by now to learn something of their language. The couple appears more than a bit xenophobic in their strange new world, however, and they tend to focus inward to the heart of the cabin rather than outward to possibilities.

From this setting alone we might extrapolate the perfect example of the individual lost in the inward, common routine, the individual without essence. The poem is not merely a descriptive discussion of the cabin by smoke and fog. It is itself an intelligent dialogue between two characters on the scene, observing. What they have to tell the reader in their representative roles is important. In the poem smoke from the cabin chimney and mist from the surrounding fields represent the vaporous, hazy unknown that envelops the couple's unknowing.[9]

When Mist opens the dialogue by observing that the couple in the cabin doesn't know where they are, the comment goes two ways. Of course the couple knows where they are. They are, in the present moment, in a cabin in the woods. Thus, they could answer, "We are being here." Such in effect is Smoke's view. Smoke points out that they are clearing back the forest, have set a path, and have located themselves. Smoke's voice, however, originates from within the cabin itself. Necessarily, Smoke speaks with the "inside" voice, interior to the couple, and thereby Smoke misses the implications of Mist's question.

Mist, which is the more widespread, generalized Spirit emanating from the earth itself, specifies the point of the question in lines 22 and following. Smoke tips the reflection by saying that the couple could ask the Red Man where they are. But Smoke still thinks in terms of *locale*. Cued by the reference to the Red Man to think of a living heritage, Mist worries that all the couple will ever know is "accumulated fact." Acquiring knowledge, says Mist, is itself "a part of their religion." Instead of entering into a place and a tradition by a self-assertive act of the individual will, the couple will forever be ruled by facticity.

Smoke accedes to a degree. In Smoke's important response in lines 29–33, Smoke points out that the couple must first find out *who* they are, in order that "they may know better where they are." While the existentialists have it that existence precedes essence, Frost supplies the important counterpart here: essence—knowing who one is—will determine how one exists in this world and in one's traditions. Adroitly, he transmutes the existentialist cliché into an ethical statement in this important poem. Who one is affects how one lives and acts.

Smoke nearly apologizes for the radical nature of its claim, saying it is "too much to believe." They are "too sudden to be credible," Smoke says, which does not at all deny the validity of the prior claim. Any individual, at any "where"—any moment of self-identity and expression—will certainly be "too sudden to be credible."

Then Mist and Smoke do a wise thing. Instead of talking about the couple in the cabin, they will coil about the cabin itself—to eavesdrop on the murmuring of the couple inside, they say. And that is wise—to go to the source. But the inside of the cabin, where the couple murmurs, is here (39) described for the first time as a "haze." It could be quiet talk, or earnest discussion, or fear. Whichever, it now links the couple with Smoke and Mist as they wrap themselves protectively about the house.

Just as we observed the limitations of a theological ethics in understanding Frost's work, finding that ethics finally unsatisfying as a guide, here too we recognize profound difficulties of an existential ethics as taught by the likes of Heidegger, Sartre, and de Beauvoir. It is true that in *Being and Nothingness* Sartre makes a distinction between freedom as responsibility versus freedom as the "Cult of Personality," but this is far from a plenary qualification of his fundamental views. At best, one might call it cautionary advice. The individual does indeed come first.

Often what we find in Frost's work is an abhorrence of isolation. Our choices, even the most individual ones, necessarily affect others. It is doubtful that Frost would agree with Sartre's assessment in *Being and Nothingness* that humanity is a "degenerate, degraded thing." Nor would he agree with Sartre's polemical rejection of God. While these are characteristics that Sartre handed down to later existentialists, and to postmodernism, there are other areas generally where we might find Frost in disagreement. As we have seen in the poems examined in this chapter, it may be observed that individualism that makes freedom the absolute good has no principle for unifying society. Second, existentialism seeks liberation but provides little government. Such was Frost's concern with New Dealism. Whether from his native conservatism or from his regional conservatism, Frost often fretted to friends that big government was virtually no government. Third, and perhaps most troubling, the existential ethics provide no stopgap to despair, crime, and suffering. Finally, but related to the third point, is the fact that an existential ethics provides little positive agenda by which to address social ills.

If we find the rationalist ethics rejected, and neither the theological nor the existential ethics fully satisfying, then, we have to search out some middle ground between these opposites, something that partakes a bit of each in fact. From the theological ethics we observed that although a divinely ordained body of laws, given as ethical guides, does not appear in Frost's poems, a keen sense of the divine does. And from the existential ethics we observed that although Frost rejects the radical individualism that may work to separate humanity, he does nonetheless emphasize the necessary freedom of individual choice as a means of affirming the individual. We search out that middle ground, then, by examining the presence of a deontological ethics in Frost's work.

6

The Undeniable "Ought":
Deontological Ethics

INSTEAD OF ASKING THE FAMILIAR ETHICAL QUESTION OF WHAT IS the right or wrong choice, the deontological ethics asks where one obtains a sense of rightness or wrongness itself. Is it simply a utilitarian pattern, or a cultural norm? If one feels that certain acts are right (compassion for the needy) and certain others are wrong (genocide of a needy people), how do we know we ought to do one and not the other? To extend the issue, why do we see the genocidal tyrant as an aberration of some moral quality, not just doing wrong but being evil? Deontological ethics begins with an investigation of where the "oughtness" behind right and wrong human actions originates. Furthermore, the investigation has clear implications for how we know we bear responsibilities to fellow humans, nature, and the divine. If Heideggerian and Sartrean ethics are predicated upon a phenomenology, deontological ethics is predicated upon an epistemology.

Deontological ethics began as a response to both Universal Principle and also Utilitarian theories of the "right act." Universal Principle ethics asks whether there are obligations or "principles" that are not relative to individuals, situations, or cultures, but are valid for all humanity. Some of these might be to avoid harm to others and to exercise compassion to relieve suffering wherever possible. To cause harm to another, or to ignore suffering, then, are ethical wrongs. Utilitarian ethics builds upon this theory by insisting that right acts are those that produce the greatest good; thus it is often referred to as the "ethics of benevolence." Two schools of utilitarians diverge in this crowded woods. The first, the "hedonistic utilitarians" insist that good is defined in terms of pleasure and happiness. The problem here is self-evident. If wealth gives me great pleasure, I may have stabbed others in the back to acquire it.

Therefore, the "ideal utilitarians" temper their hedonistic breth-
ren by speaking of friendship, love, beauty, and such as acts that
bring pleasure *and* produce the greatest good.

Deontological ethics recognizes the naturalistic quality in both of
these camps. Indeed, it might share some of the ideals, but it is less
optimistic about humanity achieving them through a naturalistic
process that is evoked through human thinking. In his own odd
way, Immanuel Kant straddles the divide between naturalistic and
deontological camps. In *The Critique of Pure Reason*, Kant performed his miracle of transformation by marrying Rationalism and
Empiricism. Reason and experience are necessary for knowledge.
He also recognized that his work dealt only with epistemological
realities. How about moral, ethical, abstract values? Thus, in *The
Critique of Practical Reason* Kant argues that every human has a
sense of "oughtness," or what he calls the "Categorical Imperative," the "thou ought." Humanity needs this to make sense and
order out of life, to validate an ethical existence. Therefore, Kant
postulates these universals derived from his Categorical Imperative: That everyone has freedom to seek the universal; that everyone has a soul that is free and that seeks; and that this soul has an
underlying cause that is God. It is an odd little triumvirate, where
Kant still clings to rational intuition (or apprehension of the *a pri-
ori*) but nonetheless grants importance to moral duty. Moreover,
he also grants the background cause of this sense of ethical duty to
God (something that does not appear in *Pure Reason*).[1] The cause
for human knowledge in ethical choices lies *outside* of the natural
world.

For the deontologist these ethical values are not merely good
suggestions, however. They are obligations morally required of us.
The right act, then, is to say this ought to be done. But how do we
know that? One option derives from H. A. Pritchard's 1909 essay,
"Does Moral Philosophy Rest on a Mistake?" in which he argues
that we apprehend what we ought to do intuitionally. We can see
immediately or intuitively that certain actions are right without
having to examine these acts as utilitarian. The source of "oughtness," then, is intuition, an innate quality of human nature itself.
The problem, if this originates in human nature, is that the "right
thing" is not always clear. Therefore, a second camp corrects this
by the guideline of "disinterestedness." We are to be interested in
the consequences of our actions upon others; we are disinterested

in that we refuse to allow personal interests to outweigh the good of others.[2]

FROST AND THE DEONTOLOGICAL ETHICS

Most pertinent among these options in a study of Frost's work is the deontological intuitive ethics. Characters or narrators ponder what ought to be done; right or wrong acts are a necessary byproduct when a decision on the oughtness is made. In both interpersonal and nature relationships, however, the pattern is that a certain propriety of action derives from the intuited ought and is restorative of wholeness in those relationships.

In one of his more barbed poems, "To a Thinker," Frost poses a dialectic between the analytic intelligence and the intuition of the poet. Originally titled "To a Thinker in Office" in its 11 January 1936 publication in *The Saturday Review*, Frost emended the title for inclusion in *A Further Range*. The implications of the original title and the political issues of the time did not escape early readers, however.[3] Many immediately saw Roosevelt and the New Deal as the target. The poem acquired a fair degree of infamy when a reporter for the *Baltimore Sun* managed to corner Frost in an impromptu interview at the railroad station as Frost was about to leave town. Run under the headline "Latest Poem by Robert Frost Versifies New Deal is Lost," the brief interview, which includes the full text of the poem, was also accompanied by editorial commentary when it appeared in the 26 February 1936 issue of the *Sun*. Regardless of the fact that Frost allied himself with the Democratic party, (his objection was with New Dealism and with the fact that it did not attend to the need of farmers), the interview sparked considerable controversy.[4] Most pointedly, readers observed that the first twelve lines of the poem could be read as a mockery of Roosevelt's increasing infirmity.

A follow-up editorial in the next issue of the *Sun* raised a larger question: Should a poet be meddling in political affairs at all? Again, on 28 February 1936, *The New York Times* published an editorial under the title, "Poet in Politics." The reading here is more astute, observing that "A statesman who has his feet on the ground can't very well have his head in the clouds" (*Selected Prose* 86). Nonetheless, the editorial accuses Frost of being self-contradictory and too harsh in his jabs at the government. Things came to a head for Frost when Henry Goddard Leach asked to reprint the poem in *The Forum*. In his response to Leach, dated 15 March 1936, Frost called it the "offending poem." He had changed the title (from "To a Thinker in Office" to "To a Thinker") to emphasize that it "was aimed at the heads of the easy despairers of the republic and of parliamentary forms of government" (*Selected Prose* 88). In no way, he insists, was it directed at Roosevelt's personal infirmities. It is possible of course that Frost is covering himself as well and fast as he could. Perhaps, however, it might also be profitable to take the poet at his word, for in this case it neatly divides the moral ought-ness derived through rational scrutiny and committee analysis from the intuited oughtness of the individual.

Certainly a tone of mockery pervades the first twelve lines, where even as natural an act as walking is dissected analytically. Lines 8–12 move from the back and forth action of walking to the exaggerated action of writing poetry. Line seven, "Or weaving like a stabled horse," is end-stopped by a colon, a punctuation that frequently signals further illustration in Frost's works. Although ostensibly about the erratic actions of the "Thinker," a quick eye will spot several of Frost's poetic peeves:

> From force to matter and back to force,
> From form to content and back to form,
> From norm to crazy and back to norm,
> From bound to free and back to bound,
> From sound to sense and back to sound.

The lines themselves incarnate a tour de force. The virtuosity of internal and end rhyme at once carries a hobbyhorse rhythm ("weaving like a stabled colt") and tense inner contradictions that belie the rhythm. For example, Frost's poetics championed sound to sense; here it deadens to sound only. Frost marries form and content; here there is only form without content. It is an elaborate and powerful piece of satire, the point of which is that poetry or government can be reduced to a merely mechanical act when governed by analysis rather than intuition and reflection.

Lines 13–24 are almost certainly directed at big government in general and Roosevelt in particular. They are presented here as examples of the contradiction in the first twelve lines, those who have departed from a natural "democracy." Line 24, however, raises the disturbing thought that "you've no direction in you." By "direction" it is clear that Frost means an overriding and guiding moral premise, for he observes in line 28 that the only option left open then is to "sway with reason more or less." Such people simply continue to plod through their programs like the analytic but soulless minds of the first 12 lines. In the final lines, the poet has his final play with the programmers. Although he pointedly does not ally himself with the "reformer or reformed," he does affirm both the need and place of conversion in the grand scheme of grace: "And yet conversion has its place / Not halfway down the scale of grace" (31–32). If the politicians should consider that, Frost entreats them not to "use your mind too hard, / But trust my instinct." Grace is intuited, not boxed categorically in a neat package.

Although the poem has its acerbic moments indeed, and probably warranted the controversy it stirred through some of its ungenerous lines, one is mistaken to understand it as a broadside against Roosevelt or the government per se. More precisely—and profoundly—the poem contrasts the analytic mind attempting to arrive at moral solutions with the intuitive mind grasping and enacting grace. As the final line has it, Frost as the bard links himself with intuition to arrive at the best solution.

This sense of moral oughtness, however, often bewilders humankind. Not the possible breaking of or according with a divinely-given law, nor the uncertainty of self-fulfillment, but the sheer perplexity of translating the intuited ought into deeds frets the characters of Frost's poems. His common pattern sets forth the possibilities and then leaves them ambiguously unresolved for the reader's reflection.

It bears mentioning that this ethical pattern wholly accords with Frost's views on metaphor in the poem and the poem itself as metaphor. Frost's most salient commentary on metaphor appears in his address "Education by Poetry," delivered at Amherst College in 1931. The address contrasts the concrete thinker who would rid the college curriculum of poetry, to the subversive notion that taste and judgment—developed through literature generally—are necessary elements in education. It was the 1930s equivalent to the contemporary conflict in higher education between technical skills and liberal arts.

Frost argues the essentiality of poetry in the curriculum because it trains us in human nature through metaphor. Some of his most famous quotations appear here—"I would be willing to throw away everything else but that: enthusiasm tamed by metaphor" (*Selected Prose* 36). But at the heart of it lies his firm assertion that metaphor enables us to understand human nature and "figurative values" that grant one safety (personhood) in life not found in other disciplines. Metaphor takes one beyond the triviality of mere discipline and opens speculative thinking, wondering about implications and significance.

Frost has one more step to take in his argument, and it is a bold one. Having asserted the importance of metaphor as intellectual training, having set forth poetry as the means for learning about and understanding human nature, he closes the address with his powerful appeal that to get close to poetry is also to "know more about *belief* than anybody else knows, even in religion nowadays" (*Selected Prose* 44). Writing poetry is more than skill in a craft; it is an incarnation (metaphorically?) of belief. Frost then distinguishes certain beliefs we have; that is, they are an intrinsic part of our individual beings. The beliefs climb a ladder, from the very simple, adolescent "self-belief," to a belief in art, and finally a belief in God, "a relationship you enter into with Him to bring about the future" (*Selected Prose* 45). The one pattern of belief that Frost dismisses is national belief, which, in his view, is nearly always divisive and destructive of personal human nature.

This important document ties directly to the ethics under examination here. It transcends an existential ethic, which would be encapsulated in "self-love." But, while not denying it, the address does not affirm God directly reaching out to humanity. Nor, for example, does Frost's lengthy investigation of faith in "Kitty Hawk":

> Someone says the Lord
> Says our reaching toward
> Is its own reward.
> One would like to know
> Where God says it, though.

The lines linguistically incarnate the ethical and religious ambiguity. Just as an argument by removal—reference to second and third-hand accounts—diminishes the philosophical argument, so too here the references diminish. "Someone says"—but who and where? And this unknown "Someone" says that "the Lord / Says." The narrator is right to think that one would like to know where

God says it. The following line in the poem, "We don't like that much," refers pointedly to this lack of specific information and affirmation. The reason we don't like it is clear in the poem: it casts us adrift in ambiguity.

The poem does, however, affirm humanity reaching out to God (and, religiously, the expectation of a hereafter with him).[5] Frost also suggests that the means for searching out the ladder of love is through metaphor, the same by which we search out meaning in the poem. In this sense the ethical and the poetic act merge. It might be expected that this could be demonstrated through those poems of Frost that deal directly with human relationships and how the divine impinges upon decisions to be made in those relationships. It seems wiser, however, to examine the anterior issue; that is, the poems that search out this oughtness, located intuitively through the metaphor itself. To that end, it is helpful to examine the succession of "star poems" Frost crafted during his lifetime, most of which are highly metaphorical for a human positioning before the undeniable ought.

After one has read carefully in Frost's collected works, one can't help speculating about the lifelong interest in stars, an interest appearing frequently from the earliest to latest poems. One answer is simply that Frost paid keen attention to all of nature, stars being one part of it. They enter his poems as easily as paths, woods, brooks, and the like. Another answer, however, separates the unknowable or only partly knowable stars from the taxonomy of present natural objects. The stars are only what they reveal of themselves, not what we can subject to evidentiary and rational scrutiny. As such, many of the star poems are themselves metaphors of humanity's desire to *know* what is known in part. In them, the narrator or character peers hard into the transcendent in order to see how it relates to this present life. Both of these answers, moreover, tie directly to events of Frost's own life.

With the changing view from the Enlightenment's acceptance of an orderly nature according to Deistic laws to the post-Romantic view of nature as a chaotic power in its own right, Frost was early and deeply influenced by his readings in evolutionary theory. Already during his sophomore year at Lawrence, his friend Carl Burell introduced him to such writers as Huxley and Spencer. Then one of those life-changing works came into his possession. Jay Parini describes it:

About this time Frost inherited a copy of *Our Place Among Infinities*, by Richard A. Proctor. Though its primary subject is the evolution of the universe, it also takes up the related issues of theology and cosmology—subjects that would continue to fascinate Frost to the end of his life. It was in Proctor that he first came across the "argument from design," which became a subject in "Design," one of his most ferocious, and original, poems—although his reading of Darwin was perhaps more important here, since Darwin's principle of natural selection deeply altered the argument.[6]

Parini demonstrates the enduring effect of the book on Frost by quoting a 1935 letter by Elinor Frost to Edna Davis Romig:

> One of the books longest in his possession came to him from a friend of his father's in San Francisco, who died in the early eighties— Proctor's *Our Place Among the* [sic] *Infinities*. He read it several times about 1890 and got a telescope through the Youth's Companion. He has been astronomical ever since.[7]

Frost's early reading of Proctor opened wide the doors to Darwin and the claims of evolution. It also opened the doors of astronomy to his far-reaching imagination. Frost walked through the doors and wandered about the room the rest of his life.

Frost's earliest star poem, "Stars," appears already in *A Boy's Will*. Read in the context of the volume as a whole, detailing the stages of a boy's will, "Stars" is glossed in the table of contents as "There is no oversight of human affairs," and it follows the pattern of the boy's confrontation with his own isolation and loneliness. "Stars" also certainly embodies Frost's personal pain, first drafted as it was near the time of the death of his young son Elliott (8 July 1900).

Here the overhead stars are mirrored by the blank, cold snowfall on earth, as if a cold vacancy lay between them. The snow is "tumultuous," drifted by "wintery winds." The metaphor of the poem, in which humanity and snow merge, appears in the second quatrain:

> As if with keenness for our fate,
> Our faltering few steps on
> To white rest, and a place of rest
> Invisible at dawn. . . .

Like the snow, humanity wanders, wind-blown, in uncertain direction. Humanity's "faltering few steps" wind directionless through the effacing snow. While "Design" questions the presence of any directing power at work in the universe, "Stars" assumes random chaos. How can one account for the sudden death of a son of typhoid fever during the early morning hours while two parents stand grieving?

The final cryptic stanza emphasizes humanity's aloneness. The stars are too remote to give guidance. Like the statue of Minerva, goddess of wisdom, they may bear wisdom, but it is veiled. The stars have no sight, nor a means to communicate wisdom to us.

Almost a universe of difference exists between the early "Stars" and Frost's next major poem on the subject, "A Star in a Stoneboat," collected in *New Hampshire* (1923). Here we see the more speculative and playful side of Frost in a scene reminiscent of "Mending Wall." As so often happens, however, that playfulness is undercut by ambiguity and irony. The laborer who loads the heavy meteorite into a stoneboat, then lugs it away for building stone, contrasts sharply with the more speculative narrator. One's vision is all practicality and pragmatic labor; the other flinches from the concrete to symbolically-held meaning that the concrete object embodies. The poem accords well with Anna Juhnke's argument that "The speaker in the poetry keeps alive the possibility that something greater than man sustains order and purpose in the universe and may sometime break through man's isolation to reveal itself. It may even alleviate his inner uncertainty and fear about his final destiny."[8]

The narrator observes at the poem's outset that stars "slip from" heaven and are then used for such practical things as building a wall. The transcendent commingles with earthly stones. The difference lies in how one looks at them, what one is willing to behold. In stanzas 2–4 Frost gives us one of his prototypical laborers, a man intent on getting his job done and one for whom a stone is just a stone, regardless of its origin. Yet the narrator sees in it an essence, the "one thing palpable beside the soul" that can traverse space.

Stanzas 5–8 amplify those qualities the narrator apprehends by the imagination, contrasted throughout by what the laborer does not see. The narrator sees the meteor falling toward earth like a dazzling "Bird of Paradise," trailing the one glowing "wing" of its plume. It is an ecstatic portrait, touched with hints of glory. Having landed burning in the field, however, the now meteorite has burned out to an apparently lifeless coal. Yet, for all that its glory is not spent. It depends upon how one perceives the event. The laborer lifts the stone with his crowbar and topples it into the stoneboat. The narrator, dismayed by the transcendent beauty that he has imagined now being dragged through the fields, vows in line 36 "To right the wrong." But what is the wrong? Is it wrong for the laborer to build walls with materials at hand? The narrator himself confesses that he doesn't know where it could better go. It is, after all, only a stone.

Righting the wrong, however, lies specifically in that act of imagination that sees beyond mere physicality to spirituality. Dragging the stone through the field is a profanation of such possibilities as the narrator held forth in lines 12–24.[9] In lines 40 and following the narrator claims that such imaginative apprehension puts one in relationship with the transcendent. Although others may seek transcendent answers in school or church, the narrator is content here to search it out himself, be he "fool or wise."

Thereby also the poem establishes an ironic tension between imagination and practicality, paralleled by the perfectly rhymed tercets. The masculine end rhymes distinctly chop off the flow of each line, yet the majority of the lines use enjambment so that not just the punctuation but the meaning itself carries to the following. In the first stanza the enjambment forces a restrictive clause with further restrictions upon that:

> Never tell me that not one star of all
> That slip from heaven at night and softly fall
> Has been picked up with stones to build a wall.

The two negatives in the first line chart a course of deliberate assertion. This is the transcendent sphere. The last line, however, gives the verb of the first noun clause in the passive voice. This is the more indeterminate sphere of human action. This is the great "if," and it is the postulate for the poem in how we view the laborer. The passive voice ironically undercuts the certitude of the initial claim; so too do earthly matters tend to undercut our beliefs in the divine.

That same irony plays in counter meanings throughout the poem. Lines 31–33 force together the laborer's movement with celestial movements:

> He dragged it through the plowed ground at a pace
> But faintly reminiscent of the race
> Of jostling rock in interstellar space.

From the earthward vision, the laborer dragged the meteorite. Moreover, he does not drag it *over* the ground, but *through* it—the weight of the stone miring the boat in earth. In space the rocks race, but they do collide, hurtling this meteorite to earth. The grandeur and force of the heavens redounds to the plod of earthbound humans weighted by the gravity of their labor.

Despite the ironies of the poem, however, it is crucial to note that the narrator, who is also caught in earthbound seeing, constantly apprises earthbound things with the imagination, searching for transcendent signs. In lines 40–42, the narrator confesses that

> From following walls I never lift my eye
> Except at night to places in the sky
> Where showers of charted meteors let fly.

From the man-made walls, where a meteorite may be enclosed, he turns his vision heavenward where the meteors glow and flow.

"The Star-Splitter" from the same volume slightly turns the tables on this intuitive apprehension of the transcendent, however. Brad McLaughlin gets tired of Orion sneaking up on him when he works to get overdue jobs done. He wonders if these "forces" have any obligation to human rights. To look for an answer Brad burns down his house to collect the fire insurance and buys a telescope. Despite the whimsicality of his character, Brad is not altogether unlike the laborer of "A Star in a Stoneboat." He wants to bring Orion down into his lap to study it, rather than reach out to it with the imagination as does the narrator of "A Star in a Stoneboat."

But Brad becomes a curiosity in the town. His behavior is too outlandish, even when he buys his six-hundred dollar telescope that he can use during his new job as an under-ticket-agent on the railroad. During his spare time he plants his telescope the way he once planted crops. And one night he invites the narrator to come out with him to watch the stars separate into focus through the powerful lens. It is a powerful experience, the narrator agrees, but then he wonders—what does it all mean? In the end, "Do we know any better where we are. . . ?" There is something altogether different between the personal kinship Brad has with Orion at the outset of the poem, and the objectifying scientism of the telescopic view.[10]

The *New Hampshire* volume contains a third poem in a star sequence, "I Will Sing You One-O," that many readers have understood as one of Frost's most explicit investigations of humanity and
the divine. It is certainly the most cosmically transcendent of
Frost's poems, in which he outwardly ponders the One behind the
All. What is truly important about this poem, however, is not just
Frost's grappling with the fundamental issue of Aristotle's metaphysics, but the impact of that grappling upon the decidedly personal narrator of the poem. The poem does not so much expand
the human imagination beyond the material world as other star
poems do, but bounces that imagination off the most distant One
and back to humanity.

The first lengthy stanza (1–24) provides a clear and uncluttered
setting, matched by the two-foot lines. The narrator lies awake
long into the night, listening to the contrary winds (11–15) of a
snowstorm. The bleak, desolate scene heightens the individual
loneliness of the speaker. In this state he wishes for some definitive
marker, be it only the striking of the clock tower to tell him what
time it is.

Then, like the two contrary winds colliding in the village street,
two markers—the clock tower and church steeple—echo off each
other in their announcement of the time. And like the winds com-
mingling, here too the plural commingles into one. Hearing the
one o'clock rattled against the window, the sleepless narrator is left
to ponder the significance of the "grave One." The combination of
words is peculiar. It may well be the gravity of the tolling bells. The
first hour of the day peals outward to the city, then to outer space
in lines 39 and following. But if one holds in mind the ending of
the poem, the grave One also suggests a devolution, a beginning
toward death. (I cannot agree with those readers who, because
One is capitalized here, see it as synonymous with God, who is
mentioned in line 52. The language is far too ambiguous here, and
the speculation that follows is entirely the narrator's lonely imagination searching for some source of meaning.)

The narrator's imagination rockets outward, past planets and
galaxies. To these "man sends his / Speculation." But at that point
beyond which his imagination can no longer go, like Aristotle's
"Unmoved Mover," we place God (52). The clockwork movements
of the tolling bells, however, evoke another image—the utmost star
that lies so far out that its "whirling frenzies" make it appear to
stand still. In fact, it is an exploding star, writhing in its own extra-

terrestrial death throes as a nova. The bright light seen today issued millions of years previously. While it appears to us as bright, the star is nonetheless cold and dead.

In "I Will Sing You One-O" the narrator's imagination recedes from the limits of its investigation not with any clear sense of a divine "ought" ("God" is merely one more item, albeit abstract, in a universe representing the limits of human imagination) nor yet a deontological "ought." Rather, the lesson from the star, like its long-past light striking earth, is a negative one for ethical consideration. Here three patterns of the poem fuse. The two contrary winds collide and combine into one gust in the street. The tower and steeple bells collide and fuse as one. Now the imagination collides with the dead star and perceives the one lesson: all life is now in a state of devolution. The "One-O" echo of the star is enacted on earth since creation, when "man began / To drag down man / and nation nation."

"I Will Sing You One-O" is one of Frost's bleaker poems, both in mood and subject. (It may be fruitful to contrast a later star poem, "Skeptic," to this one.) If we are to trust in the intuitive imagination for a sense of oughtness in ethical decisions, the somber closing lines of the poem admit little hope. Is our self-destructive tendency as inevitable as the flaring death of the nova?

One answer might appear in one of Frost's most ambiguous poems, "All Revelation." In some ways this poem may play off the early "Revelation," from *A Boy's Will*. There Frost makes distinctions among three kinds of speech. "Light words" in the first stanza are often used to hide our own inner selves. They are defenses lest our true nature be found out. The "literal" word of the second stanza is used to simplify and clarify. Frost admits that it is a "pity" to use such speech, for it fails to reveal the deeper emotions of the heart. The final stanza suggests metaphorical speech, a means that mysteriously unites us as "babes" to "God afar." Metaphor in "Revelation," then, is the poetic speech of intuition and insight that allows us glimpses of something larger than ourselves.

"All Revelation" replays the effort to see, but does so in a way circuitous with irony and ambiguity. Jay Parini observes that Frost's poems "would live on that perilous fault line between skepticism and faith. At times these contrarieties would merge in moments of complicated, synthetic vision, as in 'All Revelation.' "[11] Immediately upon reading the first line, "A head thrusts in as for the view," one is confronted with the complexity. Many construe the work as either a sexual fantasy (from the point of view of the penis) or a birth image. In the first vein, Richard Poirier argues that sexuality

> is syntactically and in every other way made continuous with the general human thrust toward penetration and creativity. Thus, what "can of its comings come" is kept from being quite as specific as it might sound by the initial uncertainty about whether in the first stanza a phallus is exploring a vagina or a child's head is emerging to look into the world.[12]

On the other side, Frank Lentricchia has argued that "His subject is the act of the mind, the dynamic thrust of consciousness, which he evokes in his metaphor of the cathode ray . . . [which] emerges as a metaphor for the tendency of human consciousness to be excursive, to reach out, to grasp, and shape its world. . . ."[13] Reuben Brower gives the poem extensive discussion along similar lines of the mind acquiring knowledge. He is quite accurate, I believe, in his assessment that "In this dark lyric as in the simpler poems it is *poetic* revelation that brings imaginative assent—the co-operation between metaphors of cave, geode, ray, and eye that we may accurately call 'symbolic.' "[14]

Perhaps the most imaginative reading of the poem, however, is given by Peter Hays, who argues that the mysterious crystals and ray cathode, by which the geode is perceived, refers to the earliest advent of television about the time the poem was first published (as "Geode" in the *Yale Review*, 1938). As Hays points out, television was established by this time, although commercial broadcasting didn't begin until 1941. Thus, for Hays, "Eyes seeking for truth and human contact . . . have turned toward the actors and scenes of television."[15] It has become a wholly mechanical process, and it squares into a small box the human seeking for some significance larger than itself. Hays concludes that "The questions asked in the first two stanzas—where, what, whither—are the basic questions of existence: where have we come from, what is our purpose here, whither do we go after death? As 'The Star-Splitter' acknowledges, we have 'a life-long curiosity / About our place among the infinities, / a curiosity about / questions that have no reply.' "[16]

When "all revelation" is ours, humanity has lost its capacity for metaphor and mystery. If there is, as a number of critics have observed, a bleakness to the poem, it is because humanity will also have lost its desire to explore something or someone transcending itself. Humanity will then be thrown onto that Cyb'laean (goddess of earth) avenue, wondering "what can of its coming come."

In two poems, then—"I Will Sing You One-O" and "All Revelation"—we find two negative patterns. In one the heavens reward the narrator's searching with a message of devolution into blackness. In the other, humanity itself has turned from searching the heavens for any sign and, whatever the many possible readings of the poem, is trapped in defining for itself all revelation. As one probes further into the star poems, one finds a variety of treatments. For example, in several poems Frost treats his star subjects simply as objects or events. Such is the case in the playful "Canis Major," where the narrator romps and barks in the dark with "the great Overdog." So too, in "On Looking Up by Chance at the Constellations" the unchangeability of celestial courses reminds the narrator of patience in human affairs. "Lost in Heaven" might best take its place among Frost's pastoral works, where he welcomes the opportunity to be lost in the landscape of heaven.

The observation of "There Are Roughly Zones" plays behind such poems as a *leit motif*. Although not properly a star poem at all, it does raise similar questions. From inside the haven of a house, a group of friends watches a vicious storm batter the landscape. Particularly threatened is a peach tree, and all agree that if the tree dies, this storm would be the cause of it. At that point the narrator muses on the fact that they have just switched from a physical topic (the storm) to a metaphysical one (the death of the tree). He wonders what it is in humanity that refuses to be confined to strict limits and boundaries. Human ambition—and imagination—forever searches out a "zone" beyond the immediate existential one. Then the narrator observes that though there is no fixed line between wrong and right, there are roughly zones whose laws must be obeyed. As with the tree, however, we don't know the consequence of any one deed, at any one place and time. We act within the zones, and then, also like the tree, leave it to destiny to see if our actions will bear fruit.

As does "There are Roughly Zones," the delightful letter from the tramp in "An Unstamped Letter in our Rural Letter Box" affirms a mysterious link between one person's deepest self and the activity of heaven. Aware of the fact that the farmer's dog had been barking all night, the tramp feels compelled to drop a letter in the box that it was only he sleeping at the edge of the field and not some burglar the dog was warning off. The tramp had found a good spot under a protecting juniper and rolled into his blanket. Around 2:00 A.M. a protruding rock caused him to awaken, just in time to witness a meteor blazing across the western sky. Having seen the rupture in "Heaven's firm-set firmament," the quixotic tramp feels a comparable response in his brain. Like two stars colliding to catapult the meteor, two memories collide and fuse in his brain. We are not told what those are, but the tone of the lines certainly suggests that the experience of them has been healing.

We come then to Frost's most famous star poem, "Choose Something Like a Star," to which he himself gave special notice by placing it, along with the selected "From Plane to Plane," to conclude *The Complete Poems*. (The afterword from the 1949 Henry Holt edition of *The Complete Poems* initially included "Closed for Good." That work was incorporated into *In the Clearing* (1962), which now appears after them in *The Complete Poems*.) "Choose Something Like a Star" not only enfolds the collected works, it also resolves the ambiguities and contrary pulls of the star poems.

The poem is poetically situated as an apostrophe, hailing "O Star." As such, the words and thoughts, while bestowed upon the star, are entirely the narrator's own. Moreover, they project fully outward, unlike other star poems, where the transcendent is seen through earthward metaphors and actions. The narrator affirms that the star is the "fairest one in sight," but its very distance necessitates some hiddenness. The narrator "knows" it only in darkness; that is, with the limitation of human seeing. Yet, that is when its splendor shines most brightly. Again, the narrator grants that some mystery lies inherent in a body so proud, yet he yearns for some direct revelation, something "we can learn." Instead of lofty wonder, the narrator would like for once to have direct revelation: "Say something to us we can learn."

But if the star did speak, what would it say? It would define itself by its own nature, not human nature. Therefore, its words would be "I burn." The words evoke those of Yahweh to Moses: I am that I am (Ex. 3:14). In this theophany God says in effect that I have no need to identify myself by anything other than my own being. Nonetheless, the narrator here pleads for categories that make sense to human calculation. If you say you burn, put it in specific degrees of heat. Such is precisely the pattern in those star poems that stumble on humanity's own unknowing. We still want to contain and quantify that which can only be apprehended by faith, intuition, and the imagination. Of the poem, Robert Faggen points out that "the star, and the power and force it embodies, 'does tell us something in the end.' The something is a moral rebuke to our narcissism and our demands that the world conform to images, measurements, and metaphors appealing to our sensibilities."[17]

Strangely, in this case we know the star by what it asks of us. Being what it is, in and of itself, it embodies certain lessons. The primary lesson is stated as steadfastness in line 18, in a reference to both the star of this poem and the "Bright star" of John Keats's sonnet by that title. The first quatrain of Keats's poem is fairly well echoed in Frost's. There the bright star watches like a "sleepless Eremite," and Keats wishes that he were as steadfast as the star. Keats's longing, as it so often was, turned in his poem to Fanny Brawne. The narrator of "Take Something Like a Star" is less singular in directing his lesson.

If we come to know the nature of the star by what it asks of us (20), here we have the essential ethical summary of the star poems. It is not simply a matter of what one knows; rather, a matter of what one feels obligated to do. The star here asks of humanity a certain state of being not entirely unlike itself as a star: "It asks of us a certain height," so that at times when we are beset by a mob frenzy, or praise, or blame that can tip our personal equilibrium, we can "stay our minds" on the star. As the star holds sway far above us, so humanity has to hold to values above the sway of emotional aberration. Holding steadfast in an unsettled world mirrors the stately steadfastness of the bright star in a dark heavens.

"Choose Something Like a Star" is very nearly a perfect poem in its subject and expression. Although some readers have observed some bitterness in the narrator—"Say Something!"—this is precisely how it should be. Even that all-too-human persistence is absolved in general affirmation. No less important is the poem to understanding Frost's ethics, particularly as it comports with a deontological ethics. For the imagination that probes to the star—which always remains partially veiled by its very nature—intuits lessons from that star about human living. In this one particular instance the lessons include to remain above the fray of public opinion and to be reserved in both giving and receiving praise or blame. Above all, be steadfast.

7

Ethics in Society

In his loose-ranging account of conversations with Robert Frost, Baird Whitlock reports the poet saying, " 'To be a poet you have to believe something so hard that it would break your head if it wasn't true.' "[1] In the case of Frost's ethical beliefs, we have determined several premises. While neither orthodox nor church-affiliated in his religious beliefs, he did nonetheless locate himself in the Judeo-Christian tradition. As Andrew Angyal has pointed out, "Frost remained a lone believer, isolated from any denomination, an outsider by choice from religious institutions that had lost their spirit while retaining their outward forms."[2] It is fair to say, furthermore, that Frost leaned more toward the prophetic qualities of the Old Testament than the more charismatic qualities of the New. Invariably, when the name God enters his poetry or letters it refers to Jehovah. With the significant exception of *A Masque of Mercy*, Christ is seldom mentioned at all.[3] That fact, combined with his native reticence and New England conservatism, effectively prohibited an open expression of personal belief.

From this religious positioning, however, we inquired how it affected the poet's sense of right and wrong action in the midst of others. Any presuppositional belief framework affects the way one acts. Since Sartre was an atheist, he wanted to discover a means for knowing proper actions apart from God. At the same time, an agnostic such as Camus (his agnosticism may be argued from such texts as *The Plague*, *The Myth of Sisyphus*, and *Resistance, Rebellion, and Death*) searches for an act that he can *know* is right. In *The Plague*, the novel that would center Camus's ethics, that act is self-sacrificial love. In a World War II letter to a German friend, Camus writes: "I continue to believe that this world has no ultimate meaning. But I know that something in it has a meaning, and that is man, because he is the only creature to insist on having one."[4] If

146

such is the case, argues Camus, justice is the demand of humanity generally, and the individual response is love.

We inquire, then, what presuppositional frames direct Frost's ethics. Specific evidence of a theological ethics does not appear in Frost's works (not to be confused with poems that mention God, or even, to a large extent, those peripherally about God). Frost the believer must be dissociated to a large degree from Frost the poet when we scan the poems for a systematic ethical system. Necessarily, one is compelled to discard a theological ethics by virtue of its own definition—no directive law of right and wrong behavior emanating from the mandates of a deity appears.

A fascinating case could be made for Frost's placement in an existential ethics, particularly as we become absorbed in those poems of intensifying personal ambiguity. Here an important qualification prevails, however. The existentialist—Camus taken as example in the foregoing quotation—sees the world as having "no ultimate meaning." Accepting this premise, the existential ethics focuses upon identification of self in this bewildering world. Frost's ambiguity differs markedly. For his bewildered narrators, the issue is not that the world lacks ultimate meaning, but that the narrator himself lacks continuity with that meaning or feels alienated from it. In fact, the net effect of such poems as we examined serves only to emphasize an ultimacy in the world's pattern with which the narrator is despairingly out of touch.

The deontological ethics supplies something of a middle road in this diverse wood, and clearly it is the belief system where we may most comfortably situate Frost. Without the need to specify a legislative mandate from a divine authority (and also without the need to deny such), the deontological ethics powerfully appeals to the poet's intuitive sense of moral oughtness. As in Frost's poem "The Sound of Trees," one acquires "a listening air." The reader discovers in the poem that the narrator increasingly moves in rhythm and in knowledge with the tree. Nonetheless, as in "The Oven Bird," we see that even as the narrator does this, it is not the tree speaking (no more than the oven bird) but the narrator making sense out of some universal language that flows all around him. The emphasis upon the "oughtness" certainly attracts the poet, but the ethical "deed" it evokes is a sense of unity with the universe about him. Dorothy Judd Hall, whose focus is primarily the manifestation of Frost's religious beliefs in his poetry, observes that "There is an overriding consciousness of design in his poetry that is apparently a synecdochic expression of his faith in the possibility of universal form and meaning. It links the artist in him to what he intuitively perceives as a comprehensive, if sometimes incongruous, cosmic structure."[5] If one were to trace the many comments Frost made about his own poetic craft, and the significance of design—rhyme, meter, stanza—in it, Hall's point acquires credibility. But it is only partially accurate in terms of Frost's ethics.

When that presumed unity breaks down, however, and when the voices about him are not of universal harmony but discordant, then the narrator is thrust back upon his own voice. Often it is a whimpering lifted toward storms and dark skies. Then what Hall calls a poetic ambiguity derived by holding something in reserve becomes an ethical ambiguity of the narrator's incongruity in the universe. That Emersonian harmony Frost so deliciously tasted of becomes bitter fruit, emphasizing the dissociative character of the narrator's own self. Ambiguity is all one finds in lostness. One cannot choose to act in such an ethical and moral state simply because one doesn't discern any choices, therefore is immobilized to inaction, and in the inability to act or choose further descends into a state where no ethical anchors at all seem viable.

The ethical paralysis of this state severs the individual from that most fundamental of ethical communities—the society in which he or she is situated. As we examine the final steps of Frost's ethics, it is fitting then to consider the poet's sense of social obligations. Such do not necessarily stave off the personal ambiguity, nor do they represent a means to remedy it. In fact, social obligations often exacerbate the personal ambiguity. "This is what I should be doing" is the deontological urging. "This is where I should be doing it" is the social urging. At times, these social issues whirl maddeningly behind the narrative ambiguity in the poem.

That ethical choices are enacted in society—determined by one's understanding of and attitude toward others—is a fundamental premise of all ethicists. John Donne's sentiment that "No man is an island, entire of itself. . . ." (Meditation 17) only affirms what had been argued for over two thousand years. The foundational work on ethics in the western world, Aristotle's *Nichomachean Ethics*, divides nearly evenly between what makes a person good and how a good person works good in the world. What Aristotle does not tackle, however, is the issue of attitudes toward others, this sense of how one "holds" others.[6] Certainly, it was not the issue in his age that it has become in the twentieth century. Aristotle's ethics is analytic, defining the particularities of what constitutes a just or an unjust action, for example. The twentieth-century ethical mind also wants to impose a synthetic grid upon such issues and question how they affect the "personhood" or the value and integrity of an individual or social group.

In this regard, ethics is not simply an issue of right or wrong actions. In their search for ethical norms that hold in all places at all times, ethicists turn from the particular *act* to how one *holds* society generally. That includes one's personal belief system, but places it in the larger framework of how one sees oneself in the midst of others, and how one sees those others influencing oneself. It is not merely an issue of what one believes, but also how those beliefs and the beliefs of others affect society.

In his *Ethical Reflections,* Henry Stob points out that we too easily and conveniently define ethics as "the science of morality." Stob grants the foundational issues of his science; for example, that human actions unavoidably affect others, that humanity has "not ultimate privacy," that one's moral behavior is shaped within community. Stob also points out, however, that individuals are free "to transcend the social matrix." Therefore, he asserts that "This feature of man's existence also provides a charter for that department of ethics which has come to be called personal. Personal ethics cannot be finally isolated from social ethics, but . . . it does not concentrate on collectives and communities or on impersonal structures and arrangements. It concentrates instead upon the individual moral agent who lies behind and participates in these."[7] The importance of the distinction lies essentially upon the significance of the person making choices and acting upon them, but with full awareness of the consequences of such choices and actions. This, however, is not the end of the matter for Stob. If he argues that ethics cannot be restricted to the moral agent alone, he also argues that ethics "must contemplate the person in his attitudes and actions toward others."[8]

The twist that Stob gives to traditional ethics lies in that word *attitudes*. Responsible ethics moves beyond an issue of right and wrong choices and actions in a social context, to a "holding" of those others—and oneself—in that context. Do I, for example, hold myself as an ethically responsible self for the choices I make? And do I hold others with ethical responsibility when I make my choices? Consider Chaucer's inimitable Pardoner. He makes a career out of being a duplicitous lout, and prides himself in it. But

on what grounds may we call him unethical? Just because he bilks
every gullible fool, of which the medieval and modern world are
crammed, out of every penny he can? Not necessarily. We regard
the Pardoner at the ethical level of sewer scum precisely because
that is how he regards all of humanity.

And how do we consider Robert Frost's social ethics? Perhaps
first among our concerns is to recognize that Frost could hardly be
accused of being a moral crusader. Although an ethical belief system is clearly seen in both the man and his art, he refused to make
that art didactic or propagandizing. His native reticence about religious matters corresponds to that of his own ethical values in social
contexts. When forced into the role, it was more by accident than
design. His sally into political criticism with "To a Thinker" may
have upset him as much as others. It certainly had him covering
his tracks quicker than a broom-sweep. His reading tour to the Soviet Union and his personal visit with Khrushchev came with few
political pretensions on Frost's part. When we examine one focused area of Frost's social ethics, then, it is not with the intent of
claiming a systematic ethical view. What it does do is to position
him ethically in one historic moment.

One of the more fascinating avenues by which to trace Frost's
social ethics is by considering the role of female characters in several of his works. During the last decade, sustained attention has
been given to the topic, but not in a strictly ethical sense. That is to
say, studies that will be noted in the following pages have analyzed
certain female characters in the works, have considered female/
masculine conflicts, and have brought Frost's personal relationships (Elinor and Kay Morrison in particular) to bear upon an understanding of the works. But is there any ethical imprint upon
these works? What conclusions can one form? Final answers remain elusive; nonetheless, one can detect some fundamental attitudes by considering Frost's poetic relationships with several
significant women in his life. Furthermore, it is worthwhile to consider representative examples of recent approaches to the question
of Frost and gender. Finally, we will examine several poems closely
tied to the issue of Frost's social ethics.

In *A Masque of Reason* God finds himself intrigued by Thyatira
and asks Job what her interests are. "Witch-women's rights," Job
responds. He goes on to explain that Thyatira suspects that God is
"no feminist" and that she would like to know God's reaction to a
prayer that started off with "Lord God of Hostesses." It is an amus-

ing little scene that Frost paints, but God's response is ambiguous: "I'm charmed with her" (182). Other than that, he is indifferent—or he has not disclosed the difference he makes. The response is not surprising in a poem about ethical stasis, where the characters seem stuck in what Kierkegaard calls in *The Present Age*, "the mudbanks of reason." But can one legitimately extrapolate anything about the way Frost holds women from the poem? Or do we simply leave the narcoleptic Thyatira to her dramatic domain in the *Masque*?

Two decades prior to *A Masque of Reason* (17 April 1926), Frost had occasion to write his daughter Lesley from the University of Michigan. Frost, who was never terribly patient with students, reflected with more than his usual share of acrimony on the growing feminist spirit on campus. He wrote:

> The young assertiveness prevailing everywhere east and west seems a little more crude and impolite out west. And I find I'm not fond of teaching girls in their new state of mind. They started out escorting me home from night classes and proposing canoe rides and when I blocked that turned on me in some sort of sex resentment and gave me one of the worst classes of wrangle and flat contradictions I ever had. The same critic missies have sat mum at the Whimsies and never helped with an observation or comparison in the five years I have done my best to entertain them; much less have they ever started any subject of their own. Suddenly out of some sex mischief they break loose and storm me not with subjects, observations and comparisons (such would be welcome) but with contradictions and abuse. (*Family Letters* 112)

As if to check himself, however, Frost quickly added, "I'm willing to grant their equality if thats [sic] all they are fighting for" (112). What disturbs him, it appears, is the aggressiveness of their approach, which denied *him* his own individuality and humanity.

The two instances demonstrate the dangers of taking isolated examples and stirring them together into a muddled ethics. Out of the stirred-up pot we can drag forth virtually anything—from a brutish misogynist to a man starved for the love and comfort of a woman. In this regard, a valuable service has been done by scholarly research into unpublished correspondence with a number of women.

It is unusual that in this time of burgeoning feminist studies relatively little has been written on Frost's *professional* relationships with women. *English Literary Studies* published a special issue on

Frost in 1994, devoted to Frost's influence upon other artists. The volume is startling for its complete lack of any entries representing women. The ten essays consider only male relationships. But what of Frost's relationship, for example, with Amy Lowell? Why did he express appreciation for Elizabeth Bishop and Edna St. Vincent Millay's poetry, including them in a group of seven poets "most likely to last"?[9] One must grant that most of Frost's friends were in fact male, that the influences upon him were traditionally male, that personally he felt more comfortable in male circles. But with the great strides women writers were making in the early twentieth century, one begins to suspect that the influences extend more broadly. Fortunately, some recent studies have balanced the picture somewhat.

Working with a small collection of letters between Frost and Marie A. Hodge, held by the Mugar Memorial Library, Special Collections, of Boston University, Donald Sheehy has pieced together a bit of literary history influencing the recognition and dissemination of *A Boy's Will* early in Frost's career. When the book was published, Frost confessed in a letter to John Bartlett that "I am in mortal fear now lest the reviewers should fail to take any notice of it" (*Selected Letters* 70). The fear was legitimate, of course, since Frost had received scant poetic recognition this side of the Atlantic. Marie Hodge had a hand in first providing that American recognition.

During the year Frost spent in Plymouth teaching at the Pinkerton Academy, he and Elinor apparently first made acquaintance with Hodge. Her duties as Preceptress of Normal Hall ranged widely in what Sheehy describes as a *loco parentis* role. A former teacher herself, a future librarian, an author of several local histories, and a sometime poet, Hodge was clearly the very sort of intelligent, multitalented person that would attract the Frosts. Hodge's historical influence, however, extends beyond friendship. When *A Boy's Will* first appeared in England, Mrs. Hodge arranged orders for the Pinkerton students wishing to purchase the book. The orders grew larger than Frost expected. In one letter he dated 8 June 1913, he observes, "This is growing into a business between us—I mean in regard to the books. I feel as if you deserved a commission" (*Selected Letters* 86). In a letter dated 10 October 1913, Frost thanked her for the additional orders.

Marie Hodge's influence extended further than distributing Frost's work, however. A poet also needs exposure. Readers want to know the person behind the pen. After the Frosts returned to Franconia, Hodge set up something of a "triumphant" reading at Pinkerton in July, 1916. Apparently the return took two directions—a private reading for Hodge's literary club and a week of lectures and readings at the Academy under the direction of the principal, Ernest Silver. What we lack in terms of specific details of the events, however, seems to be requited in Marie Hodge's "An Appreciation," published in the June, 1916, issue of the school magazine, *The Prospect*. Anticipating the poet's imminent visit, Hodge celebrates this way: "One cannot remain long in the presence of Mr. Frost without discovering the elements of poetic genius which have found expression in the two volumes of poems lately published by him" (*Selected Letters* 84). In fact, reading the whole of Hodge's brief commentary, one finds it an astutely penetrating insight into the nature of the poet as a person at this time in his career.

Frost's early relationship with Harriet Monroe, the well-known founder and editor of *Poetry: A Magazine of Verse*, went in two distinct directions. She not only published several of Frost's early works, bringing them before prominent readers, but she also, at Frost's gentle urging, published several poems by Frost's friend Edward Thomas.[10] In "Between Poets: Robert Frost and Harriet Monroe," Frost's granddaughter, Lesley Lee Francis, uncovered a remarkably detailed history of the correspondence and relationship. Throughout this history, the profound and mutual admiration between Frost and Monroe becomes clear. Lesley Francis remarks that "Frost admired Monroe as 'the most esthetic intellectual of her sex' and was generous in acknowledging the importance of her contribution to poetry through her magazine. He became impatient at times with her form of aesthetic idealism and her predilection for Imagism and free verse. But because he and the other poets of his generation—as poets and not as editors or critics—championed a common cause, he could tell her in all sincerity: 'Never mind.' "[11] Although one might view the phrase "of her sex" as depreciatory and sexist, it should be seen in the evidence of their long friendship of a mutually high regard.

They ran into some conflict in 1917 over Monroe's increasing interest in Ezra Pound's *Cantos*—and Pound did have considerable influence upon *Poetry*. Frost, however, was apparently sufficiently alienated from Pound by this point that he found it difficult to champion any work of his.[12] When Monroe asked Frost's opinion of the "Three Cantos," Frost equivocated in terms like this: "I can't say that I don't like it."[13]

But the fact remained that Monroe published several of Frost's works before an important audience, that she paid him handsomely for those works at a time when he was on the edge of financial disaster, and that she arranged readings for him in Chicago for which he was not only paid well but where he also met many of the leading young American poets of the day. It is not surprising, then, that with *Poetry's* tenth anniversary celebration, Frost wrote to Monroe acknowledging "*Poetry's* decade as 'the best ten years of literature any Magazine has had in America and the best boost poetry has ever had from a poet.' "[14]

Although Frost wrote in 1935 to Morton Zabel, associate editor of *Poetry*, "*Poetry* is one of the few places it would seriously bother me to be left out of for good and all," it was clear that he was by then distancing himself from the journal.[15] "The Witch of Coös" was published in *Poetry* in 1922, and received the $200 Magazine Prize for that year. In the April, 1936, issue he allowed *Poetry* to publish seven of his poems that would be collected in *A Witness Tree*. Six of the poems were included in the brief "Ten Mills" section.[16] By 1936, however, Frost's need for *Poetry* had been outgrown. He was now publishing his work in wider circulation journals—*The Atlantic Monthly*, *The Saturday Review of Literature*, and the like. Both Monroe and Morton Zabel wrote him often for poems to publish; Frost's responses, when he did respond, were polite but noncommittal. It is possible that other factors entered into Frost's distancing himself from *Poetry*. Although Monroe always praised Frost's blank verse, she made no secret of the fact that she preferred *vers libre*—the "new poetry" as she termed it in her anthology. Of her contributors, Pound was the chief proponent of free verse. The relationship ended altogether when Harriet Monroe died of a cerebral hemorrhage on 26 September 1936 while traveling in Peru.

Frost's relationship with another accomplished author and editor, Susan Hayes Ward, would prove to be not only more intimate but also more enduring. The relationship started early, when Ward, as literary editor of *The New York Independent*, accepted Frost's poem "My Butterfly: An Elegy" in 1894. The lofty sentiments and gooey archaisms of the poem, collected in *A Boy's Will*, did not in the least daunt Frost's celebration of having had it published. The Ward family, who published *The Independent*, was a

well-known, religiously grounded, and intelligent trio, and encouragement from such quarters was vital to Frost. The very lofti-
ness of the poem—in language and sentiment—that William Hayes
Ward (Susan's brother) so admired would turn against Frost. For
one thing, Ward thought it was in the style of Sidney Lanier, whom
Frost claimed he had not read at this point in his life, and for another thing, when Frost started writing in the blank verse and
"sound sense" that he was pioneering, Ward thought it was flat
and inferior.

Susan, as Lesley Lee Francis demonstrated in "Robert Frost and
Susan Hayes Ward," had, however, a keener insight into Frost's
talent, and also the ability to encourage him. In her review, "A
Decade of Poetry: 1889–1899," Ward singled out several still relatively obscure poets. She had this to say about Frost: " 'My Butterfly' (November 8, 1894), which reads as if written with a practiced
pen, was, I believe, the first poem its author, Robert Lee Frost,
ever offered for publication. He was hardly past boyhood at the
time, and the poem was written, he says, when it first dawned upon
him that poetry 'ought to sound well.' "[17] It is a sensitive comment
pertaining to a young poet, and one in a pattern of encouragement
Frost would receive as their friendship grew. It would be fair to say
that what Monroe did for Frost by giving him public exposure,
Ward did by giving him personal encouragement.

Ward and the Frost family visited several times, and the correspondence between Frost and Ward became the casual sort that we
see among only a half dozen or so of his epistolary relationships.
Significantly, in a 1911 letter, while he was at Pinkerton Academy,
and while ostensibly pressing her for an opportunity to visit, Frost
made the rare move of sending her a sizable number of unpublished poems:

> Frost forwarded a packet of 17 of his unpublished poems folded into
> sheets stitched together in a heavy blue binding. The as-yet-unrecog-
> nized poet referred to his offering as from a "minor poet" and candidly
> critiqued its significance: "It represents, needless to tell *you*, not the
> long deferred forward movement you are living in wait for, but only
> the grim stand it was necessary for me to make until I should gather
> myself together. The forward movement is to begin next year," he an-
> nounced prophetically.[18]

Not surprisingly, when *A Boy's Will* was published one of the first
copies was sent to Susan Ward.

A final coil in the skein of this relationship occurred shortly before Susan's death. During a visit to the Ward household in South
Berwick, "Frost was importuned by Miss Ward to compose a poem
based on some childhood memory of her about a 'little boyish girl'
who couldn't let go of the birch tree while trying to reach the fox
grapes growing there."[19] Although Frost typically refused all such
requests, he honored this one from his longtime friend. The ensu-
ing poem, "Wild Grapes," was published in the December, 1920,
issue of *Harper's Magazine*.[20]

A fourth significant relationship, both personal and poetic, arose
between Frost and Amy Lowell. It started almost accidentally, as
Lesley Lee Francis has demonstrated in her study "A Decade of
'Stirring Times': Robert Frost and Amy Lowell." Intrigued by the
Imagist movement led by Ezra Pound, Amy traveled to England
where she happened across a copy of Frost's *North of Boston*. Struck
by the power of Frost's blank verse, she reviewed the book for the
20 February 1915 issue of *New Republic* upon returning home. As
in the case of Susan Hayes Ward, the friendship between Frost and
Lowell grew rapidly and quickly included the Frost family. Also
like Ward, but to a still greater extent, Amy came from an illustri-
ous family that had the wealth and authority for her to influence
the causes she believed in.

Her own poetry and artistic beliefs, however, did not entirely
comport with Frost's. Somewhat alienated from Pound by this
point, Lowell prepared her own anthology entitled *Some Imagist
Poets* containing her set of Imagist beliefs that Pound quickly called
"Amygist." Not only did the volume conflict with Pound, however,
but also with Harriet Monroe's work with *Poetry*. As the debate between east coast and midwest sharpened, Frost wrote to Harriet
Monroe that "he was tempted to title his next book 'Upper Right
Hand Corner.' "[21] The fundamental disagreement between Frost
and Lowell, however, rested solidly upon their differing views of
the "verse form" of poetry. That disagreement, early in his own
career, helped Frost shape and sharpen his own poetic "voice."

Just as with Harriet Monroe, Frost had already begun formulat-
ing his ideas of "sound sense." In his relationship with Amy Lowell, he deepened his already strong belief in the traditional forms
of poetic expression. The Imagist poetry, as it developed in the
modernist era, strove for a sensuality and immediacy. The image
was intended to locate the reader in the poem by an emotional
power acquired through description, language sounds, and musi-

cal pattern. *Intended* is an ambivalent word here, for the poem is also organic, ameliorating and modifying the artist's rational state with the emotional state. To Frost this sounded a bit too much like artistic abandonment. He cherished artistic control over his poem and believed he could arrive at the same ends Lowell sought—engagement or illumination of the reader—using traditional versification and melodic techniques.

Disagreement over poetic technique can no doubt be helpful to any emerging poet, testing his or her own choices and craft against those of others. The disagreements with Lowell took a slightly different turn, however, when she published her *Tendencies in Modern American Poetry* in 1917, devoting a section of critical appraisal to Frost. Although she found much to praise in Frost's artistry, she saw *North of Boston* as a nearly unmitigated assimilation of bleak portraits.[22] Whereas Frost saw real people, Lowell saw ideas masquerading as people. Similarly, while Frost believed he used authentic speech, Lowell heard only a coarse dialect. They inhabited two different worlds—the poet mining his rustic culture for authenticity; Lowell holding forth as one of the Bostonian cultural elite.

Yet, they did agree, emphatically, upon the significance of drama in poetry. Characters in confrontation and situations demanding choices mark the art of each. In "A Decade of Stirring Times," Francis recounts a commentary by Frost at one of his readings:

> I knew Amy Lowell very well and she said one night to me in her great house in Brookline, she said: "After all, what's the difference between your stories about New England and mine?" I said: "Amy, you're more like Shakespeare. You can't have a tragedy without a villain and I do it without a villain." She said: "You don't like mine?" And I said, "Yes, Amy, you're more like Shakespeare."[23]

Despite the substantial differences, and occasional slight agreement, the relationship remained a cordial and friendly one. Frost felt a rare freedom to write to her with a tone of levity and wit. He intervened to arrange a visit by his daughter Lesley with her, advising Lesley to read a volume of Amy's poems with the hope that she would "find something to like." Whatever the case, Frost promised Lesley "She'll be interesting" (*Family Letters* 21). Moreover, in Amy Lowell, Frost found a first-class intellect who could do the kind of witty verbal sparring he so delighted in. Their noto-rious joint reading at the University of Michigan in 1922 is legend-ary (see "Stirring Times" 520, and Meyers 168–69, and others). It was a most unusual friendship, enduring profound disagreements but nonetheless marked by a high and mutual respect.

Other relations between Frost and women that influenced his life and work could be examined.[24] In the case at hand, however, we discover divergent relationships. Marie Hodge had almost a motherly influence upon Frost; nonetheless, one has to wonder what the shape of his career would have been had she not so assid-uously championed his work—preparing a place for him—before he returned to the States from England. Similarly, Susan Hayes Ward, in addition to publishing and praising Frost's early poem, provided him the encouragement he so desperately needed at the threshold of his career. It is fair to say that Harriet Monroe's *Poetry* revolutionized poetry at the start of the century. It is one of the signal markers on the modernist highway. Her introduction of Frost to a literary elite and her early—and emphatic—endorsement of his work provided him an imprimatur he very much needed to scramble out of the field of unknowns. Perhaps in many ways the most valuable relationship was Frost's strange but powerful relationship with Amy Lowell. They respected each other sufficiently that they could freely disagree. Lowell's wide-reaching literary influence helped establish Frost's place. They were, above all, friends—personalities altogether different but oddly enough altogether in accord. They were as unlike as Amy's imagism and Frost's blank verse, yet similar in their attention to poetry as an aesthetic form.

One may conclude from such evidence that Frost's circle of in-fluence was much broader than many assume. At the same time, he was sharp with his tongue in an equal opportunity way. Although notoriously acerbic in his critical judgments, belying the avuncular image many assumed, those judgments almost always focused on the *work* of a poet, not on the poet him- or herself. Considering that broader social ethics introduces new issues to Frost's attitudes toward women. In particular, revisionist literary criticism of gen-der issues has opened different ways of seeing how Frost holds so-ciety in his poetic works. Instead of seeing the presence of humanity generally in the poetry, such studies see conflicts be-tween the sexes and look for responses to the conflicts.

An example of one such study is James Dawes's "Masculinity and

Transgression in Robert Frost." Developing earlier work by Philip
Gerber and Richard Poirier, Dawes focuses upon the central issue
of what men can be to each other, considering the patterns of ho-
mosocial (the broad range of interaction between men in all society), homophobic, and homosexual relations that he discovers in
the poetry. "The Grindstone," for example, is for Dawes an overt
example of the psychology of homophobia. His premise is that
Frost describes work in two different ways. "Mowing," for Dawes,
displays heterosexual images. But "work that has become sick and
ugly, leading to domination and humiliation rather than revitaliza-
tion, is . . . best expressed through images of the homosexual."[25]
These we find in "The Grindstone." Dawes concludes the contrast
between "Mowing" and "The Grindstone":

> If "Mowing" is a glorification of heterosexual love, "The Grindstone"
> is a virulent denigration of homosexuality. Through his use of imag-
> ery, the speaker here suggests that *unnatural* homosexual love is, at
> best, only a grotesque parody of *real* love; sterile and destructive, ho-
> mosexual love grinds away precious blade rather than creating it.[26]

Many readers have difficulty with the overtness and assertive-
ness of Dawes's claims. Is "Mowing" a glorification of heterosexual
love? No, it is not. It is a poem about a narrator mowing a swale
with a scythe. That is the "is-ness" of the poem. It suggests, as I
have argued earlier, an act of writing poetry, even as the poem is
written. Could it also suggest something of what Dawes speculates?
Of course, but the distinction between overt declaration—which
Frost abhorred—and suggestiveness of metaphor is not always
carefully observed in Dawes's study. Such a qualification is not to
deny the essay's contribution, particularly in the framework of this
study where we are trying to lay hold of Frost's ethics in general
and his social ethics and gendered ethical position in particular.
    Similarly, Dawes's application of Coppelia Kahn's Jungian views
of the animus/anima relationships to Frost's works is thoroughly
entertaining even while the reader might be uneasy with some of
the conclusions. Dawes argues that "Male fear of being dominated
by men is, essentially, the fear of being feminized, or made into a
homosexual—at heart, homophobia."[27] In such poems as "From
Plane to Plane," "Mending Wall," and "The Code," according to
Dawes, this fear manifests itself in powerful competition. In such a
poem as "A Hundred Collars" the fear of domination is overpow-

ering. The reader can't help feeling the Doctor's fear before the huge Lafe. Frost evokes a fear that nearly every person (except the Lafes), male or female, has known. His power as artist, as we have seen before, is to engage the reader, to bring the reader inside the drama. But rather than seeing Lafe as a ruthless, homosexual predator, it might also be possible to see him as a man with a sense of self-humor proportionate to his physical bulk, a man merely tweaking the suspicions of his more learned and wealthier roommate. He reminds one, more than anything, of Queequeg in Melville's *Moby Dick*.

In "The Place is the Asylum: Women and Nature in Robert Frost's Poetry," an essay as intriguing as Dawes's and also heavily reliant upon symbolic interpretation, Katherine Kearns switches the focus to women's freedom, dominance, and entrapment in Frost's poetry. Taking "A Servant to Servants" as her point of departure, Kearns postulates that

> Men and women possess the power to make each other mad, yet it is the man in "A Servant to Servants" who must be locked away. Women are powerful, active, magnetic in their madness, which is manifested in escape from the asylum of households into nature. Men are rendered impotent; they can only pursue unsuccessfully or withdraw into themselves. They have nowhere else to go, because Frost's world is controlled by a powerful femininity.[28]

Moreover, since the household often appears sexually sterile, Frost's women—albeit longing for the security of a home—are pulled to the more sensuous world of nature. Kearns reminds us that "The woods in Frost's poetry are indeed 'lovely, dark, and deep,' and while his households are often left cold and vacant, his nature is enticing, provocative at once of both desire and death."[29] It is important to be aware of what Kearns is *not* claiming in her essay. She is not claiming, for example, that all of Frost's narrators or protagonists are misogynistic luddites, although in some cases this might be true. Nor is she claiming gendered domination and repression, which also upon occasion might be true. What she does clarify is that in the ethical stances held between men and women dissonance arises by virtue of gender. These are not irreconcilable; in fact, in some instances Frost points toward reconciliation. Such a view comports with my own—that while conflict inevitably arises among Frost's poetic characters, his social ethics works toward (not always successfully) a harmony that subsumes dissonance. Recognizing fundamental contrarieties of point of view and nature, Frost nonetheless attempts to balance these in an ethical harmony.

Rather than examine the dialectics, paradoxes, and ironies of a gendered poetics, Karen Kilcup turns her eye in *Robert Frost and Feminine Literary Tradition* to correspondences in voices and values between Frost and both earlier and contemporary female writers. Her aim, she says is "frankly and unapologetically to recuperate the poet, and by extension other male poets, as a positive model for readers who have been troubled by depictions of him as almost inevitable masculine and misogynous."[30] While granting (of necessity) that Frost himself was not a feminist, Kilcup sets for herself the ambitious task of finding links with a feminine tradition. Kilcup points to Rita Felski's argument in *The Gender of Modernity* that "gender is continually in process, an identity that is performed and actualized over time within given social constructs" to explore her premise that Frost's own views of social gender were continually in process.[31] Thus, she examines Frost's poems not in a strictly chronological order but by "representations" in different volumes. In doing so, and by process of careful definitions, Kilcup legitimates the use of such terms as "sentimental" and "emotional" as well as "intellectual" in the evocative construct of Frost's art. Particularly effective in the study is Kilcup's analysis of Thyatira in *A Masque of Reason*, which, along with *Masque of Mercy*, she rightfully reads, I believe, as "very funny poems."

In a study of ambiguity in the poetic text—both in Frost's imaginative power and the reader's imaginative perception, Patricia Wallace points out that the female outsider figure in Frost's poems often "works to displace and disrupt the very order which the poetic text attempts to create."[32] Thus a metatext appears questioning the reasons for the displacement itself rather than what some critics have seen as female hysteria or depression.[33] In fact, Wallace claims that "When Frost places the figure of a woman within (and without) a figure of a man he *marries* the distinctions between outsider/insider, order/disorder, and writes about the figure of a woman as if he did not fear her, or the imaginative power she represents."[34]

Having considered Frost's social and personal relationships with several remarkable women, and having considered how several recent studies have dealt with issues of gender in Frost's work, consider finally evidence from the work itself. Frost's social ethics receive clarification by contrasting "Home Burial" and "The Hill Wife."

"Home Burial," which might easily be—and frequently is—read as a poem of marital discord, may also be understood as a poem in which understanding opens, dissonances dissolve, and the order/disorder conflict begins resolution. In the opening lines the husband's actions are ambiguous, subject to interpretation as either gentle or dominating. Amy comes down the stairs from the window, her fear evident on her face. Simultaneously the husband climbs up, wondering what it is that so besets her. At once the mercy/domination images collide. His voice is gentle enough, "You must tell me, dear," yet she "cowers" under him, her face now gone "dull." While the interior world carries the tension here, the husband now looks out the window where her gaze has swept so often and now admits "that I see." Furthermore, he admits that it is a wonder that he had not really seen the small, hillside family burial plot framed by the window before. That is, he had previously seen it according to custom; now he sees it through the eyes of his wife's particular tragedy in the loss of their child.

It seems for a moment that their mutual perspective from inside and out through the window might be restorative, but suddenly Amy darts down the stairs, ready to run out of the house. As she stands with hand on the door, the husband begs her not to leave. He confesses his own lack of understanding—how to communicate with her—and says "I might be taught, / I should suppose." But he qualifies it, uncertain how that could be, and wondering whether "A man must partly give up being / With womenfolk." Nonetheless, he begs for a chance, asking to be let "into your grief" so that he might understand.

Amy won't have it, however. For her the time of understanding has passed. Husband and wife have moved into their own separate spheres as means of coping individually with the death of their child. The husband represents the fundamental pragmatist, and rightly so. There was this thing to do—a grave to be dug and a child to be laid in it. This is what pragmatism serves. At the time, Amy sat behind the window looking outward, allowing her own glass wall to grow between them. Amy, on the other hand, represents the emotional response to a tragic situation, and rightly so. She is a mother grieving; there are tears to be shed. In his ruthless pragmatism, her husband also failed to enter into, or even notice, her world of tears. Now, long after the burial, he remains outside the window; she sits on the inside. Their roles precisely reverse at the close—the husband sitting disconsolate on the stairs, Amy turning to the door with her husband vowing to bring her back by force. Amy, in the view of Katherine Kearns, "is crossing the threshold from marital asylum into freedom. The house is suffocating her."[35] It is the first time, really, that the husband's emotions have truly surfaced in this scene.

The poem is beautifully and powerfully crafted, justly deserving the accolades given it. The subtle changes in character, the reversals of both physical positions and psychological roles, enhance the drama of the tragedy. At the outset of the poem, Amy huddles on the step by the window as her husband enters; at the close he sits where she had been, and Amy is now at the door, preparing to leave. At the outset she charges him with being incapable of emotion; at the end he is overcome with emotion, pleading with her to stay. If we see this poem only in the negative and disruptive sense—frustrated woman leaves husband frustrated—we seem either to be depreciating Frost's artistry or to be putting a late twentieth-century spin on it that might not have been fully there in Frost's conception. Here, as in many of Frost's male/female, husband/wife poems, there often seems to be a larger metatext that is ethical in nature.

Amy's clear charge against her husband is that "You *couldn't* care!" The evidence in the poem, however, is not that the husband is uncaring but that he has not discovered communal means for caring. He has, for example, equated caring in a marriage with sexuality (11.50–55), but also expresses a willingness to forego that. The heart of the matter, however, lies in Amy's discourse on friendship (97–f). Friendships, even the best of them, fail in her view. True community of spirit is a pretense. The reality of life is a daunting, individual loneliness. Proclaiming that "The world is evil," Amy tries to flee from that fact. Her flight is not merely from her husband; it is from the torment of loneliness, unassuaged by anything that society, including marriage, has to offer.

Seen in such a light, the poem falls solidly in accord with those poems of personal ambiguity that we examined earlier. Loneliness was the chief despair of Frost's life, and grief was like unto it. Disruption of the ties of community bore the shape of tragedy. *If* Amy leaves, and tellingly we don't know if she does, she joins one more of Frost's characters acquainted with the night. The significant ethical implication of the poem, however, is the redemptive power of community and friendship: What is heard most powerfully in this poem is not the lamentation of what has passed, but the crying out of two people for reconciliation and restoration.

In "Home Burial" the reader is never sure of Amy's departure. Nor is one sure of what would happen if she remained. Is the husband's proclamation that he will bring her back by force an expression of his long pent-up emotional need for her, or simply an expression of his marital domination and bull-headed resolve to keep Amy caged in domestic asylum? Because the poem is so heavily laden with ethical implications of duty to self and duty to community, Frost, as in other poems, suspends direct answers in ambiguity. Rather than a concrete answer—this happened; this was the effect—Frost engages the reader in such a way that the reader is forced to determine answers. Does one side with Amy or her husband, pitting one over against the other, or does one embrace the tragedy of both, pitying the loneliness each feels?

Far different is "The Hill Wife," for here the rupture seems irremediable. Unlike the couple together in their lonely cottage in "Smoke and Mist," the loneliness here grows between husband and wife themselves. The rhymed lyrics by themselves are not unusual, but the shifting point of view emphasizes the dissonance of the marriage and within the wife. She speaks the first and third "poems" in the sequence of five. The others are narrated by some other deeply intimate voice—one intimate with the situation and the reader. That second voice brings a drama of credibility to the scene, and also creates an objective, albeit all-seeing, eye that frames the wife's thoughts and actions.

In the wife's first poem, "Loneliness," it is uncertain to whom she directs her comments. She mentions a "you" that joins her, but it certainly would not be her husband on this remote farm. Is it, then, the reader, or another self she has created to assuage her loneliness? Or indeed it might well be an apostrophe to the bird she views through her window, for the bird exemplifies the positive counter to all the things she lacks. What emerges is that she cares deeply—and wishes that she did not have to—about the actions of the birds. They freely come and go. They freely sing. They freely nest and "fill their breasts / But with each other. . . ." Each observation plays a deep counterpart to the life she leads— isolated, childless, and apparently loveless.

The outside narrator appears in part 2, "House Fear," with commentary that further emphasizes the wife's loneliness. The wife speaks from inside the house; the narrator from outside. What the narrator sees is a "lonely house." Here the couple returns from some event to the house unlit and with cold ashes in the fireplace. Dank and desolate this house is; nonetheless, they rattle the door in the event a burglar might be within. These four walls hold fear.

In part 3, "The Smile," the imagined burglar becomes an actual tramp that has stopped by to beg food. Although nothing overtly sinister appears about the tramp—he smiles and leaves—the wife's increasingly twisted psyche interprets his every action in sinister terms. The tramp's smile becomes a mocking sneer of the couple's evident poverty and newlywed status. Or it might come from his sense of power over her. She begins to wonder with some desperation how far down the road he is—or whether he is watching from the woods.

The woods of part 3 switches to a particular "dark pine" in part 4. Immediately the pine is associated with the same invasive and predatory aura of the tramp. The hill wife curses the pine not just for rubbing against the bedroom window, but for trying the latch, trying to enter. In many of Frost's poems earth and tree imagery carry sexual connotations, and something of that pervasive fear of the pine operates here. It is a nightmare the hill wife only has abed, of course. In the morning she speaks of the tree as ineffectual, its hands making "futile" passes. She reduces the threat to the image of a little bird flying against the window. The return of the bird figure, however, echoes the first part, where the sight of the nesting birds heightens the wife's sense of desolation. The childless household seems, especially with the figure of the tree's futile passes, to be sexually sterile as well. The tree, here closely allied with male sexuality, has never been inside the room, however. She is the only one in the room afraid "Of what the tree might do."[36]

Since we have not heard from, nor indeed even seen, the husband of the poem, our conclusions as we enter part 5 are solely through her voice and the eyes of the narrator. She suffers under an inconsolable loneliness for several reasons. Her compelling attraction to the nesting birds heightens her lonely childlessness. The house she lives in is remote and isolated, carrying with it a host of fears that she inhabits. Furthermore, even though it is not overtly mentioned, part 4 suggests a deep fear of sexuality, projected upon the phallic symbol of the pine tree fumbling at her window latch.

All such items might serve to make her cower ever inward. Or

they might serve to spring her from the very fear and loneliness
that bind her. We do remember that the tramp, even though
frightening to the wife, had the freedom to go wherever he
wanted, even *into* the woods.

Part 5, "The Impulse," captures her own urgent impulse to simply walk away. It is no rational flight; indeed, she first walks away,
remarkably ill-equipped, as if on a Sunday stroll. The outside narrator reiterates the reasons—the loneliness of the house, the lack
of children, her lack of work. She follows her husband on his farm
chores one day, a nonparticipant to them, until she finds a felled
log to rest on. She is near the mysterious woods now, where she
dreamed the tramp lurking. When her husband calls, instead of
coming dutifully she simply slips away into the fern. Perhaps the
most poignant picture is that of the distraught husband. He now
experiences her loneliness, to which we must assume he had been
unaware. He searches everywhere but discovers only "finalities /
besides the grave."

As in "Home Burial" Frost holds things in reserve. As so often
happens with Frost's tactical ambiguity, the reader is left with the
task of juggling possibilities. The wife is simply gone; the conflict
left in tension. At the same time, however, "The Hill Wife" sharpens the ethical theme of "Home Burial." Loneliness drives her
away, but conversely the poem emphasizes the need for community. Moreover, it recognizes the place of a woman in that community. Cast into merely domesticated roles is to kill something of a
woman's vital spirit, forcing her escape to freedom.

Freedom, as Frost testifies often, is humanity's highest value. In
his careful essay "On Emerson," a sort of autobiography of the
growth of his own ethics, Frost says that "I owe more to Emerson
than anyone else for troubled thoughts about freedom" (*Selected
Prose* 115). Citing Emerson's lines that God "Would take the sun
out of the skies / Ere freedom out of a man," Frost proclaims himself on the side of this freedom. Importantly, Frost points out that
the issue is not that the truth will make me free, but that "My truth
will bind you slave to me" (*Selected Prose* 115). That is to say, authentic personal freedom allows others the freedom to personally
choose their authenticity. This ethics, Frost reminds us, demands
high courage, since it entails a letting go of one's own demands. "I
am on record," Frost stated, "as saying that freedom is nothing but
departure—setting forth—leaving things behind, brave origina-
tion of the courage to be new" (*Selected Prose* 115). The brave deter-

mination of many of Frost's female characters casts them as ethical heroes in his scheme. If community is the cherished stay against loneliness, courage is nonetheless often required to make all things new in that community—or to depart from it altogether.

All too often Frost's poems provide a bleak landscape of empty homes and ruined farms. Cellars that once held canned goods lie open like pits under broken fortress walls. The playthings of the past are scattered to the winds. Even the memory of hopes perishes. While such portraits surely dotted Frost's physical and emotional landscape, his depiction of them seems to punctuate his ethics. The loneliness of loss is ruin. In "The Need of Being Versed in Country Things" such collapse of buildings and family and community appears as a wound on some larger natural plan. There the birds that nest in the ruins of the old barn—even while they nest toward new life—appear to weep for the loss about them. The eye that sees the phoebe for what it is—a bird rejoicing in its nesting—will not see this. It is versed in country things and knows the reality. Yet the reality of loss is also poignant. One almost believes the phoebes mourn.

So too Frost appears to mourn the breakdown in community, and particularly so in that community between male and female. Each must "hold" each other in trust and freedom. There can be no trust, of course, without the freedom to violate the trust. That is the sublime ethical paradox. But that risk also undergirds Frost's social ethics.

Conclusion: Letting Frost be Frost

İN A JOINT REVIEW OF WILLIAM PRITCHARD'S REVISIONIST BIOGRAPHY of Frost and Dorothy Judd Hall's *Robert Frost: Contours of Belief*, Philip Gerber finds some significant links between both works. Pritchard set for himself the task of salvaging Frost's humanity from what he believed to be Lawrance Thompson's presentation of "a species of monster in human form."[1] In Gerber's view, Pritchard's revisionist attack upon Thompson in itself weakens his own work. According to Gerber, "having set up the Thompson straw man, Pritchard too often in demolishing his target succumbs to the obvious risk of swinging too far in his corrective position, giving Frost the benefit of the doubt at every turning."[2] It bears the curious effect, as Gerber muses, "That Pritchard himself quite often 'lifts the rock' to view Frost's hidden life, and each time that he does so, he reveals enough pettiness and spite to excite precisely the effect he has disowned."[3] Gerber strikes a significant and seldom spoken message, one that applies not only to Frost but also to many modern writers that we may hold dear or casually loathe for our own personal reasons. Gerber reminds us once again of this salient fact: "Why can't we accept Frost for what he so obviously was, a human being with huge virtues and considerable faults, and go on from there?"[4]

In one tight statement from his essay on Frost in *Remembering Poets*, Donald Hall brings those faults and virtues together with the force of a collision:

> He was vain, he was cruel, he was rivalrous with all other men; but he could also be generous and warm—when he could satisfy himself that his motives were dubious. He was a man possessed by guilt, by knowledge that he was "God," by craving for love, by the necessity to reject love—and by desire for fame which no amount of celebrity could satisfy.[5]

In the wreckage of those colliding virtues and flaws, one wonders if the poet was ever whole. The larger issue for scholarship, however, is the "wholeness" of the verse.

The difference between Frost and many modern writers, Philip Gerber contends, is that Frost was "very successful in preventing his worst traits from coloring his verse." Perhaps we should include his "best traits" also, for while his verse was often intensely personal in *tone*, it seldom was by way of didactic message. To know Frost is to accept that there is a hidden Frost, and that the poetry too is veiled of personally overt statement. As Gerber points out, "It is the poetry that is our ultimate concern; the rest is gossip."[6]

Dorothy Judd Hall, on the other hand, focuses almost exclusively upon the poetry in her study of Frost's religious beliefs. One might point out that she is writing a form of literary criticism, and not biography. Beyond several of the obligatory references to Frost's personal statements of belief, however, Hall roams pretty decisively within the world of poetry itself. Gerber recognizes, as Hall most certainly does, that this is necessarily so simply because of the marked ambiguities and hiddenness in Frost's life—but that hiddenness also pervades the work.

In the introductory chapter to this study, we examined some possible connections between George Santayana's aesthetics and Frost's work. It is useful to reemphasize one point from that. The study of aesthetics differs markedly from literary critical study. The latter might, for example, entertain such a topic as "The Use of Irony between Speakers in Frost's Narrative Poems." A study in aesthetics wants to know that too, but it wants to press the issue: Why use irony at all? How does it enrich or detract from the quality of the work as a whole? What are its implications for allied issues or themes in the poem? These are essentially aesthetic questions, and not necessarily those of literary criticism.

The implication for a study of Frost's ethics, then, is a necessary balance between the man's personal and public statements and the work. It seems to me that Frost held a systematic, clear, and persistent ethical belief framework throughout his life. We can surmise a number of particulars about his religious grounding. There is ample evidence for such. Yet his fundamental ethical positioning must be understood, to a large degree, apart from his religious beliefs. That is to say, his ethical positioning is primarily deontological, operating from an intuited sense of moral oughtness. This accounts both for a personal sense of right and wrong actions and also for the way he "holds" others, evidenced in his view of women. Furthermore, it accounts for his belief in freedom, and his consequent effort to engage the reader in the drama of the work rather than to exhort the reader to "right" judgments. It also, therefore, accounts for his personal ambiguity and also that ambiguity that infiltrates a large body of his poetry. Consider the multifaceted implications of this in one of his most widely discussed and possibly most ambiguous poems, "Stopping by Woods on a Snowy Evening." In this case, I would like to depart somewhat from the standard procedures of analysis employed in this study, and risk contextualizing the poem to a classroom setting.

In *A Living Voice*, Reginald Cook records Frost saying about the poem: "That one I've been more bothered with than anybody has ever been with any poem in just the pressing it far more than it should be pressed for."[7] For a poet who loathed obscurantism in his art, the message is clear. Yet, perhaps the poem has been pressed "far more than it should be" simply because of its perfection of form and suggestiveness. Indeed, despite his arch tone in the previous comment, "Stopping by Woods" captures nearly everything Frost sought in his art.

Reginald Cook's record is not the only evasive commentary of Frost on the poem. During his reading, "On Taking Poetry," at Bread Loaf on 30 June 1955, Frost read the poem and commented at length on it. He prefaced the reading by saying, "I've got to say old ones, familiar ones, to some of you, for what I've heard people make of it."[8] Such is tantamount to announcing, now I'm going to clear the record. Here's what the poem is really *about*. But what the poem is about, we understand, is only its "aboutness"—that is, the event that occurred in the woods one night. The poem is not a tool to get a chore done, nor a means for proving or disproving anything. A poem is about itself.

Therefore, after reading the poem, Frost declared, "Now, you see, the first thing about that is to take it right between the eyes just as it is . . . take it right between the eyes like a little blow and not, you know, take it in center sort of."[9] A slight opening occurs here. If the reader takes the poem right between the eyes, the blow also sparks attention and reflection. In effect, the reader takes the poem into him or herself, owning it personally. Frost himself, however, playfully avoids taking sides. In the humor-studded commentary that followed at quite some length, he merely described the physical elements that went into the poem. After all, the physical elements—the cold, the trees, and so forth—constitute the "aboutness" of the poem. Allow me to contextualize this personally.

During the years that I have taught modern poetry, I have discovered that my task is to teach the students how to read (or engage) the poem as much as how to analyze and discuss it. That is to say, many students today, even the brightest ones, are fairly ignorant of the intricate play of form and language in the work. In Frost's terms, they all want to play tennis with the net down and then talk about how good the game was. As they acquire the formal expertise the students more readily adapt differing critical methodologies to the work, and begin to identify their own emerging critical premises. But Frost's "Stopping by Woods" allows this instructor the opportunity to drop a little bombshell in the neat intellectual patterns. If not always instructive to them, it is always such to me.

The second fundamental lesson for the students is to work from the inside out of the poem. Before analysis or interpretation begins, the reader is obligated to locate character and setting, form and tonalities of language—in short, the "aboutness" of the poem. In the particular case of "Stopping by Woods," however, I depart from the standard procedure by asking six or seven students to provide an interpretation of the meaning of the work immediately upon my reading the poem aloud. They are also required to provide a one-sentence statement of support from the poem for their interpretation. Thereby I short-circuit the second fundamental lesson, momentarily disabusing them of what I have been trying to teach.

Some interpretations are predictable and come quickly. The poem is a contemplation of death. Why? Because of the symbolism of snow as cold and deathlike, the darkness of the trees, and so forth. Quickly the students are on to my game. If you can say a poem is about death, flip the coin and say it is about life. Why? Because he has promises to keep. Somewhere in there someone suggests that it is a poem about suicide because of the pervasive tone of sadness. The vowel sounds in the rhymes, after all, are all weighty, sinking sounds. Obviously the poet is profoundly depressed. Another person senses the need for a change. The poem is about a harried businessman, she says, having to keep promises when he would rather enjoy the beauty of the snow. Another, it's about Santa Claus. Why? Well, he has his sleigh and reindeer-horse, and the date is December 22, the winter solstice. Santa has these promises to keep before Christmas. And so it goes.[10]

Is the poem then an open invitation to see anything we want?

Does the ambiguity into which Frost casts his ethical views permit us to push them any way we want? I think not. I think those views have to be thrust against ethics itself as a discipline, and then located in consistent patterns in the work. Doing so, we may fairly locate Frost's personal ethics as deontological, an intuited sense of moral oughtness, and his social ethics as a delicate blend of freedom and trust.

Before I leave "Stopping by Woods" in the classroom, I always tell the students a story. It is related by N. Arthur Bleau in *Centennial Essays III*, entitled—dangerously—"Robert Frost's Favorite Poem." So unusual is the story that it required an afterword note of authenticity by Lesley Frost. Lesley recalled her father telling the story behind the poem during the forties, remembering how Eunice—the little horse—stopped "a hundred yards or so south of our farm on the Wyndham Road." And she adds, remembering her father's words: " 'A man has as much right as a woman to a good cry now and again. The snow gave me its shelter; the horse understood and gave me the time.' "[11] So, what private story lies behind this so public a poem that it has entered the American consciousness as one of our literary jewels?

In brief, the story is easy to relate. Arthur Bleau was in the audience at Bowdoin College in 1947 for one of Frost's presentations. When Frost asked for questions at the conclusion, Bleau asked, " 'Mr. Frost, what is your favorite poem?' " Frost responded as most any writer would: "They're all my favorites. It's difficult to single out one over another."[12] After the session concluded, however, Frost signaled Bleau and asked him to remain. Then, in the privacy of the empty room, Frost told why "Stopping by Woods" was his favorite poem.

The poem, first published in *The New Republic* in July, 1920, recalled an earlier history in subject matter. It recalled the young Frost having moved from California to New England during desperate financial times. As he looked toward Christmas, he felt he had to do something to insure some cheer in the household. He put some of their farm produce on the wagon, hitched up Eunice, and headed into town. And there he sat throughout the day. Everyone else was affected by the tough times also. He sold nothing. Realizing finally that there would be no presents in the Frost household, he turned homeward. The horse knew the way, and the boy gave him his head. But as the horse reached the fork, he seemed to understand the despair in the boy. The horse slowed, stopped, and the boy "just sat there and bawled like a baby." Then, as suddenly, the horse shook its harness, jingling the bells, and turned down the road homeward.

While classroom students (and scholars) may bring multilayered meanings to bear upon the "aboutness" of the poem, for the poet in this case the poem was quite simply about the relationship between human and animal. A deep, primordial understanding connected them that night. It is interesting, moreover, how Frost worked toward this connectedness through various drafts of the poem. For example, one draft variant of line 5 reads "My steaming horse." That would be literally true, as the labored animal paused in the cold air. But the revision to "My little horse" creates an entirely different quality. It opens that emotional quality of affection between them. Interestingly, however, Frost had a hard time deciding on the gender of Eunice for the poem-horse. Line 9 shifted in draft from "he" to "she" to "he."

All of this is not to say that Frost's view of the aboutness of the work is right, and everybody else is wrong. In fact, such a statement would violate everything Frost stood for poetically and ethically. In both instances, as I have argued throughout this text, the genius of Frost is to leave sufficiently structured ambiguity, with a fairly concrete grounding, that the reader is free to contemplate the structure in his or her own way.

Notes

INTRODUCTION

1. George W. Nitchie, *Human Values in the Poetry of Robert Frost* (Durham: Duke University Press, 1960), 7.

2. Judith Oster, *Toward Robert Frost: The Reader and the Poet* (Athens, GA: University of Georgia Press, 1991), xiv.

CHAPTER ONE: AESTHETICS AND ETHICS

1. Any argument that Santayana's aesthetic theories influenced Frost is admittedly circumstantial, resting largely upon Frost's attendance at Harvard during the time that *The Sense of Beauty* was first published. In his sophomore year (1898) at Harvard, Frost enrolled in the History of Philosophy course taught by Santayana. According to Jeffery Meyers, "Frost was shocked by Santayana's sarcastic and even blasphemous attitude toward religion" (45). Similarly, Jay Parini observes that "Frost always kept a wary distance between himself and Santayana, remaining canny if not coy when it came to his own religious views" (63). Whatever the case at that time, Frost later kept four of Santayana's books in his personal library—*Character and Opinion in the United States, Poems, Skepticism and Animal Faith*, and *Soliloquies in England and Later Soliloquies*.

The Sense of Beauty earned Santayana his reputation, and remained his best-selling book throughout his lifetime. According to Arthur C. Danto's introduction to the M.I.T. Critical Edition (1988), Santayana wrote the text simply as an extrapolation from the aesthetics course he taught at Harvard from 1892–95, and in order to secure his tenure as quickly as possible. Danto recalls a conversation he had with Santayana in 1950: He was teaching at Harvard; it was a good job; he wanted to keep it; but "They let me know through the ladies [the secretaries] that I had better publish a book. On what? "On art of course. So I wrote this wretched potboiler" (xvi). The derogatory comment was not unusual. Throughout his life Santayana often spoke with disaffection of both the book and also the field of aesthetics.

However, Danto also addresses the question of why Santayana held such an attitude. He finds the answer in Santayana's 1904 essay, "What is Aesthetics?" There Santayana laments a cleavage between human history and art. Art, he argues, is not separable from human experience. To study aesthetics as some separable field, apart from any other human endeavor, is unreasonable, for in "moral

174

philosophy . . . there is as little room for a special discipline called 'Aesthetics' as there is among the natural sciences" (xvi).

2. George Santayana, *The Sense of Beauty* (Cambridge: MIT Press, 1988), 13.

3. Ibid.

4. The very diversity of this seminal work in the modern philosophy of aesthetics leads Santayana to occasional equivocation. In part 4, "Expression," Santayana returns to the issue of morality and aesthetics. He raises a series of probable artistic subjects, then admits that, "All these matters, however, belong to the sphere of ethics, nor should we give them here even a passing notice, but for the influence which moral ideas exact over aesthetic judgements" (*Beauty* 137). Ethics, morality, and criteria of aesthetic excellence are all intimately interwoven in Santayana's theories.

5. Santayana perceived Rationalism of the order that Pope represented as a serious threat to human values. It abstracted, in his view, human experience from emotions and consequences. Taken to its extreme, Rationalism deprives humanity of values: "No event would be repulsive, no situation terrible. We might, in a word, have a world of idea without a world of will" (*Beauty* 15).

6. Here lies a major difference between Santayana and the young modernists whom he influenced. One of the traits of modernism was to use art as a means of cultural protest. To them, World War I proved definitive evidence of the moral bankruptcy of the west, but that became only a platform for protest at other cultural deficiencies.

7. Santayana, *Beauty*, 17.

8. Ibid., 19.

9. Ibid., 18–19.

10. Jeffery Meyers, *Robert Frost: A Biography* (New York: Houghton Mifflin, 1996), 16.

11. George Santayana, *Essays of George Santayana in Literature*, Ed. Irving Singer (New York: Charles Scribner's Sons, 1956), 282.

12. *Ibid.*, 283.

13. In her essay "Education by Poetry," Joan Peters has extensively developed the possible relationships between Frost's ideas of metaphor and Eliot's of the objective correlative. Significant to our argument here, moreover, Peters demonstrates Frost's emphasis "on the close, metaphorical relationship of art to life, at a time when poets and critics were generally anxious to obscure that connection" (27). In Frost's views on metaphor, then, Peters sees him deliberately distancing himself from the modernist mainstream. In a similar way, Robert Kern in his "Frost and Modernism" provides a convincing study of variations between Frost's idea and use of the image and that of other modernist authors.

14. Frost's letters to Lesley while she was a student at Barnard College are intriguing simply because Frost felt free to drop any and all of a series of epistolary masks he often wore. In 1934 he wrote her a candid letter confessing to his own negative feelings about Eliot, but admonishing, "Don't take anyone *alive* seriously" (*Family Letters* 160). That letter also reveals his exasperation with Pound for abandoning verse and meter in order to strip the materials of the poem back until only the image stands. Thus, Frost's famous retort in the same letter, "For my part I should be satisfied to play tennis with the net down as to write verse with no verse form set to stay me" (Family Letters 161).

15. Santayana, *Essays*, 288.
16. Ibid., 290.
17. Ibid., 293.
18. Ibid.
19. See David Perkins, "Robert Frost and Romantic Irony," *South Carolina Review* 22 (1989), 33–37.
20. In *The Ordeal of Robert Frost*, Mark Richardson contrasts the works of Frost and Pound in terms of audience:
Part of the difference between Pound and Frost derives from a simple fact. Pound writes for a rather restricted audience that takes for granted the claims and demands of his art, whereas Frost almost never does. Frost explained in a 1913 letter to John Bartlett that he hoped to reach "the general reader who buys books in their thousands. . . . I want to be a poet for all sorts and kinds" (*Collected Poetry, Prose & Plays* 667–68). This aspiration required him to hold together constituencies so various as to be in certain respects incompatible. To write compellingly for "all sorts and kinds" is admirable, but also uncommonly difficult (21).
21. Robert Francis, *A Time to Talk* (Amherst: University of Massachusetts Press, 1972), 30.
22. Claudia Roth Pierpont, "The Mother of Confusion," *The New Yorker* (11 May 1998), 80.

CHAPTER TWO: PERSONAL AMBIGUITIES: SUSPENDED ACTION

1. Mark Richardson, "Robert Frost and the Motive of Poetry," *Essays in Literature* 20 (fall 1993), 278.
2. Jay Parini, *Robert Frost: A Life* (New York: Henry Holt, 1999), 78.
3. Katherine Kearns, *Robert Frost and a Poetics of Appetite* (New York: Cambridge University Press, 1994), 112.
4. See Robert Faggen, *Robert Frost and the Challenge of Darwin* (Ann Arbor: University of Michigan Press, 1997), 46–47.
5. Oster, *Toward Robert Frost*, 66.
6. In his careful discussion of Frost's method of romantic illumination, Sheldon Liebman concludes that "Frost was not a sentimental escapist, a brooding nihilist, or a pragmatic Greek who courageously faced chaos in order to impose meaning on it. As a romantic, he did not believe that truth is simply willed into being; nor did he believe that beauty is merely created. According to his own testimony, truth and beauty are discoverable in reality. They come into being when thinker and artist transcend their ordinary selves and allow experience to complete itself" (433).
7. See Roger Tory Peterson's authoritative *Eastern Birds* for further information on the oven bird.
8. Frost's prayer-like supplication "May no fate willfully misunderstand me" (50) has proved troublesome to readers. In the context it emphasizes his "full" wish to swing back to earth rather than departing it altogether. "Fate" itself may receive some clarification, however, from Emerson's essay by that title. After distinguishing fate from several other influences upon humanity, Emerson says that "Whatever limits us we call Fate." But he expands on this—somewhat illogi-

cally—to say that if fate is all, then "a part of Fate is the freedom of man. Forever wells up the impulse of choosing and acting in the soul. Intellect annuls Fate." Thus Emerson holds forth humanity's freedom to choose, basically its ethical positioning, above fate. So too in "Birches," with its evocative freedom of imagination, Frost chooses to return to earth where hard choices are necessary.

9. The quotation from Wittgenstein is from his *Philosophical Investigations*, section 129.

10. Ibid., 30.

11. In her study, "Frost's Last Three Visits to Michigan," Dorothy Tyler locates the physical placement of the tower clock: "The big illuminated clock on the Michigan Central Station . . . was in the valley on the old stone building. It was just around the corner from the house on Pontiac Road where the Frost family lived in 1925, down the hill and over the railroad bridge he must have crossed many times" (521). Thus, contrary to a popular opinion that the "luminary tower" is the moon, the clock tower is an actual one in the city. Such a view seems to me to be in keeping with the densely earthbound quality of the poem. See also C. Himes Edwards's essay on the topic, "The Clock in Frost's 'Acquainted with the Night.' "

12. Parini, *Robert Frost*, 246.

13. The earliest recognition of the Hawthorne link with the poem was by James Ellis in his essay "Frost's 'Secret Places' and Hawthorne." Several essays in *Frost Centennial Essays* affirm and develop the relationship. In " 'Nothing That Is': A Study of Frost's 'Secret Places' " Albert Von Frank argues that the poem "retains a large measure of the ambivalence of the germ in Hawthorne" (122). In "Other 'Deserted Places': Frost and Hawthorne," Edward Stone also finds ties to other poems, and in "Hawthorne and Frost: The Making of a Poem" J. Donald Crowley examines the influence of Hawthorne on "The Wood-Pile."

14. See David Tutein, *Robert Frost's Reading An Annotated Bibliography* (Lewiston, NY: Edwin Mellen Press, 1997), 21.

15. Frost's religious beliefs and biblical allusions continue to be a source of scholarly investigation. In "If I Had To Perish Twice: Robert Frost and the Aesthetics of Apocalypse," Edward Ingebretsen shows how Frost drew upon several apocalyptic resources in his work. In particular, "Frost moves by way of analogy from a collapsing cosmos to the collapsing world of human meaning" (37). Several studies apply views presumed of Frost directly to explication of the text. For example, in "Dark Climber: Robert Frost's Spiritual Ambivalence in 'Birches,' " Larry Islitt argues that, " 'Birches' lies somewhere in the middle of his sceptical spectrum, somewhere between the overt pessimism of 'Despair,' and the religious pessimism of *A Masque of Reason* and *A Masque of Mercy*. . . ." (14). In "Looking Through the Glass: Frost's 'After Apple-Picking' and Paul's 1 Corinthians," David Sanders provides a detailed analysis of allusions from Paul's epistle. The poem is, Sanders writes, "theological from the start" (13).

16. Dorothy Judd Hall, *Robert Frost: Contours of Belief* (Athens: Ohio University Press, 1984), xviii.

17. Ibid.

18. The investigation into the ethics of literature is hampered by the lack of current terminology to address the issue. Yet, it is quickly becoming one of the more prominent methods of discourse about literature in recent years. In a spe-

cial issue of PMLA (January, 1999) devoted to the topic of Ethics and Literary Study, general coordinator Lawrence Buell observes in his introduction that "Ethics has gained new resonance in literary studies during the past half dozen years, even if it has not—at least yet—become the paradigm-defining concept that textuality was for the 1970s and historicism was for the 1980s" (7). Consequently, Buell points out that "As with any groundswell, particularly when the central term of reference already belongs to common usage, the challenge of pinning down what counts as ethics intensifies as more people lay claim to it" (7).

19. Clarence Walhout, "The End of Literature: Reflections on Literature and Ethics," *Christianity and Literature* 47 (1998), 459.

20. See also Jeffrey Stout, who in *Ethics after Babel: The Languages of Morals and Their Discontents*, similarly argues that the *telos* need not be "a fixed conception of the good, derived once and for all from a philosophical view of the human essence" (237). For Stout, the *telos* is only worthwhile if it is in fact attainable in human affairs.

21. Walhout, "The End of Literature," 461.

22. In *The Company We Keep: An Ethics of Fiction*, Wayne C. Booth contends that "Every appraisal of narrative is implicitly a comparison between the always complex experience we have had in its presence and what we have known before" (71).

23. Walhout, "The End of Literature," 472–73.

24. Ibid., 473.

Chapter Three: Rationalist Ethics

1. James Boswell, *Life of Johnson* (London: Oxford University Press, 1953, 1970), 561.

2. Benjamin Franklin, *The Autobiography* (New York: The Library of America, 1987), 1384.

3. David Hume, *An Inquiry Concerning Human Understanding* (New York: Bobbs-Merrill, 1955), 118.

4. Ibid., 138.

5. Ibid., 139.

6. Faggen, *Robert Frost*, 7–8.

7. Ibid., 8.

8. Ibid., 304.

9. Nathan Scott, *The Broken Center* (New Haven: Yale University Press, 1966), 11.

10. Robert Langbaum, *The Poetry of Experience* (New York: W. W. Norton, 1963), 16.

11. For a substantially detailed biographical accounting of "The Road Not Taken," see Larry Finger, "Frost's Reading of 'The Road Not Taken' " in the 1997 issue of *Robert Frost Review*.

12. William S. Doxey, "Whistling in the Dark: Robert Frost's Modernist Quest for Meaning," *West Georgia College Review* 23 (May 1993), 31.

13. Mordecai Marcus, *The Poems of Robert Frost: An Explication* (Boston: G. K. Hall, 1991), 231.

14. Reuben A. Brower, *The Poetry of Robert Frost: Constellations of Intention* (New York: Oxford University Press, 1963), 210.

15. Ibid.

16. Hall, *Robert Frost*, 40.

17. Peter J. Stanlis, "Robert Frost's Masques and the Classic American Tradition," *Frost: Centennial Essays III* (Jackson: University Press of Mississippi, 1974), 444.

18. Peter D. Poland, "Frost's 'Neither Out Far Nor In Deep,' " *Explicator* 52, (winter 1994), 96.

19. Beyond question, the most significant work in this area has been done by Alvin Plantinga, called by John Stackhouse, Jr., writing in *Christianity Today* (June 2001), "arguably the greatest philosopher of the last century."

20. Thyatira was one of the seven churches to whom Jesus dictated a letter through John in the book of Revelation. In general Jesus praises the church but he condemned a prophetess named Jezebel (see *Masque of Mercy*) who had led many people into idolatry, Satan-worship, and sexual immorality. A very helpful resource for following the allusions in the two poems is Laurence Perrine's "A Set of Notes for Frost's Two Masques."

21. Faggen, *Robert Frost*, 3.

22. John Robert Doyle, Jr., *The Poetry of Robert Frost: An Analysis* (New York: Hafner, 1965), 241. Frost's treatment of the nature of God in *A Masque of Reason* has elicited highly varied, sometimes diametrical, views. John Ciardi took the humanized God as one more sign that Frost had abandoned religion altogether. In "Robert Frost and His Use of Barriers: Man vs. Nature Toward God," Marion Montgomery turns the tables on humanity, arguing that the presumptive scene of God on the plywood throne actually incarnates humanity's failed understanding of God. In "The Bleak Landscape of Robert Frost," Roberta Borkat argues that "Frost is trying to show not man's misunderstanding of God, but God's lack of superhuman perfection" (458). Borkat's argument might be more persuasive if she had made such necessary distinctions as suprahuman versus superhuman; the latter, of course, God never claimed for himself.

23. This is not the only place in Frost's poetry where he struggles with a hidden God and the burning bush image (he also spoke occasionally of his poetry being hidden like God). In "Sitting by a Bush in Broad Sunlight," Frost asserts that:

> There was one time and only the one
> When dust really took in the sun;
> And from that one intake of fire
> All creatures still warmly aspire.

From the experience, Frost concludes, two things endure:

> One impulse persists as our breath;
> The other persists as our faith.

24. For a careful discussion of constraints upon God's power, see Nelson Pike, "Omnipotence and God's Inability to Sin."

25. Stanlis, "Robert Frost's Masques," 456.

26. Paola Loreto, "A Man in Front of His God, A Man in Front of Himself: The (Post) Modernity of Frost's *A Masque of Reason*," *Robert Frost Review* (fall 1999), 29.

27. The obvious biblical allusion for Jesse Bel is to the wicked Queen Jezebel of first and second Kings, although in the book of Revelation she is also depicted as an archetypal figure of evil, destroyed at the Second Coming. However, it is also possible that a very early run-in that Frost had with the poet and anthologist Jessie Belle Rittenhouse (1869–1948), may have played a minor role. In a letter to Sidney Cox in 1915, Frost halfheartedly dismissed the "temperate praise" in her review of *North of Boston* (*The New York Times*, 16 May 1915). But his full irritation erupts when he encounters her rejection of the rave reviews he had received in England: "The only nastiness in Jessie B.'s article is the first part where she speaks of the English reviews as fulsome. There she speaks dishonestly out of complete ignorance—out of some sort of malice or envy I should infer. Her anthology with the silly name [*The Little Book of Modern Verse: A Selection from the Works of Contemporaneous American Poets*] made a very bad miss in England" (Friendship 69).

28. Dallas Willard, *The Divine Conspiracy* (San Francisco: HarperCollins, 1998), 383.

29. Ibid., 383–84.

30. An interesting echo arises here from the poem, "I Years had been From Home" (J609), by Emily Dickinson, a poet whom Frost greatly admired. In the poem Dickinson imagines herself before the "Door" (of heaven), fearful to knock in case a "Face" should answer and ask her what her business was there. As such the poem is closely related to Dickinson's others, which use the poetic imagination to probe what lies beyond this side of life. Yet it intensifies here: "I laughed a crumbling laugh / That I should fear a Door." She reaches for the latch, trembling, "Lest back the awful Door should spring / And leave me in the Floor—." In Dickinson's poem, the narrator flees the house "like a thief." Jonah is unable to do so. All the doors to the outside are locked. Instead, the blow of the cellar door and the repulse "Crumple him on the floor" (518).

31. See Anna K. Juhnke, "Religion in Robert Frost's Poetry: The Play for Self-Possession," *American Literature* 36 (May 1964), 163. The poem "To Prayer I Think I Go," appears on pp. 130–31, 136, and 331 of *The Letters of Robert Frost to Louis Untermeyer*. The poem, which is not collected in *The Poetry of Robert Frost* but is included in its 1942 variant in *Collected Poems, Prose & Plays* (550), appears in variant forms, gathering lines through later versions. Common to each version is the image of going to prayer compared to descending a stair of self-abasement.

CHAPTER FOUR: THEOLOGICAL ETHICS

1. George Patrick, *Introduction to Philosophy* (Boston: Houghton Mifflin, 1924), 402.

2. Plato, *The Republic*, Trans. Francis MacDonald Cornford (New York: Oxford University Press, 1964), 139.

3. Ibid., 129.

4. See *The Republic*, "We shall conclude that a man is just in the same way that a state was just. And we have surely not forgotten that justice in the state meant

that each of the three orders in it was doing its own proper work. So we may henceforth bear in mind that each one of us likewise will be a just person, fulfilling his proper nature, only if the several parts of our nature fulfill theirs" (139–40).

5. In his always valuable study, *The Story of Philosophy*, Will Durant observes, "Justice is a *taxis kai kosmos*—an order and beauty—of the parts of the soul; it is to the soul as health is to the body. All evil is disharmony: between man and nature, or man and men, or man and himself" (33).

6. See Plotinus, "If he is nowhere, he has not just happened anywhere, and if he is everywhere, then 'everywhere' is the same size as he is: so he is the 'everywhere' and in 'every way' Himself and not in the 'everywhere.' He is that everywhere Himself and gives other things their being, neighboring each other in the everywhere" (*Enneads* Ed. A. R. Armstrong (New York: Macmillan Collier), VI, 8, 16).

7. *Enneads*, VI, 9, 3.

8. See Plotinus, "The One produces Nous without any movement or change in itself by a sort of emanation or radiation" (Enneads V, 1, 6).

Plotinus writes in reaction to the Gnostic view that the world is trapped in darkness and evil and that only special knowledge delivers humanity. In Ennead IV Plotinus follows the Platonic model to explain the human capacity for evil. The soul experiences a severing from the all-soul by its "enchaining in the body." Furthermore, "It is a captive; this is the burial, the encavernment, of the soul" (Ennead IV, 8, 4). In spite of this, however, the soul always retains something of the transcendent, that "something" being the "Nous." In later Christian philosphy, starting already with Augustine, that Nous is identified as the *Imago Dei*—the image of the Creator God in the creation he has made.

9. Augustine, *The City of God* (Garden City: Doubleday Image, 1958), viii, 3.

10. Book 8 of *City of God* deals in particular with Plato. Here Augustine argues that God manifested himself to Plato through ideas or works of the classical and Hebraic worlds.

11. Augustine, *The City of God*, 7, 9: The Isaiah passage is subject to various linguistic interpretations and translations. The Revised Standard Version renders it, "If you will not believe, surely you shall not be established," which although stated in the negative implies the positive. The wordplay in the Hebrew is nearly impossible to capture in the English. Another way to consider it is, "If you don't have faith, you won't have steadfastness [of understanding]."

12. Although not directly addressing Augustinian epistemology, an extremely helpful analysis appears is Alvin Plantinga's essay "Necessary Being." Addressing the question "Why does God exist?" Plantinga points out that "Outside of theism . . . the question is nonsensical and inside of theism, the question is never asked" (106). But more directly to the subject here, Plantinga adds that "Essential to theism is an assertion to the effect that there is a connection between God and all other beings, a connection in virtue of which these others are causally dependent upon God" (107).

13. For a careful discussion of dualism in Frost's thinking, see Peter J. Stanlis, "Dualism: The Basis of Robert Frost's Philosophy," *The Robert Frost Review* (fall 1994), 33–46.

14. The letter to the student newspaper, dated 25 March 1935, was a reply to

their congratulations to him on his sixtieth birthday. After a whimsical opening paragraph on their congratulations, Frost uses the occasion for one of his more reflective and careful statements of philosophical belief.

15. Randall Jarrell, "To the Laodiceans," *Kenyon Review* 14 (1952), 554.

16. Nitchie, *Human Values*, 144.

17. Mark Richardson, *The Ordeal of Robert Frost: The Poet and His Poetics* (Urbana: University of Illinois Press, 1987), 255.

18. Ibid., 256.

19. Guarding the doors of the Chapel Perilous stand two rampant stone lions, also Lancelot's personal herald. The symbolism is obvious. Lancelot must overcome himself, or, more precisely, entirely forsake his former self, before he can climb toward redemption.

20. See Hall, *Robert Frost*, 109.

21. Ibid., 113.

CHAPTER FIVE: EXISTENTIAL ETHICS

1. Martin Heidegger, *Being and Time* (New York: Harper & Row, 1962), 42.

2. Ibid.

3. Robert Solomon, *From Rationalism to Existentialism: The Existentialists and Their Nineteenth-Century Backgrounds* (New York: Harper & Row, 1972), 227–28.

4. Therein also lies the logical conundrum of existential ethics. If my individual essence is determined by the freedom to choose, and if, therefore, freedom is the highest ethical value, why ought I respect the freedom of others? Hence, Iris Murdoch, in *The Sovereignty of Good*, observes that "Existentialism, in both its Continental and Anglo-Saxon versions, is an attempt to solve the problem without really facing it. . . ." (27). Having severed any link to a theologically revealed ethic, there is no divine source for respecting the freedom of fellow humans. They are simply other time/place particles of being. If there is some cultural norm that determines this right or wrong, then I am in fact not free at all. If I am, as de Beauvoir insists, acting in a bad faith whenever I follow the dictates and will of others, and authenticity lies in free choice apart from the influence of others, can I ever know my essence as one human among many? Is there no longer a call for such prior normative values as compassion, loving-kindness, and self-giving?

5. Arnold Bartini, "Robert Frost and Moral Neutrality," *CEA Critic* 38 (1976), 22.

6. Richard Poirier, *Robert Frost: The Work of Knowing* (New York: Oxford University Press, 1974), 135.

7. Frank Lentricchia, *Robert Frost: Modern Poetics and the Landscapes of Self* (Durham: Duke University Press, 1975), 181. The "brook poems" refer to chapter 2 of Lentricchia's study in which he argues that "These brooks belong personally to Robert Frost—by bathing them in his consciousness he has created them as metaphors of self" (45). Similarly, the "house poems" form the subject of chapter 3, where they represent patterns of self-enclosure.

8. Oster, *Toward Robert Frost*, 93.

9. In his "Love's Sentence: Domesticity as Religious Discourse in Robert Frost's Poetry," Edward Ingebretsen points out that Mist "resembles Milton's

Satan, who in *Paradise Lost* sneaks into the Garden in the form of a ground mist. Frost develops what Milton implies, namely that Satan spies upon Adam and Eve because he envies their good fortune—chiefly their bodies and the place they have in which to live" (56). It is an interesting speculation, and one might indeed detect a note of envy in Mist. However, Mist is more benevolent in Frost's poem, and, importantly, comments: "No one—not I—would give them up for lost." Mist's interest lies in the couple finding themselves, not in destroying the domesticity they have.

CHAPTER SIX: DEONTOLOGICAL ETHICS

1. Frost held *The Critique of Pure Reason* in his personal library and heralded Aristotle and Kant as two of the greatest intellects of all time.
2. The constraints of space necessarily prevent a full development of contemporary deontological ethics beyond the historical backdrop I have provided here. For further reading see particularly Charles Fried, *Right and Wrong*; John Rawls, *A Theory of Justice*; and Nancy Davis, "Contemporary Deontology," *A Companion to Ethics*.
3. In his essay "The Politics of Robert Frost," Andy Moore maintains that Frost's primary concern, specifically in "In Divés' Dive," "is not with who runs the government or what the authoritative element is; his concern is with the role of the individual in the scheme of things. Frost wants his share of what belongs to him, and he wants no less for other people. One reason Frost was not a radical in political opinions, then, was his belief in each man's minding his own business" (4).
4. For a detailed analysis of Frost's sociopolitical thought, see Peter J. Stanlis, "Robert Frost: Politics in Theory and Practice," *Centennial Essays, II*.
5. Once again we confront here the tension between Frost's public persona and the private man. The four loves searched out by poetic metaphor work nicely in his argument here. Whether they held any validity in his personal life, apart from the artistic life, is, as we have seen, open to question. In his discussion of Frost in "The New England Tradition," Hayden Carruth might very well overemphasize the negative side of Frost:

> Perhaps Frost asked too much, of love and of the world; it is an inferable proposition. But this was his radicalism, his almost total abnegation springing from an almost total lack of faith: not just religious faith, nor even faith in humanity, but faith in any reality—he was the agonized total skeptic. Nor was he the first New Englander to find himself in such a fix, or the last. Many of his own people, the characters of his poems, were thus beset, and were driven to violence and madness because of it; but he himself chose another way out, the way of continued thinking, writing, enduring, the way of unexplainable heroism—unless the explanation lies in his creative power, secondarily over his characters, primarily over himself. (947)

Nonetheless, Carruth argues, Frost is the very "embodiment" of the New England tradition.
6. Parini, *Robert Frost*, 25.
7. Ibid.

8. Anna Juhnke, "Religion in Robert Frost's Poetry," 153.

9. The idea here correlates with Frost's discussion of Emerson's "Brahma" in his essay "The Prerequisites." Imagining a young reader (perhaps himself) encountering the enigmatic last lines of the poem, Frost speculates, "He didn't want the wrong kind of help. The heart sinks when robbed of the chance to see for itself what a poem is all about" (*Selected Prose* 96).

10. One should not deduce from this poem that Frost opposed scientific methods in and of themselves. At about the same time that *New Hampshire* was published, Frost made it clear in an interview with Allen Shoenfield for *The Detroit News* that science and art were separate disciplines and that the poet had nothing to fear from science. In fact, he points out that "Life has lost none of its mystery and its romance." Although this may, at times, kindle fear, fear is "a great stimulus to man's imagination" (Interviews 64). One might say then that science and poetry are two different ways of exploring mysteries.

Moreover, in 1959, Frost participated in a symposium on the topic "The Future of Man" that touched frequently upon the roles of science and the arts in contemporary life. There Frost made a comment that could almost serve as a gloss on the final stanza of "Star-Splitter": "Who are we? Science can't describe us; it contributes very little to our description. . . . The wonderful description of us is the humanities. . . ." (*Interviews* 209).

11. Parini, *Robert Frost*, 19.

12. Poirier, *Robert Frost*, 22.

13. Frank Lentricchia, "Robert Frost and Modern Poetic Theory," *Frost Centennial Essays III* (Jackson: University Press of Mississippi, 1974), 317.

14. Brower, *The Poetry of Robert Frost*, 143.

15. Peter L. Hays, "Frost and the Critics: More Revelation on 'All Revelation,' " *English Language Notes* 18 (June 1981), 289.

16. Ibid.

17. Faggen, *Robert Frost*, 24.

Chapter Seven: Ethics in Society

1. Baird Whitlock, "Conversations With Robert Frost," *Xavier Review* 3 (1983), 16.

2. Andrew Angyal, "From Swedenborg to William James: The Shaping of Robert Frost's Religious Beliefs," *Robert Frost Review* (fall 1994), 74–75.

3. By claiming that Frost's religious beliefs were largely Old Testamental, I do not mean to imply that he denied the divinity of Christ, nor his atonement. Baird Whitlock records one conversation that arose during a talk Frost gave in 1961 at Case-Western Reserve University: "His main thesis in that talk was that science was the only human enterprise—'a descent into matter' " (13). When a Catholic priest rose to challenge that proposition, Frost responded with these words: "God seemed to feel this way too—the center of Christianity was God's descent into matter. Wasn't that what the Incarnation was about?" (14). It may be, of course, that Frost was simply responding to the priest apropos of his calling; nonetheless, the comment also indicates Frost's understanding of and sensitivity toward New Testament doctrine.

4. Albert Camus, *Resistance, Rebellion, and Death* (New York: Modern Library, 1963), 22. Clearly, Camus's definitive text on his agnosticism is the essay "The Unbeliever and the Christian," collected in *Resistance, Rebellion, and Death*. In this profoundly interesting essay, Camus establishes his agnostic premises, but then explores the ethical implications of any presuppositional belief system (he assumes that atheism is presuppositional while agnosticism is not). Moreover, he outlines the shared ethical tasks of unbelievers and Christians alike, demonstrating a certain ethical deontology in which certain things are done because our human intuition tells us they are the right things to do.

5. Hall, *Robert Frost*, xix.

6. A fair example of Aristotle's tenaciously limiting his ethics to proper or improper actions for the individual occurs in his discussion on moral weakness and self-indulgence. "A morally weak man is the kind of person who pursues bodily pleasures to excess and contrary to right reason, though he is not persuaded [that he ought to do so]; the self-indulgent, on the other hand, is persuaded to pursue them because he is the kind of man who does so" (*Ethics* 198). Superficially, the statement is satisfactory; it is merely incomplete. In Aristotle's time also there was the case of the alcoholic committing crimes to get his drink. What does society do with him? What does a just man do with the man who sells his cheap wine at inflated prices? Does he hate both, love both, or find some ambivalent compromise? Admittedly, Aristotle does broach such issues in chapters 8–10 in his discussion of friendship, but even here the issue is more what friendship can do for the individual rather than for society.

7. Henry Stob, *Ethical Reflections: Essays on Moral Themes* (Grand Rapids, MI, Wm. B. Eerdmans, 1978), 3.

8. Ibid., 4.

9. See Meyers, *Robert Frost*, p. 297.

10. Harriet Monroe was herself of course a prominent poet in Chicago circles when she started *Poetry*. She was invited to write the dedication poem for the Columbian exhibition in Chicago. She published several volumes, two of them before she founded *Poetry*. The impact of *Poetry* was immediate and powerful, as she brought to print such poets as Frost, Sandburg, Lindsay, Kilmer, and others. Edward Thomas's poems were sent to her anonymously. Frost encouraged her interest, referring to his friend by his pseudonym, Edward Eastway. Several of Thomas's poems were published in the February, 1917, issue.

11. Lesley Lee Francis, "Between Poets: Robert Frost and Harriet Monroe," *The South Carolina Review* 19 (summer 1987), 12.

12. The legendary disaffection between Frost and Pound started in England already. In a 1913 letter to Marie Hodge, Frost wrote:

Ezra Pound . . . is six inches taller for his hair and hides his lower jaw in a delicate gold filigree of almost masculine beard. His coat is of heavy black velvet. He lives in Grub Street, rich one day and poor the next. His friends are the duchesses. And he swears like a pirate and he writes what is known as vers libre and he translates from French, Provencal, Latin, and Italian. He and I have tried to be friends because he was one of the first to review me well, but we don't hit it off very well together. (Sheehy 87)

13. Francis, "Between Poets," 6.

14. Ibid., 8.

15. Ibid., 7.
16. In addition to "At Woodward's Garden," the other poems included "Precaution," "Pertinax," "Waspish," "The Hardship of Authority," "Not all There," and "In Divés' Dive."
17. Lesley Lee Francis, "Robert Frost and Susan Hayes Ward," *The Massachusetts Review* 26 (summer/autumn 1985), 343.
18. Ibid., 346.
19. Ibid., 349.
20. In *Robert Frost and the Challenge of Darwin*, Robert Faggen provides a rather extensive reading of "Wild Grapes" as influenced by Darwinian views on the origins of the sexes and also an Edenic view of acquisition of knowledge (195–203). Accordingly, "Wild Grapes" explores the uncertainty about origins and about the conflict of sexes, particularly the power of females to choose and the power of men to attempt to exercise control over that choice (196). See Frost's "The Way There" where he tells the story of Ward's request for the poem (*Collected Poems, Prose & Plays* 847–48).
21. Lesley Lee Francis, "A Decade of Stirring Times: Robert Frost and Amy Lowell," *The New England Quarterly* 59 (December 1986), 513.
22. See Amy Lowell, *Tendencies in Modern American Poetry* (New York: Macmillan, 1917), 105–8.
23. Francis, "Decade of Stirring Times," 517.
24. See, for example, Lesley Lee Francis, "Robert Frost and Helen Thomas Revisited," *The Robert Frost Review* (fall 1993), 77–85. The study provides a fascinating completion to Frost's deep friendship with Edward Thomas in a 1957 meeting with his widow and daughter.
25. James R. Dawes, "Masculinity and Transgression in Robert Frost," *American Literature* 65 (June 1993), 299. Several examples of Dawes's symbolic readings to demonstrate his tripartite schemata may be helpful. Of "The Grindstone" he points out that "Phallic, masturbatory, and ultimately homosexual images accumulate to describe this futile struggle" (299). The older and younger men "struggle" or work against each other in their labor. Dawes cites supporting lines from the poem: "All day I drove it hard, / And someone mounted on it and rode it hard." Similarly, Baptiste's handling of the ax in "The Ax-Helve" simulates a masturbatory act, particularly with his closing comment: "See how she's cock her head!" Certainly, there is no shortage of sexually suggestive lines in the poem (2:76–78, 95–96), but one should be aware of the narrator's announced perception of the event in two ways. His French neighbor is trying to demonstrate his worth and locate a friend in this Yankee community (39–45) and, second, the pleasure of knowledge found outside the school system (82–83). It's probably worth remembering that Baptiste's wife is sitting in the room the whole time also.
26. Ibid., 299.
27. Ibid., 303–4.
28. Katherine Kearns, "The Place is the Asylum: Women and Nature in Robert Frost's Poetry," *American Literature* 59 (May 1987), 191.
29. Ibid., 191.
30. Karen L. Kilcup, *Robert Frost and Feminine Literary Tradition* (Ann Arbor: University of Michigan Press), 3.
31. Rita Felski, *The Gender of Modernity* (Cambridge: Harvard University Press, 1995), 5.

32. Patricia Wallace, "The 'Estranged Point of View': The Thematics of Imagination in Frost's Poetry," *Frost: Centennial Essays II* (Jackson: University Press of Mississippi, 1976), 178.

33. For other such views, see Elaine Barry, *Robert Frost*; James Cox, "*Robert Frost and the Edge of the Clearing.*" Many readers would place the wife of "Home Burial" in this category, a placement that I believe does a disservice to the poem which may be seen as constructing images of continuity rather than dissonance.

34. Wallace, "The 'Estranged Point of View,' " 194.

35. Kearns, "The Place is the Asylum," 182.

36. In "The Place is the Asylum," Katherine Kearns explores the significance of tree imagery and sexuality in Frost's poetry. Her observation in the following, for example, might well apply to "The Hill Wife": "Frost's speakers are then justifiably preoccupied with entry into woods, for this movement is fraught with potential ecstasy and equivalent danger; the woods are emblematic of sexual knowledge and thus of death, and while rebirth is a natural consequence in this fallen Eden it is seldom a convincing apotheosis" (203).

Conclusion: Letting Frost be Frost

1. William Pritchard, *Frost: A Literary Life Reconsidered* (New York: Oxford University Press, 1984), xii.

2. Philip L. Gerber, "Frost the Man, Frost the Believer," *Contemporary Literature* 27 (spring 1986), 135.

3. Ibid.

4. Ibid.

5. Donald Hall, *Remembering Poets: Reminiscences and Opinions* (New York: Harper Colophon, 1979), 41.

6. Gerber, 135.

7. Reginald Cook, *Robert Frost: A Living Voice* (Amherst: University of Massachusetts Press, 1974), 52. For some of the many differing critical discussions of "Stopping by Woods," see James Armstrong, "The 'Death Wish' in 'Stopping by Woods,' " which links the pattern to other poems of Frost; John Ciardi's "Robert Frost: The Way to the Poem" also focuses on the "death wish" theme, and William Shurr's "Once More to the Woods: A New Point of Entry into Frost's Most Famous Poem," summarizes critical views to date (1974) and relates the poem to a sense of religious abandonment. In "The Slant of Christmas Past," Herbert Coursen parodies interpretations and offers the Santa Claus narrator pattern.

8. Robert Frost, "On Taking Poetry," *Collected Poems, Prose, & Plays* (New York: Library Classics, 1995), 822.

9. Ibid.

10. For an amusing discussion of John Ciardi's long analysis of the poem in *The Saturday Review*, see "Ciardi on Frost: An Interview" with Edward Cifelli in *Centennial Essays I*, 471–95.

11. N. Arthur Bleau, "Robert Frost's Favorite Poem," *Centennial Essays III* (Jackson: University Press of Mississippi, 1978), 177.

12. Ibid., 174.

Selected Bibliography

PRIMARY WORKS

Biography

Francis, Lesley Lee. *The Frost Family's Adventure in Poetry: Sheer Morning Gladness at the Brim*. Columbia: University of Missouri Press, 1994.

Meyers, Jeffery. *Robert Frost: A Biography*. New York: Houghton Mifflin, 1996.

Parini, Jay. *Robert Frost: A Life*. New York: Henry Holt, 1999.

Pritchard, William. *Frost: A Literary Life Reconsidered*. New York: Oxford University Press, 1984.

Thompson, Lawrance. *Robert Frost: The Early Years*, 1874–1915. New York: Holt, Rinehart and Winston, 1966.

———. *Robert Frost: The Years of Triumph, 1915–1938*. New York: Holt, Rinehart and Winston, 1970.

———, and R. J. Winnick. *Robert Frost: The Later Years, 1938–1963*. New York: Holt, Rinehart and Winston, 1976.

Walsh, John Evangelist. *Into My Own: The English Years of Robert Frost*. New York: Grove Press, 1988.

b. Works of Robert Frost

POETRY AND PROSE

Frost, Robert. *Collected Poems, Prose, & Plays*. Edited by Richard Poirier and Mark Richardson. New York: Library Classics, 1995.

———. "My Favorite Books." *Chicago Sunday Tribune*. 20 November 1958, 4:28.

———. *The Poetry of Robert Frost: The Collected Poems, Complete and Unabridged*. Edited by Edward Connery Lathem. New York: Henry Holt and Co., 1979.

———. *Selected Prose of Robert Frost*. Edited by Hyde Cox and Edward Connery Lathem. New York: Collier, 1968.

LETTERS

Robert Frost. *Family Letters of Robert and Elinor Frost*. Edited by Arnold Grade. Albany: State University of New York, 1972.

————. *The Letters of Robert Frost to Louis Untermeyer*. Edited by Louis Untermeyer. New York: Holt, Rinehart and Winston, 1963.

————. *Robert Frost and Sidney Cox: Forty Years of Friendship*. Edited by William R. Evans. Hanover: University Press of New England, 1981.

————. *Selected Letters of Robert Frost*. Edited by Lawrance Thompson. New York: Holt, Rinehart and Winston, 1964.

INTERVIEWS

Cook, Reginald. *Robert Frost: A Living Voice*. Amherst: University of Massachusetts Press, 1974.

Robert Frost. "Conversations with Robert Frost" with Baird W. Whitlock. *Xavier Review* 3 (1983): 1–16.

————. "An Interview with Robert Frost," with John Sherrill. *Guideposts* (August 1955): 1–5.

————. *Interviews with Robert Frost*. Edited by Edward Connery Lathem. Guilford, CT: Jeffrey Norton, 1997.

————. "*Paris Review* Interview" with Richard Poirier. *Writers at Work: The Paris Review Interviews, Second Series*. Edited by George Plimpton. New York: Viking, 1963: 11–34.

SECONDARY WORKS

Allen, Paula Gunn. *The Sacred Hoop: Recovering the Feminine in American Literary Traditions*. Boston: Beacon Press, 1986.

Angyal, Andrew J. "From Swedenborg to William James: The Shaping of Frost's Religious Beliefs." *Robert Frost Review* (fall 1994): 69–81.

Aristotle. *Nichomachean Ethics*. Trans. Martin Ostwald. Indianapolis: Bobbs-Merrill, 1963.

Armstrong, James. "The 'Death Wish' in 'Stopping by Woods.' " *College English* 25 (1964): 440, 445.

Augustine, St. *The City of God*. Ed. Vernon Bourke. Trans. Gerald G. Walsh, S. J. et. al. Garden City: Doubleday Image, 1958.

Bartini, Arnold G. "Robert Frost and Moral Neutrality." *CEA Critic* 38 (1976): 22–24.

Bieganowski, Ronald. "Robert Frost's Spiritual Realm." *Historical New Hampshire* 35.1 (spring 1980): 59–65.

Bleau, N. Arthur. "Robert Frost's Favorite Poem." *Centennial Essays III*. Jackson: University Press of Mississippi, 1978: 174–76.

Booth, Wayne C. *The Company We Keep: An Ethics of Fiction*. Berkeley: University of California Press, 1988.

Borkat, Roberta F. S. "The Bleak Landscape of Robert Frost." *Midwest Quarterly* 16 (1975): 453–67.

Borroff, Marie. *Language and the Poet: Verbal Artistry in Frost, Stevens, and Moore.* Chicago: University of Chicago Press, 1979.

Boswell, James. *Life of Johnson.* Edited by R. W. Chapman. London: Oxford University Press, 1953, 1970.

Brook, Heyward. "Robert Frost's Masques Reconsidered." *Renascence* 3 (1978): 137–51.

Brower, Reuben A. *The Poetry of Robert Frost: Constellations of Intention.* New York: Oxford University Press, 1963.

Buell, Lawrence. "In Pursuit of Ethics." PMLA 114 (January 1999): 7–19.

Camus, Albert. *Resistance, Rebellion, and Death.* Translated by Justin O'Brien. New York: Modern Library, 1963.

Carruth, Hayden. "The New England Tradition." *American Libraries* (1971): 690–700; 939–48.

Ciardi, John. "Robert Frost: The Way to the Poem." *Saturday Review of Literature* 41 (1958): 13–15, 65.

Coursen, Herbert R., Jr. "The Ghost of Christmas Past: 'Stopping by Woods on a Snowy Evening.' " *College English* 44 (1962): 236–38.

Cox, James. "Robert Frost and the Edge of the Clearing." *Virginia Quarterly Review* 35 (winter 1959): 73–88.

Crowley, J. Donald. "Hawthorne and Frost: The Making of a Poem." *Frost Centennial Essays.* Jackson: University Press of Mississippi, 1974: 288–309.

Davis, Nancy. "Contemporary Deontology." *A Companion to Ethics.* Edited by Peter Singer. Cambridge, MA: Blackwell Reference, 1991: 205–18.

Dawes, James R. "Masculinity and Transgression in Robert Frost." *American Literature* 65 (June 1993): 297–312.

Doxey, William S. "Whistling in the Dark: Robert Frost's Modernist Quest for Meaning." *West Georgia College Review* 23 (May 1993): 29–33.

Doyle, John Robert, Jr. *The Poetry of Robert Frost: An Analysis.* New York: Hafner, 1965.

Durant, Will. *The Story of Philosophy.* New York: Simon and Schuster, 1967.

Edwards, C. Hines, Jr. "The Clock in Frost's 'Acquainted with the Night.' " *Explicator* 15 (May 1985): 8–9.

Emerson, Ralph Waldo. *Emerson: Essays and Lectures.* Edited by Joel Porte. New York: Library of America, 1983.

Faggen, Robert. *Robert Frost and the Challenge of Darwin.* Ann Arbor: University of Michigan Press, 1997.

Felski, Rita. *The Gender of Modernity.* Cambridge, Harvard University Press, 1995.

Finger, Larry. "Frost's Reading of 'The Road Not Taken.' " *Robert Frost Review* (fall 1997): 73–76.

Fleissner, Robert F. "Frost as Ironist: 'After Apple-Picking' and the Preautumnal Fall." *The South Carolina Review* 20 (fall 1988): 50–57.

Francis, Lesley Lee. "Between Poets: Robert Frost and Harriet Monroe." *The South Carolina Review* 19 (summer 1987): 2–15.

———. "A Decade of 'Stirring Times': Robert Frost and Amy Lowell." *The New England Quarterly* 59 (December 1986): 508–22.

———. "Robert Frost and Helen Thomas Revisited." *The Robert Frost Review* (fall 1993): 77–85.

———. "Robert Frost and Susan Hayes Ward." *The Massachusetts Review* 26 (summer/autumn 1985): 341–50.

Francis, Robert. *A Time to Talk*. Amherst: University of Massachusetts Press, 1972.

Franklin, Benjamin. *The Autobiography*. New York: The Library of America, 1987.

Fried, Charles. *Right and Wrong*. Cambridge, MA: Harvard University Press, 1978.

Gerber, Philip L. "Frost the Man, Frost the Believer." *Contemporary Literature* 27 (spring 1986): 134–37.

———. *Robert Frost*. Boston: Twayne, 1982.

Hall, Donald. *Remembering Poets: Reminiscences and Opinions*. New York: Harper Colophon, 1979.

Hall, Dorothy Judd. *Robert Frost: Contours of Belief*. Athens: Ohio University Press, 1984.

Hawthorne, Nathaniel. *The Scarlet Letter*. Edited by Ross C. Murfin. Boston: Bedford Books, 1991.

Hays, Peter L. "Frost and the Critics: More Revelation on 'All Revelation.' " *English Language Notes* 18 (June 1981): 283–90.

Heidegger, Martin. *Being and Time*. Translated by J. Macquarrie and E. S. Robinson. New York: Harper & Row, 1962.

———. *Introduction to Metaphysics*. Translated by R. Manheim. New Haven: Yale University Press, 1959.

Hume, David. *An Inquiry Concerning Human Understanding*. Ed. Charles W. Hendel. New York: Bobbs-Merrill, 1955.

Ingebretsen, Edward J., S. J. " 'If I Had to Perish Twice': Robert Frost and the Aesthetics of Apocalypse." *Thought* 67 (March 1992): 33–46.

———."Love's Sentence: Domesticity as Religious Discourse in Robert Frost's Poetry." *Christianity and Literature* 39 (autumn 1989): 51–62.

———. *Robert Frost's Star in a Stone Boat: A Grammar of Belief*. San Francisco: Catholic Scholars Press, 1994.

Isitt, Larry. "Dark Climber: Robert Frost's Spiritual Ambivalence in 'Birches.' " *Robert Frost Review* (fall 1994): 13–16.

Jarrell, Randall. "To the Laodiceans." *Kenyon Review* 14 (1952): 535–61. Rpt. *Poetry and the Age* (Hopewell, NJ: Ecco Press, 1979).

Jost, Walter. "Civility and Madness in Robert Frost's 'Snow.' " *Texas Studies in Language and Literature* 39 (spring 1997): 27–64.

Juhnke, Anna K. "Religion in Robert Frost's Poetry: The Play for Self-Possession." *American Literature* 36 (May 1964): 153–64.

Kahn, Coppèlia. *Man's Estate: Masculine Identity in Shakespeare*. Berkeley: University of California, 1981.

Kearns, Katherine. "The Place is the Asylum: Women and Nature in Robert Frost's Poetry." *American Literature* 59 (May 1987): 190–210.

———. *Robert Frost and a Poetics of Appetite*. New York: Cambridge University Press, 1994.

Kern, Robert. "Frost and Modernism." *American Literature* 60 (March 1988): 1–16.

Kierkegaard, Søren. *The Present Age*. Translated by Alexander Dru. New York: Harper & Row, 1962.

———. *Stages on Life's Way*. Translated by Walter Lowrie. New York: Schocken Books, 1967.

Kilcup, Karen L. *Robert Frost and Feminine Literary Tradition*. Ann Arbor: University of Michigan Press, 1998.

Kjorven, Johannes. *Robert Frost's Emergent Design: The Truth of the Self In-Between Belief and Unbelief*. New Jersey: Humanities Press International, 1987.

Langbaum, Robert. *The Poetry of Experience*. New York: W. W. Norton, 1963.

Lentricchia, Frank. *Modernist Quartet*. Cambridge: Cambridge University Press, 1994.

———. "Robert Frost and Modern Poetic Theory." *Frost Centennial Essays III*. Jackson: University Press of Mississippi, 1974.

———. *Robert Frost: Modern Poetics and the Landscapes of Self*. Durham: Duke University Press, 1975.

Liebman, Sheldon W. "Robert Frost, Romantic." *Twentieth Century Literature* 42 (winter 1996): 417–37.

Loreto, Paola. "A Man in Front of His God, A Man in Front of Himself: The (Post) Modernity of Frost's *A Masque of Reason*." *Robert Frost Review* (fall 1999): 27–39.

Lowell, Amy. *Tendencies in Modern American Poetry*. New York: Macmillan, 1917.

Lowell, Robert. "Current Poetry." *Sewanee Review* 54 (1946): 151.

Lynen, John F. *The Pastoral Art of Robert Frost*. New Haven: Yale University Press, 1960.

Marcus, Mordecai. *The Poems of Robert Frost: An Explication*. Boston: G. K. Hall, 1991.

Moore, Andy. "The Politics of Robert Frost." *The Journal of American and Canadian Studies* 15 (1997): 1–15.

Murdoch, Iris. *The Sovereignty of Good*. New York: Schocken Books, 1971.

Nitchie, George. *Human Values in the Poetry of Robert Frost*. Durham: Duke University Press, 1960.

Nouwen, Henri J. M. *The Return of the Prodigal Son*. New York: Doubleday/Image, 1994.

Oster, Judith. *Toward Robert Frost: The Reader and the Poet*. Athens, GA: University of Georgia Press, 1991.

Patrick, George Thomas White. *Introduction to Philosophy*. Boston: Houghton Mifflin, 1924.

Peckham, Morse. *Victorian Revolutionaries*. New York: George Braziller, 1970.

Perkins, David. "Robert Frost and Romantic Irony." *South Carolina Review* 22 (1989): 33–37.

Perrine, Laurence. "Frost's 'Acquainted with the Night.' " *Explicator* 25 (1967): 50.

———. "A Set of Notes for Frost's Two Masques." *Resources for American Literary Study* 7 (1977): 125–33.

Peters, Joan. "Education by Poetry: Robert Frost's Departure from the Modern Critical Canon." *The South Carolina Review* 20 (fall 1988): 27–37.

Peterson, Roger Tory. *A Field Guide to the Birds of Eastern and Central North America.* 4ᵗʰ ed. Boston: Houghton Mifflin, 1980.

Pierpont, Claudia Roth. "The Mother of Confusion." *The New Yorker* (11 May 1998): 80–89.

Pike, Nelson. "Omnipotence and God's Inability to Sin." *American Philosophical Quarterly* 6 (1969): 208–16. Reprinted in *Divine Commands and Morality*, Edited by P. Helm. Oxford: Oxford University Press, 1981.

Plato. *The Republic.* Translated by Francis MacDonald Cornford. New York: Oxford University Press, 1964.

Plotinus. *Enneads.* Edited by A. H. Armstrong. New York: Macmillan Collier, 1962.

Plantinga, Alvin. *God, Freedom, and Evil.* Grand Rapids, MI: Eerdmans, 1974.

———. "Necessary Being." *Faith and Philosophical Studies in Religion and Ethics.* Edited by Alvin Plantinga. Grand Rapids, MI: Wm. B. Eerdmans, 1964: 97–108.

———. *Warranted Christian Belief.* New York: Oxford University Press, 2000.

Poirier, Richard. *Robert Frost: The Work of Knowing.* New York: Oxford University Press, 1974.

Poland, Peter D. "Frost's 'Neither Out Far Nor in Deep.' " *Explicator* 52 (winter 1994): 95–96.

Potter, James L. *Robert Frost Handbook.* College Park: Penn. State University Press, 1980.

Pritchard, H. A. "Does Moral Philosophy Rest on a Mistake?" *Moral Obligation.* Oxford: Oxford University Press, 1950.

Proctor, Richard A. *Our Place Among Infinities.* New York: Appleton, 1876.

Rawls, John. *A Theory of Justice.* Cambridge, MA: Harvard University Press, 1971.

Richardson, Mark. *The Ordeal of Robert Frost: The Poet and his Poetics.* Urbana: University of Illinois Press, 1997.

———. "Robert Frost and the Motive of Poetry." *Essays in Literature* 20 (fall 1993): 273–91.

Sanders, David. "Looking through the Glass: Frost's 'After Apple-Picking' and Paul's I Corinthians." *Robert Frost Review* (fall 1996): 12–22.

Santayana, George. *The Sense of Beauty.* Eds. Holzberger, William G. and Herman J. Saatkamp, Jr. Cambridge: MIT Press, 1988.

———. "What is Aesthetics?" *The Philosophical Review* 13.3 (1904): 320–27.

———. *Essays in Literary Criticism of George Santayana.* Edited by Irving Singer. New York: Charles Scribner's Sons, 1956.

Schorer, Mark. "A Masque of Reason." *Atlantic Monthly* 175 (March 1945): 133.

Scott, Nathan, Jr. *The Broken Center.* New Haven: Yale University Press, 1966.

Sharma, T. R. S. *Robert Frost's Poetic Style*. Delhi: Macmillan India, 1981.

Sheehy, Donald. "The Correspondence of Robert Frost and Marie A. Hodge (1913–1916)." *The Robert Frost Review* (fall 1994): 82–93.

Shurr, William H. "Once More to the Woods: A New Point of Entry into Frost's Most Famous Poem." *New England Quarterly* 47 (1974): 584–94.

Showalter, Elaine, Editor. *Speaking Gender*. New York: Routledge, Chapman and Hall, 1989.

Singer, Peter. Editor. *A Companion to Ethics*. Cambridge, MA: Blackwell Reference, 1991.

Solomon, Robert C. *From Rationalism to Existentialism: The Existentialists and their Nineteenth-Century Backgrounds*. New York: Harper & Row, 1972.

Stanlis, Peter J. "Dualism: The Basis of Robert Frost's Philosophy." *The Robert Frost Review* (fall 1994): 33–46.

———. "Robert Frost: The Individual and Society." *The Intercollegiate Review* (summer 1973): 211–34.

———. "Robert Frost's Masques and the Classic American Tradition." *Frost: Centennial Essays I*: 441–68.

———. "Robert Frost: Politics in Theory and Practice." *Frost Centennial Essays II*: 48–82.

Stob, Henry. *Ethical Reflections: Essays on Moral Themes*. Grand Rapids, MI: Wm. B. Eerdmans, 1978.

Stone, Edward. "Other 'Desert Places': Frost and Hawthorne." *Frost Centennial Essays*. Jackson: University Press of Mississippi, 1974: 275–87.

Stout, Jeffrey. *Ethics after Babel: The Languages of Morals and Their Discontents*. Boston: Beacon, 1988.

Symons, Arthur. *The Symbolist Movement in Literature*. New York: Dutton, 1919.

Tharpe, Jac. Ed. *Frost: Centennial Essays*. Jackson: University Press of Mississippi, 1974.

———. *Frost: Centennial Essays II*. Jackson: University Press of Mississippi, 1976.

———. *Frost: Centennial Essays III*. Jackson: University Press of Mississippi, 1978.

Tutein, David W. *Robert Frost's Reading: An Annotated Bibliography*. Lewiston, NY: The Edwin Mellen Press, 1997.

Tyler, Dorothy. "Frost's Last Three Visits to Michigan." *Frost Centennial Essays*. Jackson: University Press of Mississippi, 1974: 518–34.

Von Frank, Albert J. " 'Nothing That Is': A Study of Frost's 'Desert Places.' " *Frost Centennial Essays*. Jackson: University Press of Mississippi, 1974: 121–32.

Walhout, Clarence. "The End of Literature: Reflections on Literature and Ethics." *Christianity and Literature* 47 (1998): 459–76.

Wallace, Patricia. "The 'Estranged Point of View': The Thematics of Imagination in Frost's Poetry." *Frost: Centennial Essays II*. Edited by Jac Tharpe. Jackson: University Press of Mississippi, 1976: 177–95.

Wilcox, Earl J. Ed. *His "Incalculable" Influence on Others: Essays on Robert Frost in*

Our Time. English Literary Studies. Victoria, B.C.: University of Victoria Press, 1994.

Willard, Dallas. *The Divine Conspiracy*. San Francisco: HarperCollins, 1998.

Winters, Yvor. "Robert Frost: Or, the Spiritual Drifter as Poet." *Sewanee Review* 56 (1948): 564–96.

Index